Hidden Nature

Hidden Nature

The Startling Insights of Victor Schauberger

Alick Bartholomew

Foreword by David Bellamy, OBE

First published in 2003 by Floris Books

British Library CIP Data available

ISBN 0-86315-432-8

Printed in Poland

To Callum Coats, my partner in the great Schauberger book project, without whose inspiration this book would not have been possible, and to Gareth Mills, bookman *extraordinaire,* who suggested it.

Author's note on capitalization

It seems mean not to give Sun, Earth and Moon the dignity of initial capitals; the planets get them by being named after gods. While Gaia is usually accorded a capital, I feel that Nature, which we call the fountain of life, deserves similar recognition. As a first step in deflating the human ego, we should also give Nature and Cosmos appropriate identities. When talking of Gaia, most use the personal pronoun. I have done the same for Nature, without imputing anthropomorphism.

Acknowledgments

I am grateful to Gill and Macmillan for permission to quote from *Living Water*, from *Living Energies* and from Viktor Schauberger's *Eco-Technology* series.

For the illustrations, most of which first appeared in *Living Energies*, I extend thanks to Callum Coats and to his publishers Gill and Macmillan. Specifically to the late Richard C. Feieraband for permission to use pictures of the Repulsine prototypes.

I honour my wife Mari, acknowledging her patience with my preoccupation for several years with the Schauberger project.

Christopher Moore of Floris Books has been a most creative editor in helping to make the text more navigable, and his genuine interest in the material is much appreciated.

And, not least, I am grateful to David Bellamy for his encouragement and for his Foreword.

Contents

Foreword

Water is the commonest substance on the face of the Earth, yet we really know very little about this essential source of life. We do know that without it there would be no life — indeed there would be little in the way of chemical reaction, for water is the universal catalyst. Water is also our potential nemesis, for today it is widely agreed that if there is another world war, it will be waged over this precious resource. Water in a state fit enough for human consumption or for succouring the life cycle of the brown trout is now in short supply and its availability is diminishing every day

Before Austria had stripped her mountains of all her old growth forests, Viktor Schauberger, a forester, observing how a trout could maintain its station in the midst of a turbulent stream, discovered the secret of living water. Distilled from the sea and leaving most of its burden of salt behind, it droppeth as the gentle rain from heaven, taking up kinetic energy as it makes its way back to ordnance datum (standard sea level), itself controlled by the balance of the global greenhouse.

En route this living water absorbs minerals from both soil and bedrock sufficient to nurture the pulse of life itself, tiny herbs, some full of the power of healing, and the natural vegetation that generates organic soil. The trees, reaching up to the Sun, power houses for transforming energy, are driven by living water, ameliorating the climate near the ground, controlling erosion and helping to maintain the life-giving water cycle.

If this cycle gets out of balance in any way, the consequences are dire, as insurance companies are now discovering. Drought, floods, winds and wild fire out of control, and perhaps worst of all, eutrophication, the clever name for too many nutrients choking the very arteries through which living water used to meander its self-cleansing way down to the sea.

There is much in Schauberger's philosophy that gets up the noses of the science that sees only financial profit at the end of their glass telescope of knowledge. Alick Bartholomew is to be congratulated for bringing Schauberger's vision into focus in this book at the most opportune time. Wave power is beginning to come on stream with the promise of base load electricity cheap enough to split, not the polluting atom, but the water molecule, into oxygen and hydrogen — the latter to fuel the much discussed non-polluting, fuel cell-based, hydrogen economy.

Is this a wise strategy? In the absence of Schauberger as my mentor I sat beside the stream in my garden with Tornado jets making warlike passes overhead, and watched a trout enjoying what are perhaps the only real human rights, peace and access to living water.

David Bellamy,
Bedburn, February 2003

Introduction

'I no longer own my own mind. I don't own even my own thoughts. After all I've done, finally there is nothing left. I am a man with no future.'[1] These were the words of Viktor Schauberger, an Austrian naturalist, the pioneer of Eco-technology (working with Nature) who had devoted his life to demonstrating how the desecration of our environment proceeds directly from our complete ignorance of how Nature works at the energy level. His controversial credo was that humanity must begin, with humility, to study Nature and learn from it, rather than try to correct it. We have put the future of humanity at risk by the way we produce and consume energy. His aim was to liberate people from dependence on inefficient and polluting centralized energy resources and generation of power.

Viktor was communicating his distress to his son, Walter, on the plane home from Texas after a nightmare of exhausting cross-examination to extract the secrets of the devices he had developed which demonstrated free energy, anti-gravity and fuel-less flight. He died five days later on September 25, 1958, in Linz, Austria, of a broken heart. Father and son had embarked on an ambitious, but ill-conceived, scheme hatched by an American 'consortium' which probably had CIA and atomic energy connections, in order to persuade him to give up the keys to his mysterious research (see Chapter 18). Schauberger had in 1944, under threat of death, been forced to develop a flying saucer programme for the Third Reich, the secret weapon which, had it been initiated two years earlier, might well have tipped the war's balance in Germany's favour.

Schauberger's inspiration came from studying the water in fast-flowing streams in the unspoilt Austrian Alps, where he worked as a forest warden. From his astute observations he became a self-trained engineer, eventually learning, through the implosive, or centripetally moving, processes that Nature uses, how to release energy 127 times more powerful than conventional power generation. By 1937 he had developed an implosion motor that produced a thrust of 1,290m/sec, or about four times the speed of sound. In 1941 Air Marshall Udet asked him to help solve the growing energy crisis in Germany; however the research came to an end when Udet died and the plant was subsequently destroyed by Allied bombing. When in 1943 Heinrich Himmler directed Viktor to develop a new secret weapon system with a team of engineer prisoners-of-war, he had no choice but to comply.

The critical tests came just before the end of the European war. A flying disc was launched in Prague on February 19, 1945, which rose to an altitude of 15,000 metres in three minutes and attained a forward speed of 2,200kph.[2] An improved version was to be launched on May 6, the day the American forces arrived at the Leonstein factory in Upper Austria. Facing the collapse of the German armies, Field Marshal Keitel ordered all the prototypes to be destroyed.

Schauberger had moved from his apartment in Vienna to the comparative safety of Leonstein. Meanwhile the Russians pushed in from the East and captured Vienna; a special Soviet investigation team ransacked his apartment, taking away vital papers and models, and then blew it up.

The Allies seemed to be well aware of Schauberger's part in developing this secret weapon. At the end of hostilities, an American Special Forces team seized all the equipment from his Leonstein home and put him under 'protective U.S. custody' for nine months' debriefing. It seems likely that they could not fathom his strange science, for they let him go, although this group, detailed to enlist as many of the front-line German scientists as possible, took back scores of other 'enemy' scientists to give a vital boost to American industrial and military research. They forbade him from pursuing 'atomic energy' research, which would have left him free to follow his dream of fuel-less power.

For the following nine years Viktor could not continue his implosion research because the high quality materials needed for his very advanced equipment were beyond his means, and he had no sponsors. In addition, he may have been haunted by remorse for having been forced by the German SS to design machines of war. Schauberger was essentially a man of peace who, above all, wanted to help humanity become free; so he turned his attention to making the Earth more fertile, developing experimental copper ploughshares.

Levitation and resistantless movement

This strange life path had started on his return to civilian life after the First World War, when Viktor Schauberger went to work in the mountains. His experiences of unspoilt Nature were life-changing.

One such that would set him on a lonely course to change the course of human life for ever, he describes graphically:

> It was spawning time one early spring moonlit night. I was sitting beside a waterfall waiting to catch a dangerous fish poacher. Something then happened so quickly; I was hardly able to grasp it. The moonlight falling onto the crystal clear water picked up every movement of a large shoal of fish gathered in the pool. Suddenly they dispersed as a big fish swam into the pool from below, preparing to confront the waterfall. It seemed as though it wanted to scatter the other trout as it quickly darted to and fro in great twisting movements.
>
> Then, just as suddenly the large trout disappeared into the huge jet of falling water that shone like molten metal. I could see it fleetingly, under a conically shaped stream of water, dancing in a wild, spinning movement, which at that moment didn't make sense to me. When it stopped spinning it seemed then to float motionlessly upward. On reaching the lower curve of the waterfall it tumbled over and with a strong push reached behind the upper curve of the fall. There, in the fast flowing water, and with a strong movement of the tail, it disappeared.
>
> Deep in thought, I filled my pipe, and as I wended my way homewards, smoked it to the finish. Often subsequently, I witnessed the same sequence of behaviour of a trout leaping up a high waterfall. After decades of similar observations that manifested like rows of pearls on a chain, I should be able to come to some conclusion. But no scientist has been able to explain the phenomenon to me.
>
> With the right lighting, it is possible to see the path of levitational currents as an empty tube within the veil of a waterfall. It is similar to the tunnel in the middle of a circulating vortex of water plunging down a drain, which brings up a gurgling sound. This downwardly-directed whirlpool drags everything with increasing suction with it into the depths. If you can imagine this whirlpool or water-cyclone operating vertically, you get the picture of how the levitational current works and you can see how the trout appears to be floating upward in the axis of fall.[3]

Viktor used to spend hours watching fish in the streams. He was fascinated by how the trout could lie motionless in the strongest current and then, if alarmed, without warning, would dart upstream rather than be carried down with the flow. Having learned from his family about the importance of temperature on the energy potential of water, he did an experiment. He had colleagues heat up 100 litres of water that, on his signal, they poured into the fast-flowing mountain stream some 150 metres upstream from where he stood. Viktor noted how the trout he had been observing became agitated, and soon was unable to hold its station in the fast flowing stream, thrashing its tail fins to no avail. The minute, but nevertheless abnormal, rise in the average temperature of the water and the chaoticized flow that resulted, had interfered with the trout's hovering ability. Viktor searched the textbooks in vain for an explanation of this marvel.

He would often quote these experiences with the trout as having the most influence on developing his ideas, for temperature and motion were the foundations of his theories and discoveries. He subsequently developed a generator to produce energy directly from air and water, naming it the 'trout turbine' in honour of his mentor, though it was later called the 'implosion machine.'

The non-conformist

Viktor Schauberger was discredited and criticized by 'the experts,' as pioneers have been in the past, from Galileo to Max Planck. He insisted that we have betrayed our calling and our heritage, by usurping the role of God and trashing our environment. He saw that we were hell-bent on a path of self-destruction, and predicted that, within a generation, our climate would become more hostile, our food sources would dry up, there would be no healthy water, and illness, misery and violence would predominate.

Where have conventional scientists gone astray? By not observing carefully how Nature works. If they did, they would be able to formulate her laws, as Schauberger has done, and then comply with them, so that human society could come into harmony with our environment. As he so often said, "Comprehend and Copy Nature". Instead, modern scientists believe we are above Nature and are free to exploit the Earth's resources without consequence.

Schauberger spelled out clearly exactly where we have gone wrong with our technology. How can we start to put things right?

Certainly by a complete reversal of the way we do things. This can involve only a sea change in the way we regard our lives, and a personal commitment to help bring about a major shift in our society. Only through sufficient numbers joining together in common cause can these changes begin.

He criticized mainline science for its arrogance and herd instincts. He also castigated scientists for their blinkeredness, their inability to see the connections between things. Schauberger did not blame the political hierarchy for the world's woes, as we often do today. He believed that political leaders are basically opportunists and pawns of the system. It was his own adversaries, the 'techno-academic' scientists as he called them, whom he held to blame for the dangerous state of the World.[4]

Visionaries and pioneers are inevitably a challenge to the establishment in whatever field, for they pose an imagined threat to the interests of those who benefit from the status quo. The degree of vilification seems to depend on the level of rewards at stake. Thus science, as perhaps the most exclusive and arrogant of disciplines, has done so much throughout history to undermine great innovators like Copernicus, Kepler and Galileo to, in our times, the biological pioneers James Lovelock, Rupert Sheldrake and Mae-Wan Ho.

Despite, or perhaps because of, his interrupted education, Viktor retained a great thirst for knowledge. His wife found domestically disruptive his tendency to stay up all night, pouring over books of every kind, especially the more esoteric variety. There was no question that Viktor felt he had a calling. This was evident from the fact that often he seemed to write in a trance-like state, returning to normal consciousness quite surprised by what he had just written!

Schauberger was a man of unshakeable self-confidence and inner conviction about the viability of his theories, and unsurprisingly had a lifelong battle with orthodoxy. Callum Coats describes how on one occasion during the Nazi era, good fortune saved his life from being taken in a sinister way.[5] He did, however gain important support. This was inevitably from the few scientists who were not swayed by greed or jealousy and were of more independent mind. One was the Swiss Professor Werner Zimmerman, a well-known social reformer who published articles by Viktor in his ecologically oriented magazine *Tau*. Another was Felix Ehrenhaft, professor of physics at the University of Vienna, who helped with Viktor's calculations for his implosion machines. A third very loyal friend was Professor Philipp Forchheimer, a hydrologist of world repute.

Most people have heard of Viktor Schauberger only in connection with his inspired ideas about water or of the energy-saving machines that harnessed the enormous power encapsulated in lively water. They were, indeed, so fundamental and important as to justify his reputation as an ecological pioneer. However, as we are concerned with the broader challenge of restoring the damage wrought by humanity on the Earth, we shall need to present Schauberger's larger worldview of how Nature works.

Walter Schauberger, who unlike his father, had a formal education in science and was, for a time, a university lecturer in physics, worked hard to make Viktor's ideas more accessible to mainstream science. After he did a lecture tour in 1950 at a number of England's top universities, some of the distinguished scientists were asked what they thought of the Schauberger physics. While they agreed that the theories were quite convincing, the problem, it appeared, was that "it would mean rewriting all the textbooks in the world".[6]

An alternative worldview

Viktor Schauberger suffered much from the vindictiveness of the scientific establishment towards him. Nevertheless, his constant complaints about them obscure his principal message, which is far more important than academic arrogance per se. This is that our whole culture is completely under the thrall of a materialistic worldview or way of seeing; we are caught in the excitement of apparently being free to do anything we want, and by the glamour of possessing lots of riches and distractions. Our science is but the product of this worldview, as is our philosophy and education, our religion, our politics and our medicine. You don't need to subscribe to conspiracy theories to realize that all aspects of our society suffer from a grand delusion that is contributing to the breakdown of our world order and to the collapse of our ecosystems.

The real issue is that the intellectual movement of the late seventeenth century, the Enlightenment, and its equivalent in science, Rationalism, have caused a great schism in human society. The philosopher René Descartes (famous for his "I think therefore I am") has a lot to answer for. That movement put man on a pedestal, introduced the idea of humanity being apart from Nature and started to interpret all natural phenomena by a process of deduction. The effect has been a separation of thinking from experience, of head from heart. Because of the dominance of scientific determinism in our culture, the more intuitive way of knowledge is considered as suspect, but there is a new awakening taking place at all levels of society of people wanting to get in touch with their intuition, who feel that rationalism is in fact the Great Delusion.

We have experiences every day that fall outside the accepted conventions of reality; like little synchronicities, intuiting events, the sensing of different qualities of 'atmosphere' as emanations from people, situations or places, the power of thought over action, communication with a household pet. If we share these with like-minded friends we feel like conspirators discussing something taboo that the thought police might catch. At best these phenomena might be labelled woolly, like 'psychic' experiences. We are lost because there is no system or structure to 'make sense' of an important part of our lives. They are not part of conventional wisdom.

Viktor Schauberger was one of the first to put in a scientifically verifiable framework a study of natural processes set free from the constraints of rationalism. He has widened our understanding of our place in the world by describing a worldview of a natural science that includes these experiences without recourse to scientific, religious or philosophical dogma. By understanding how Nature works, we can begin to relate our experiences to a much wider and more exciting worldview. Rachel Carson, who is credited with having initiated the environmental movement with her book *Silent Spring*, was a brave woman for taking on the multinational corporations. Schauberger is all the braver for taking on our conventional worldview.

There must be a fundamental change in the way we see the world (including our environmental policies), before change is possible. Have Viktor's warnings been vindicated? It is over 45 years since his untimely death, and much of what he prophesied has come to pass even earlier than he foresaw. There was some hope before September 11, 2001, that environmental awareness was gaining ground, if slowly. Recognition of the critical imbalances we have created in our atmosphere and of the urgent need to change our priorities from consumption to conservation was starting to spread. Now we seem to have backtracked a generation and we can't even agree to implement the kind of cuts in carbon dioxide emissions that are essential to avoid catastrophic climate change.

We feel that Schauberger's perceptions are a vital key to understanding where our culture has gone wrong and that our future as a species depends on being able to reconnect with the natural processes he rediscovered. We shall, therefore, bring into twenty-first century relevance his views of how Nature works and where our society has gone wrong, to see what we can learn from his insights.

Viktor has a singular way of deprecating our culture, as the following comment on our conditioning reveals:

> Humanity has become accustomed to relate everything to itself (anthropocentrism). In the process we have failed to see that real truth is a slippery thing upon which the perpetually reformulating mind passes judgment almost imperceptibly. In the main all that is then left behind is whatever was drilled into our brain with much trouble and effort, and to which we cling. To give rein to free thought, to allow our minds to flow freely and unimpeded, is too fraught with complications. For this reason the activity arising from these notions inevitably becomes a traffic in excreta that stinks to high heaven, because its foundations were already decayed and rotten from the very beginning. It is no wonder, therefore, that everywhere everything is going wrong. Truth resides only in all-knowing Nature.[7]

Schauberger predicted that modern human culture's destruction of the creative energies of Nature would result in greater violence and depravity in society. If we were to pay heed to what Nature requires of us, would we witness a reversal of this observable deterioration, and a gradual coming back into balance of a human society that would eventually be able to live in tune with Nature?

But as in our hubris we believe we are at the peak of material human achievement, there is a reawakening of the human spirit, and a great need is being reborn to reconnect with Nature, with our source. This book attempts to encourage and nurture this need.

Towards a Science of Nature

The majority of people in the UK oppose the genetic modification of food because they know in their hearts it is against Nature. The policy is being driven by the commercial interests of big business supported by a compliant political climate. Above all, it is justified by a science with a materialist worldview that believes Nature exists to be manipulated and exploited for the imagined benefit of humanity. Accountability is apparently not an issue.

The national debate on GM held in Britain in 2003 showed that most people are deeply disturbed by the arrogance of the view that Man can do anything he wants on this Earth. But they have no science to turn to for rebuttal. What is needed is a Science of Nature to supplant the misguided science presently taught in our schools and universities. We need to work with a holistic view of Nature as omnipotent on the Earth, whose laws govern us humans as well and which we flout at our peril — in brief, a Nature with which we must learn to cooperate with humility.

What are these laws of Nature? How are we to know what is our place, and what is demanded of us? Viktor Schauberger excelled as a teacher of the science of Nature. He describes and illustrates, as few have done, how Nature works, with its marvellous and complex processes at the heart of the evolution of consciousness.

Viktor Schauberger is known at present only to a small, holistically-inclined audience that has a strong commitment to environmental issues, to organic growing or to the development of alternative energy sources. Much of the literature on Schauberger is sometimes difficult to follow for the less committed. This book draws on Callum Coats' seminal book on Viktor's work, *Living Energies*. We hope that the less technical approach of our book will facilitate for a broader audience how indispensable are Schauberger's insights if we wish to understand our present ecological predicament. The great ideological conflict of this new century will be between the very limited and flawed mechanistic/deterministic worldview and the holistic understanding of life as a wondrous, intimately interconnected and spiritual whole.

PART ONE

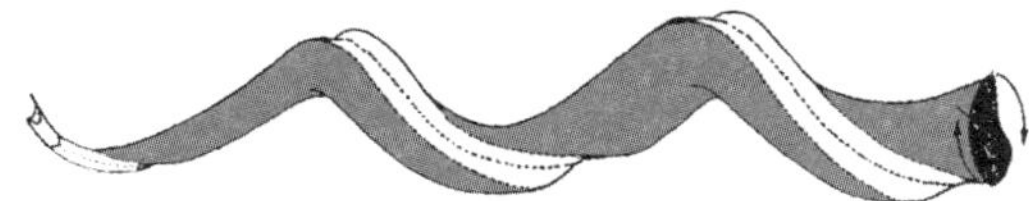

An Alternative Worldview

1. Viktor Schauberger's Vision

Our natural world is essentially an indivisible unity, but we human beings are condemned to apprehend it from two different directions — through our senses (perception) or through our minds (conceptual). A child just observes and marvels, but as our rational minds become trained we are taught to interpret what we see, usually through other people's ideas, in order to 'make sense' of our sensory experience. Both are forms of reality, but unless we are able to bring the two aspects meaningfully together, the world will present nothing but incomprehensible riddles to us. This, in fact, is the basic shortcoming of our present human society. It is the great weakness of the prevailing scientific orthodoxy. As Schauberger noted:

> The majority believes that everything hard to comprehend must be very profound. This is incorrect. What is hard to understand is what is immature, unclear and often false. The highest wisdom is simple and passes through the brain directly into the heart.[1]

Some of the pioneers of science were able to bridge this dichotomy. Their way was to immerse themselves so deeply in the world of pure observation and experience, that out of these perceptions the concepts would speak for themselves.

Viktor Schauberger (1885–1958) possessed this rare gift. As a result of this, more than anyone else of his time he foresaw, as early as the 1920s, the environmental crises in which we are now engulfed. Viktor's forebears had a long tradition of caring for the welfare of the natural forest and its wildlife in the Austrian Alps. Although he was born into a family that cherished unspoilt Nature, Viktor, like most pioneers, was the rebel amongst them.

Born one of nine children, he seemed to get on well with his siblings. His father, nicknamed after the legendary giant 'Ruebesahl,' as he was 6' 8" tall, did not relate well to the young Viktor. He resented the young man rejecting his paternal advice to improve himself with a modern academic training. His brothers acquiesced with their father. The one to whom Viktor remained closest was his mother. But he told how both his parents believed in the healing power of water, and of their insight that the quality and transportive power of water in a stream was particularly strong on a cold night, and more so under a full Moon.

Viktor was a dreamy child, but was endowed with an extraordinary quality of observation, a keen intellect, and evident intuitive and psychic abilities. As a boy he would spend hours by himself in the forests, exploring streams, watching the animals and studying the plants. He was able to experience first hand what he had first heard from his family, and more, about the life of the natural forest and its creatures. He had no interest in the academic path and declined the opportunity to go to forestry college. He did some more practical training instead, and served an apprenticeship under an older forest warden. Married young, Viktor moved to a post in a virgin forest 93 miles (150 km) south into the mountains. Four weeks after his son was born, Viktor was drafted in 1914 into the Kaiser's army.

After the war he quickly rose from junior forest warden to gamekeeper and became the head warden of the forest and hunting domain in Brunnenthal/Steyerling owned by Prince Adolf zu Schaumburg-Lippe. In this large wilderness area, almost untouched by man, Schauberger was able to study how Nature works when left undisturbed. Here biodiversity was undamaged, with many magnificent trees, an abundance of wildlife, and unspoilt streams teeming with fish and other creatures.

The water wizard

Water was always Viktor's fascination. One day, accompanied by his foresters, he came to a remote upland plateau where there was a legendary spring that emerged from a dilapidated dome-like structure. Schauberger ordered it to be pulled down for safety reasons. One of the older foresters then warned him that if the structure were removed the spring would dry up. Taking note of the old forester's advice, and as a verifying experiment, Schauberger requested that the structure be carefully dismantled, with each stone numbered and its place marked. When Viktor passed again some two weeks later, he noted that the spring had indeed dried up due to exposure to the Sun's rays. Immediately he ordered the structure to be carefully rebuilt and a few days later the spring began to flow again. This taught him that water liked to flow in cool darkness.

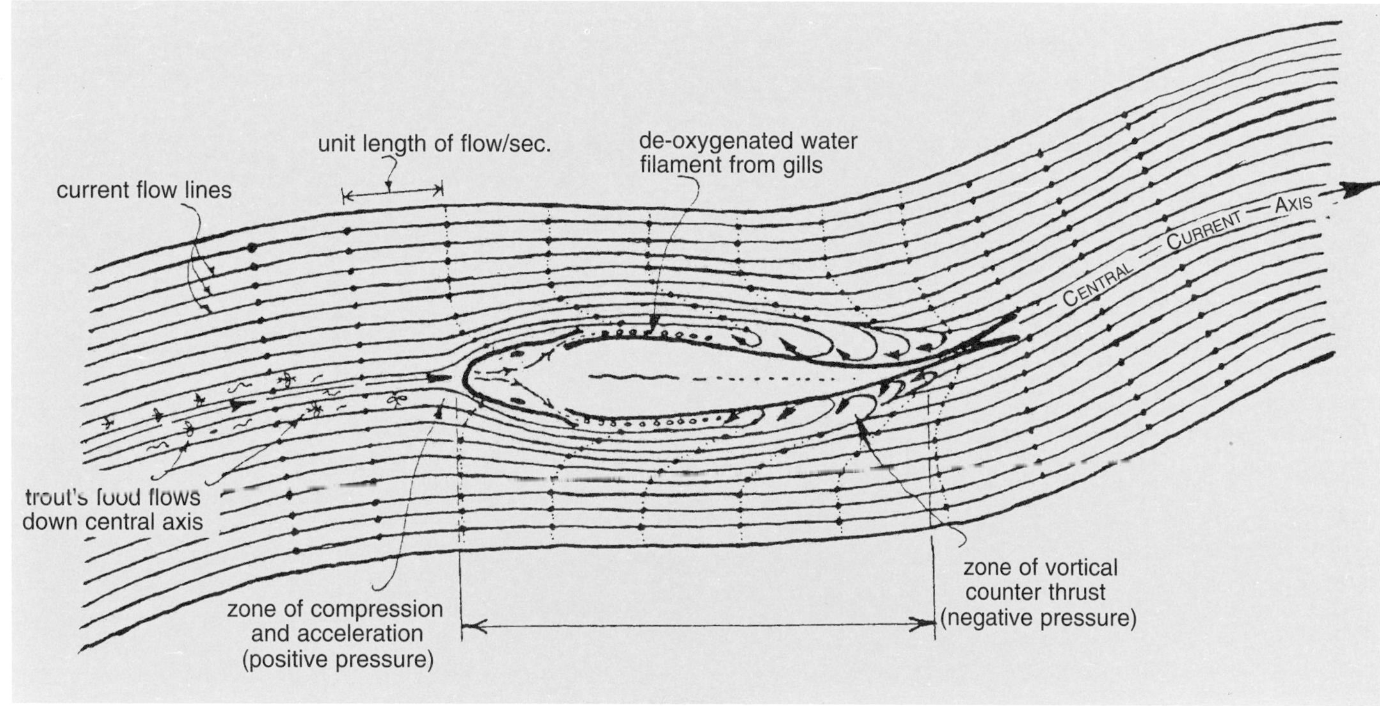

Fig. 1.1. The Stationary Trout.
The trout normally swims in the middle of the central current, where the water is densest and coldest. Its body displaces and compresses the individual water filaments causing them to accelerate. As their critical velocities are exceeded, vortices or countercurrents are formed along the rear part of the trout's body, providing a counterthrust to the current, allowing the trout to remain stationary in the fast flowing water. If it needs to accelerate, it flaps its gills, creating a further vortex train along its flanks, increasing the counterthrust upstream.

Viktor's abiding interest was to discover how to generate energy using Nature's own methods. He worked out how a trout is able to screw its way up a waterfall by hitching a ride on strong levitative currents, and using this principle, the first generator he developed was the 'trout turbine.' To perfect this he needed more precise information on how a trout is able to stand motionless in a fast moving current, and indeed how it can suddenly accelerate upstream. The above diagram illustrates this amazing phenomenon (Fig. 1.1).

The trout is holding its station in mid steam where the water is coldest, densest and has most potential energy. Viktor studied the gills of the fish and found what he thought were guide vanes which would direct the water flow into a powerful backwards vortex current. Its shiny scales minimize friction with the water, but they also create scores more of little vortices that amplify the *upstream* counter current, particularly towards the tail, which cancel out the pressure on the fish's snout. A zone of negative thrust is created along the whole of the trout's body and so it stays in the same place. These counter currents can be increased by flicks of the tail, creating negative pressure behind the fish. Flapping of the gills amplifies the vortices along its flanks, giving it a sudden push upstream. The faster the gills move the more oxygen-deficient water is expelled from the body. This combining with the free oxygen in the water, causes the water body to expand, with an effect on the fish similar to squeezing a bar of wet soap in your hand.

Another experience that Viktor often quoted as significant for his growth in understanding, occurred when he had shot a chamois buck on a frosty night under the full Moon. The buck fell into a ravine and, attempting to retrieve it, Schauberger fell down a snow chute to the bottom. In the bright light of the Moon, he became aware of movement in the stream below where he stood. Some green logs were bobbing up on the surface, then sinking to the bottom, as though they were dancing. And not only that, but a large stone began to gyrate at the bottom, and then came to the surface, where it was immediately surrounded by a halo of ice. Other stones also surfaced, and he saw that they were all egg-shaped. It seemed that no uneven or ragged stones would float in this way. Schauberger developed his ideas of different forms of motion and shapes from these observations.

Having seen how water could carry its greatest load on a cold, clear night, he made practical use of this observation. During the winter of 1918, the town of Linz was suffering a severe shortage of fuel as a result of the war when the draft animals had been commandeered. There was a small stream that ran through narrow gorges and which was considered unsuitable for transporting logs, but he wanted to try out his ideas using this stream. His offer to help being accepted by the authorities, he describes how he proceeded:

> I had observed that an increased water level after a thaw builds up sandbanks that are then partially dispersed when the water temperature drops during clear cool nights. I then waited for an increase in the strength of the water current. This takes place in the early hours of the morning, when it is coldest, and particularly at full Moon, although the volume of the water is apparently less due to its compression on cooling. I planned for the timber to be put in the stream under these conditions, and in one night 1600m^3 were brought down to the valley.

Viktor had discovered that when water was at its coldest, it had much more energy that enabled it to carry more sediment, gouging out deposits of sand, and concluded that in these conditions it would be able to carry a greater weight of logs. This was a principle that enabled him to turn upside down the current theories of hydraulics, and particularly the methods of river and flood management.

Log flumes

Schauberger was looking for a way to demonstrate to others his ideas about movement in Nature, and to discuss them with technical experts and scientists. His opportunity came in 1922 when the owner of the forest and hunting reserve on which Viktor was a junior warden, Prince Adolf zu Schaumburg-Lippe, was looking for a way to avoid bankruptcy. (His wife, the Princess, had very expensive tastes.) After World War I there was a demand by the expanding building industry for timber, and inaccessible stands of mature trees were earmarked for felling. The timber flotation methods of the time were fairly crude, straight channels running down the valleys, which caused the logs enormous damage, many being good only for firewood.

The Prince offered a prize for the construction of a flume to bring logs down from the remote areas, and Viktor eagerly submitted his plans. These were, however, rejected by the administrators of the estate as totally unworkable, as the proposed method went completely against accepted hydraulic principles. Through a chance meeting on a hunting expedition, the Princess asked Viktor what savings could be achieved through his method. On claiming that he could offer a cost of one schilling per $1m^3$ against the normal cost of 12 schillings per $1m^3$ for flotation, she offered to have his salary trebled should he succeed, despite his lack of academic qualifications. The Prince, driving a hard bargain, made a condition that Viktor should build the flume at his own expense and that it had to deliver a minimum of $1{,}000m^3$ daily.

There was much scoffing by the experts who judged Schauberger completely mad, and who made malicious predictions of the outcome; as Viktor describes:

> The construction was completed after some four months. The great timbers were in position. The day before the inauguration I tried a test. An average sized log was put into the flume. It floated down for about 100 metres and then suddenly grounded on the bottom, causing the water behind to rise and overflow the flume. I saw the scornful faces of my workers, realized that I had miscalculated and felt discouraged. The log

was taken out of the flume. I thought that there was too little water and too sharp a drop. I did not know what to do. So I sent my workers home so that I could quietly consider the problem.

The curves of the flume were correct; of that there was no doubt. So what had gone wrong? I walked slowly along the flume until I came to the trap and the sorting basins, from which a further length of flume continued. The basins were full. I sat on a rock above the water in the Sun.

Suddenly I felt something moving below my leather trousers. Jumping up I saw a coiled snake. I picked it up and threw it away; it fell into the basin and tried to get out, but the bank was too steep. As it swam back and forth I was amazed that it could swim so fast without fins. Observing it through my binoculars I saw its peculiar twisting movements in the clear water. Finally the snake reached the far bank. For some time I stood quietly and went over in my mind the snake's bodily movements of horizontal and vertical curves. Suddenly I understood how it had done it!

The snake's movement was that of a spiral space-curve twisting like the horn of a Kudu antelope. Calling back his workers, he ordered the holding basin to be emptied and the log removed. He then gave instructions to attach thin wooden slats to the curved sides of the flume walls, which would act like the rifling in a gun barrel, and would make the water rotate anti-clockwise on left hand bends and clockwise at right hand bends. Promised double wages, they worked through the night, and the adjustments were completed in time for the opening in the morning.

The inauguration of the flume was attended by the Prince and Princess, by the Chief Forestry Commissioner and a number of hydraulic specialists, the last ready to gloat over Viktor's humiliation. After greeting the royal couple and the head forester, he continued:

I opened the lock, behind which my workers started to arrange the smaller logs in the water. Unnoticed, a heavier log about 3ft (90cm) in diameter went in with the others. The senior log master shouted, 'We cannot have that one.' I gave a quick wave and the unwanted log floated high, towards the outflow. Quickly it created a blockage that raised the water level. No one said anything, staring at the log rising out of the water, waiting for the flume to overflow. Suddenly there was a gurgling noise. The heavy log swung first to the right, then to the left, twisting like a snake, its head high as it floated away quickly. A few seconds later the log slipped through the first curve and was gone.

Schauberger's flumes followed the curves of the valley, with guide vanes mounted on the curves, making the water spiral along its axis. With the careful monitoring of temperature along the route, bringing in cold water where necessary, he found it was possible to float logs under conditions regarded as impossible, using significantly less water, and achieving very high delivery rates. Parts of his flumes can still be seen in Austria today.

The flume at Steyrling was a great success, much to the chagrin of the observing hydraulic engineers who were so sure his crazy scheme would fail. Schauberger's fame quickly spread. Experts came from all over Europe to study the flume's construction. He was appointed State Consultant for Timber Flotation at a high salary. The academics were furious that he could give directives on technical questions which he could not understand with his inadequate education, and that he was paid twice as much as any of them. In the crisis that followed, Viktor resigned, and accepted a job with one of Austria's largest building contractors for whom he built installations all over Europe. If this has been his only accomplishment, Viktor Schauberger would still be known as the man who completely mastered the art of transporting timber by water.

Water, source of life

His painstaking and inspired studies of water were the source for a seminal paper that Schauberger wrote on 'Temperature and the Movement of Water.'[2] Central to these was the influence of minute differences in temperature, which are presently wholly ignored by modern hydraulics and hydrology. Natural, living, water, which is conventionally regarded as a homogenous substance, he showed to be composed of many strata or layers with subtle variations in temperature and electric charge which influence the water's motion, its form of flow and its physical properties.

Schauberger saw water as a pulsating, living substance that energizes all of life, both organic and inorganic. He called it "the life blood of the Earth". Whether as water, blood or sap (which are essentially water), it is the indispensable constituent of all life-forms, and its quality and temperature is fundamental to health. When it is healthy it has a complex structure that enables it to communicate information, carry energy, nutrients and healing, to self-cleanse and discharge wastes. He believed that one of the causes of the disintegration of our culture is our disrespect for and destruction of water, *the bringer of life*, for in doing so we destroy life itself. Viktor also profoundly believed that our dangerous technologies produce poor water that has lost its energy and its ability to pulsate — and is effectively *lifeless*. This dead water produces inadequate nutrition, and Viktor believed that its regressive energies are responsible for degenerative diseases like cancer, for lower intelligence and for community turmoil.

Natural forests (not the monoculture plantations of today) are the cradle of water and also the main source of oxygen for the planet. Their precipitate destruction, Schauberger predicted, would result in global warming, severe water shortage and the creation of deserts. He made brilliant observations of the way in which trees in a natural, diversified environment are biocondensers of energy (accumulating and storing energy from both Sun and Earth) — how the groundwater (man permitting) brings Earth's energy to the tree in order to balance the Sun's energy.

Motion is crucial

An understanding of motion may be the most important of Schauberger's discoveries. Our current technology uses the wrong form of motion. Our machines and processes channel agents such as air, water, other liquids and gases into the type of motion that Nature uses only to decompose and dissolve matter. Nature uses another form of motion for creating and rebuilding. Our technology's mode of motion creates chaos, noise and heat, bringing disease to organisms and the breakdown of structures. Visualize if you will, what happens in an explosion — matter is torn apart, fragmented and destroyed. Its effect is to create degraded energy. Through its dependence on the decomposing mode of motion our technology creates enormous energy pollution and entropy, dangerously affecting the vital biodiversity and balance of our ecosystems.

Our mechanical, technological systems of motion are nearly all heat- and friction-inducing, with the fastest movement at the

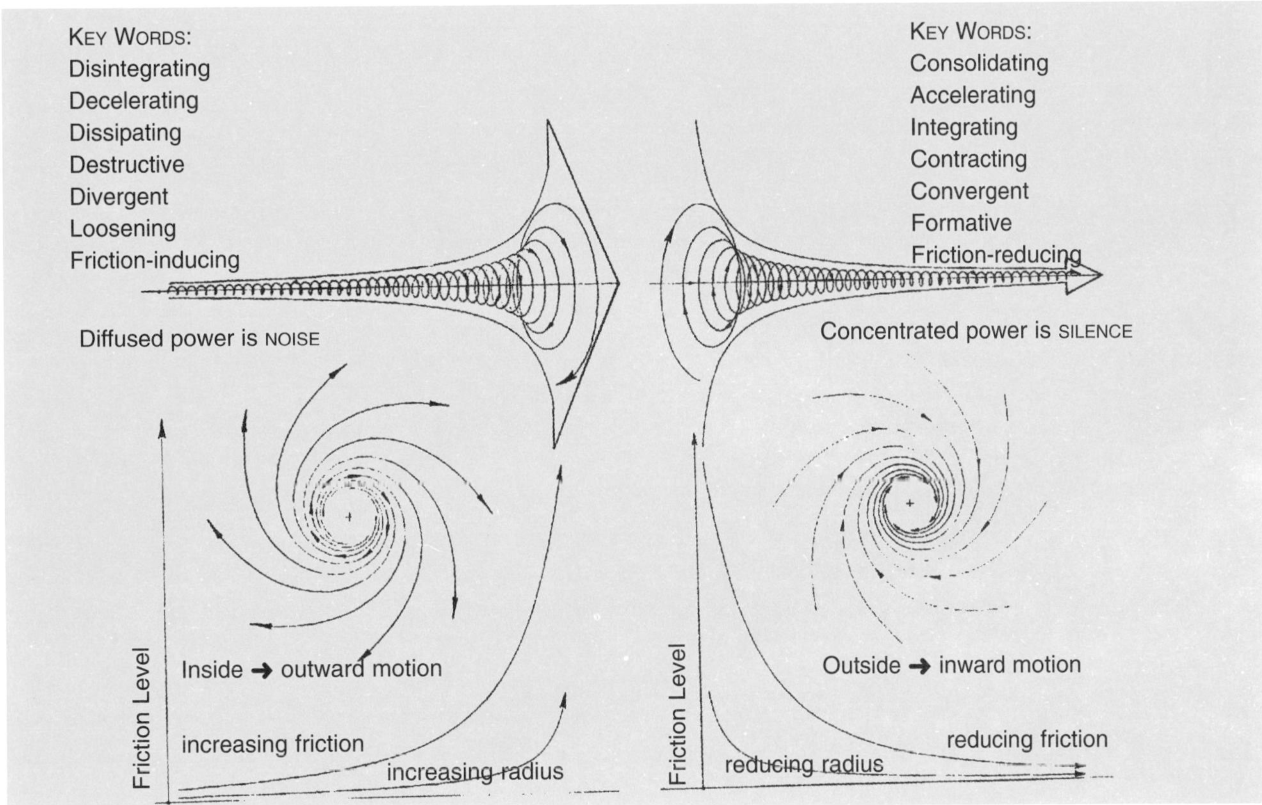

Fig. 1.2. Centrifugal and centripetal movement. *Comparison between axial>radial (inside>outwards) motion, the way our current technology works, and radial>axial (outside>inwards) motion, Nature's way of generating creative energy.*

periphery (as in a wheel), a form of motion that is disintegrative, noisy and inefficient; this is the way we generate our power — centrifugally. By contrast, Nature uses the opposite, centripetal, vortical form of motion, moving from the outside to the inside with increasing velocity, which acts to cool, to condense, to structure, assisting the emergence of higher quality and more complex systems.

Spirals are a basic form of motion in Nature, but Schauberger's recognition of the *vortex* (see p. 42) as the principal creative movement system in the Universe is at the core of his Eco-technology and the key to his valuable implosion research. From the tornado to plant growth, it is Nature's mechanism for transforming energy from one level to another (Fig. 1.2).

Asked about our technology "How else should it be done?," Viktor's answer was: "Exactly in the opposite way that it is done today". He saw that the potential for creating energy for human needs by replicating the in-winding motion of Nature was the way of the future.

Temperature controls

Another cornerstone of Viktor's ecotechnology is the importance of temperature in Nature's processes. Modern technology creates vast amounts of waste heat (entropy) which contribute to global warming, especially in cities and industrial centres (carbon dioxide from burning fossil fuels being the principal source of global warming). Increasing heat will ultimately destroy life on Earth. Nature's creativity, however, thrives on measured coolness.

Most significantly, he showed how small variations in temperature are as crucial to the healthy movement of water and sap as they are to the human blood. He identified in particular the importance for water of the temperature of +4°C (39°F), referred to physically and chemically as the 'anomaly point,' when water is at its densest and has the greatest vitality, health and energy content.

In all forms of water, in trees and other living organisms, the temperature gradient (the upward and downward movement of temperature) is active. In the natural process of synthesis and decomposition, the temperature is either approaching (positive gradient) or moving away from (negative gradient) the anomaly point. Each form of gradient has its special function in Nature's great production; the positive (cooling) temperature gradient must play the principal role if evolution is to unfold creatively. We shall be looking at this in more detail in the appropriate chapters.

Schauberger found that temperature changes according to certain patterns and cycles that activate life and death, bringing increase and decrease, decomposition and renewal. Temperature controls the innate energies that produce the pulsations that punctuate and control all life's processes. These energy pulsations which at one moment dissociate or disconnect, and at another recombine both energy and matter, are the mechanism for creating the countless individualities and qualities that make up life as we know it. Viktor said that the cyclical change of temperature creates the conditions suitable for the evolution of new individual life forms or the renewal of existing ones.

Evolution

Viktor Schauberger recognized that Nature's evolutionary purpose is to facilitate the emergence of higher life forms, to promote greater complexity of interrelationships and to raise the level of consciousness of the higher life forms, all a consequence of the continual refinement of energies.

Viktor showed that highly ordered systems lose their stability when their environment suffers deterioration. He predicted that a decrease of biodiversity in Nature would bring an increase in violence and a degeneration of spiritual qualities in the human community.

We think of evolution in terms of technological development. But if one aspect of potentiality is developed at the expense of the others, you end up with an unbalanced person, or even with a monster. This is one of the most important lessons our culture has to learn. It might well apply to the unregulated biotechnology industry. What level of crisis will be required to force us rethink our priorities and change direction?

Balance

Perhaps the most important of Schauberger's insights that we have to heed is the importance of balance in Nature. The nature of some attribute of an organism, its wholeness or unity, is composed of two seemingly opposed qualities in resonant balance. Thus, for example, both egoism and altruism are necessary as human qualities, but for evolution to proceed, altruism must be more in the ascendant. Because our culture has emphasized the coarser qualities, our creative evolution has been arrested, and we have attracted the darker energies of degeneration, with increasing disorder and violence as the outcome.

All the qualities found in Nature have a coarser physical aspect that our worldview attracts, to the discouragement of higher, more subtle energies; we shall be looking at how this impinges on the environment as a whole. In this way Nature's balance is upset, the most obvious being the supremacy today of the more aggressive energies of humankind.

Implosion

Nature's methods of producing energy are silent, but inherently far more effective and powerful than our mechanical techniques, as Schauberger was to prove with his implosion machines that produced prodigious amounts of power. The difference between the two forms of energy production is fundamental to the quality of any process in our world.

Not only does this implosion technology produce much more energy than the 'explosive' methods currently employed, but it creates no waste, pollution, global warming or other damage to Earth's fragile ecosystems. Schauberger invented a number of 'over-unity' machines that produced a substantial excess of power over input. These included means of propulsion for aircraft, submarines, and cars; different devices that produced power, coolness or heat for the home, and invaluable machines for making high quality springwater from polluted water. Unfortunately the working models were destroyed at the end of the Second World War, and his detailed drawings are missing.

His descriptions of these appliances have inspired a number of inventors searching for 'free energy' generation. It seems that no-one has quite succeeded in replicating one of Viktor's, but there are some promising devices ready to go into production. The main obstacles to their introduction include personal harassment from agents of the energy 'establishment,' the lack of imagination by politicians and investors, and the vested interests of the fossil fuel industries, whose lobbying of government is bent on delaying as long as possible the day when people will be able to gain their true independence by producing cheaply their own power needs at home, as Schauberger envisaged.

The visionary

What we have to take on board, as it were, is the extent to which the degraded energies of our present technologies are polluting the world, both from excess heat, but more particularly because they not only block or impede the natural productive and healing energies, but actually encourage degeneration. We can reduce global warming by significant reductions in CO_2 emissions. But we cannot hope for the long-term survival of humanity without ditching our current technology models for those that are wholeheartedly Nature-friendly. Schauberger shows us the way ahead. For example, ecotechnologies are being introduced into the fragile Himalayan ecosystems of Ladakh, as a means of securing economic self-sufficiency for a proud people who are losing their independence in the face of imposed economic exploitation from outside.[3]

Viktor Schauberger came from a background that was rare even a century ago. Several generations of his family had lived in the unspoilt Alpine forests. They understood many of Nature's laws. Viktor's refusal to go to college came from a fear of being indoctrinated, as he believed he would lose both his intuition and his ability to see the magical interconnections within Nature. His natural ability voluntarily to change levels of awareness was the key to his singular discoveries of how Nature works. He was able to enter a more refined state of consciousness, as when he describes how he let his awareness enter the flowing water in a stream, ready to bring back intuitions of what the water required for its health.

This book is *not* about going back to some romantic past, or about discarding science as a discipline, or technology as a means of making our lives more effective. It is about, as Schauberger used to say, "thinking an octave higher." Viktor was a supremely capable scientist, an impeccable observer, a thorough researcher and an inspired inventor. He also predicted, seventy years ago, the climate change disasters that we are now experiencing, and the moral and spiritual collapse of our civilization. But he also, supremely, gave us the keys to reclaiming our heritage as true guardians of Nature and, as we shall see, showed us how to repair the damage we have done to our precious Earth.

2. Different Kinds of Energy

Subtle energies

In the last 200 years, the application of increasingly complex technologies has accelerated enormously, overwhelming the far more subtle energy systems of Nature, with dire consequences for us all. For while some will argue that these have brought benefits to many on the material level, the quality of life on the planet has seriously deteriorated, with severe damage to ecosystems and to biodiversity.

No one explains, as convincingly as Schauberger, just how this has come about. He found that the energy our technology propagates is destructive of the evolutionary impulse in life forms, precipitating a downward spiral in the quality of organisms, and in the human quality of life. Imagine trying to be creative in a steel mill or a slaughterhouse! The pride we hold for our Machiavellian machines that pour out incessant noise and heat is based on the mistaken belief that we represent the summit of evolution.

Schauberger pointed out that, besides having the ego-centred need to control, modern science sees only the surface of things.[1] Its reductionist (everything in separate compartments) and materialistic agenda prevents an understanding of the energetic processes which, as Schauberger demonstrated, are essential for any material substance to come into being; in the same way that an idea or impulse must precede any human action. These subtle energies are essential to the increasing quality Nature demands in her evolutionary process. When these are subdued, only deterioration can result, which inevitably also affects human aspirations. So energy is cause, form is effect. An understanding of any creative process is impossible without true awareness of subtle energies.

Schauberger's worldview

Viktor Schauberger took the ancients' view of the Sun as the male inseminator of Earth to create bountiful Nature. But, also like the ancients, he saw Nature as the mirror of the Divine. Following Goethe's eighteenth century view, he conceived of God as a kind of 'Divine Weaver' of the unfolding tapestry of Evolution. It was through this vision that Viktor found common ground also with the Austrian philosopher Rudolf Steiner.

However, he saw the Earth and Nature also as part of a much larger cosmos. The visible Sun is but the kernel, the only visible part, of a much larger sun that, with its radiative body, stretches to the very limits of the solar system. The Earth is within this sun, bathed by the solar wind, spiraling with its sister planets like organs within the same body. Our own bodies too are but kernels of a much broader, invisible self that extends around us, and with which we can feel another's energy.

He was influenced by Theosophical thinking that conceives the Universe as a holistic system, and criticized contemporary thinking that cannot accept our subservience to Nature; he said that this limitation of awareness prevents us accepting our place in the Universe, of which the consciousness we call Nature is a part. This holistic view of all creation is aided by the idea of a hierarchy of energies, from the very finest that are inconceivable to humans, down to the coarse, material energies which dominate contemporary society. Schauberger would refer to these different levels as 'octaves,' but we shall describe them as 'dimensions' or domains.

Why the mystery?

His scientific contemporaries misunderstood Viktor Schauberger because his frame of reference was the subtle energies in Nature, and they hadn't a clue what he was on about. His heightened sensitivities enabled him to be aware of phenomena more subtle than most of us are able to perceive. As this was his *modus operandi*, we need to take a look at this whole question of energies.

Firstly, we need to accept that the worldview of our contemporary culture is that of the material world; that is its reference point. We don't learn about energies at school or at college, other than the purely mechanical or electrical. Any phenomenon that is nonmaterial poses a difficulty for conventional science, for it cannot be described in a manner that is familiar to its discipline. Thoughts and emotions are energies we all experience, but how do we study them in the laboratory, other than their physical effects?

The various forms of effective energy medicine such as acupuncture, homeopathy, cranial osteopathy (and others) are not understood by orthodox medicine and, for that reason, are generally dismissed and usually opposed. It is not sufficient to see that acupuncture works; or that most people are intuitive. If you can't explain it, then modern knowledge says it must be bogus. We are not talking about religion, beliefs or values, but about things that actually happen on a nonmaterial level.

Earlier cultures acknowledged the tremendous power of immaterial life-energies. The life force (*Ch'i*) that moves along the energy meridians in the human body was recognized by the Chinese several thousand years ago. To correct bioenergetic imbalances or blockages in the body, they developed acupuncture at that time, a treatment still widely used in China and now also in many Western countries by accredited practitioners and by some more open-minded physicians.

While the life sciences, for the most part, are still imprisoned in the mechanistic view of life, the physical sciences are undergoing a revolution. The study of sub-atomic phenomena has led to the development of quantum physics, in which the environment becomes unpredictable. The boundaries between energy and matter become blurred, so that the smallest constituents of matter — particles and electrons — are interchangeable. Matter becomes energy, which leads to the conclusion that everything is energy.[2] Sadly the rigid boundaries that have developed between different scientific disciplines have as yet denied these insights to the life sciences and to medicine.

As there is nowhere intellectually respectable to slot in these 'anomalous' phenomena, new labels have to be found, like 'energy medicine' or 'alternative science.' Schauberger was a pioneer of alternative science, which pushes the boundaries of what is worthy of study beyond the merely physical.

Degrees of energy

We know the ways in which energy manifests itself. We can see that flowing water is energetic. We can see that energy is associated with creating clouds. Energy is active in an engine combusting gasoline or petrol. But what is its essence, a process that always seems to be connected with movement?

When we look up at the fluffy clouds on a summer's day, we may wonder what they're made of. So wispy and light, each cloud may contain hundreds or thousands of tons of tiny individual droplets of water, invisible and in constant motion. A collection of minute, invisible, weightless things becomes large and visible. It's a question of density. Our entire universe forms in the same way.

A material object consists of billions of atoms, each composed of sub-atomic particles, each of which is a vortex of energy. Gyrating around each other in vortices, the sub-atomic particles form heavier particles of energy that become denser, eventually slowing down to the point where they may become visible or even tangible.

Water is a substance that appears in different forms according to its compactness. In its solid state, as ice, its atomic particles move the most slowly. As the ice melts, they move faster, need more space to gyrate or vibrate, creating the less dense form, liquid water. Heated up, the particles accelerate, requiring more space, and become steam or the invisible gas, water vapour. Their state and appearance differ, depending on their expression of energy as movement or vibration, and its rate of motion is called its frequency. The principles of vibration and frequency determine the countless energy forms in our world.

The material substance we see is the result of energy setting up a visible 'blur' by vibrating in and out of a physical state, with a frequency and density that makes it seem like a static whole. The forms create an illusion of being solid and static, caused by countless particles constantly accelerating and then slowing down enough for us to see them as matter. When you see that all material objects are composed of atoms and particles in constant motion, it becomes possible to understand that *everything is energy*.

The vortex as the key to creative evolution

The vortex is a window between different qualities or levels of energy. Black Holes can be thought of as vortices linking different parts of our universe or even different universes. The vortex and spiral became hallmarks for Viktor Schauberger, as for him they were the key to all creative movement. As we shall demonstrate later, the vortex is most clearly seen with water, which it uses to purify and energize itself, introducing finer energies to wipe clean the bad energies of the water's previous memory of misuse.

One could use the metaphor of a musty room that feels stale and unwelcoming. Once sunlight and fresh air are allowed to penetrate, the unpleasant atmosphere is quickly transformed. It is a natural law that the more refined energy always prevails over the coarser.[3] As Viktor Schauberger demonstrated, Nature's evolutionary imperative is continually to refine and to create greater complexity and diversity, the vortex being the key process in this endeavour.

Energies as creative process

We normally think of energy as the power to do work, as to be able to run across a busy street. But thought is also energy. For the human, creativity is dependent on thought. Between having an idea and our wish to see it fulfilled lies a complex creative process.

If I want to make an apple pie, there is first the idea, then the planning, translating this through visualization and then finally the physical creation of the pie. This is much more important than we realize. From the simplest task like tying your shoelace, to the complex challenge of becoming a tennis champion, the better the 'mind pictures' of how we are going to perform the required actions, the more successful will be the outcome. The force, the impulse, which is the motivator for us to create, is an unseen energetic process.

Viktor Schauberger shows us that we need to think of energy in Nature as the potential for creation, not as a mechanical working process. He criticized our present view of how Nature works as untenably mechanistic, which he said this is one of the main reasons why we're in such a mess. Our culture thinks of Nature as being like a big machine that can be manipulated and its resources extracted for our own greed, rather than a creative system that has a purpose.

Productive energies make it possible for life forms to arise that are appropriate to the needs of the environment. It is as if Nature has a blueprint for what is required for a balanced and diversified community. For example, a healthy river that is carrying energized water will create on its banks trees that it needs to keep it cool and protect its vitality.

James Lovelock and Lynn Margulis recognized this creativity by naming the Earth 'Gaia' after the classical Earth goddess. They described how the Earth behaves like an organism, and how the conditions for life on our planet are maintained within very narrow limits, in spite of the enormous variation in the Sun's radiation, and the effect of harmful cosmic rays. This seems to work in a similar way to the self-regulating system in the human body that maintains the blood temperature in the narrow range essential for health (around +37°C/98.4°F). A mechanistic scientist would insist that this is just a computer function, but computers don't operate with purpose and meaning.

Spiritual science

To say that purpose and meaning are more to do with belief or religion is, I believe, a mistaken view. Purpose can be ascribed to living systems. Watch a community of bees at work, and there is a significant purpose! Meaning is usually associated with sentient beings. Being creatively human is difficult without a sense of meaning in one's life. Schauberger didn't talk much about God, but as we shall see he recognized in the extraordinary fecundity of Nature, and indeed in all of her processes, an indisputable sense of meaning and purpose. If it makes more sense to you, call it 'spiritual' science.

It is not necessary to postulate a God that created every living thing and who is behind all the subtle energies in Nature. Probably the idea, found in so many religions, of God as a being like superman whose support can be called on for your little or big power plays is in much the same category as that of regarding Earth's resources as private property for exploitation. The concept of co-creation — that all of creation participates in and contributes to the creative process, is often more acceptable to the thoughtful searcher.

We are clearly influenced by the beliefs of the culture into which we are born. The worldview of contemporary Western society represents an enormous shift away from what has been the norm of human experience over its half million or so years on the Earth. The clearest modern examples of a more 'normal' worldview are the Buddhist beliefs, the Celtic, and those of the indigenous peoples worldwide who share the idea that the Great Spirit (or God) inspires and inhabits the rocks, the waters, and all living things.

In our detachment from the complete or 'real' world, we assume that it is normal to divide different 'bits' of knowledge into separate compartments or 'disciplines.' In fact it is quite abnormal. For traditional peoples, there are no barriers between cosmology, science and the spiritual, for in the interconnectedness of all Nature there is no separation; all is One.

Different dimensions

Viktor Schauberger didn't write about hierarchies of energy, but we know that he subscribed to Theosophical or Eastern concepts of energies, so we shall give an outline of these in order to understand where he was coming from.

Our physical spacetime dimension contains that spectrum of energy that vibrates at a rate low enough to support material form. This Third Dimension or domain has length, breadth and height, but it also has the three components by which humans may be conscious. These are: the physical, neutral energy through which the material world exists; the emotional, negative energy by which we receive sensory information; and the mental, positive energy by which we project our beliefs and personalities into the world. (NB: The terms negative and positive are used not in a qualitative sense, but more in the electrical sense of polarity.)

Our daily lives demonstrate the differences between these energies. The mental is the most changeable; it is harder to change our feelings, and the dense, physical form is almost impossible to change. If we move into a lower dimension, we lose one aspect of consciousness, and if we move higher, we gain one. Moving from the third to the second dimension, we lose the ability to generate original thought. Moving from the third to the fourth, we add the ability to mould time.[4]

In terms of the pure physicality of our three-dimensional world, our consciousness places and senses each lower dimension as being

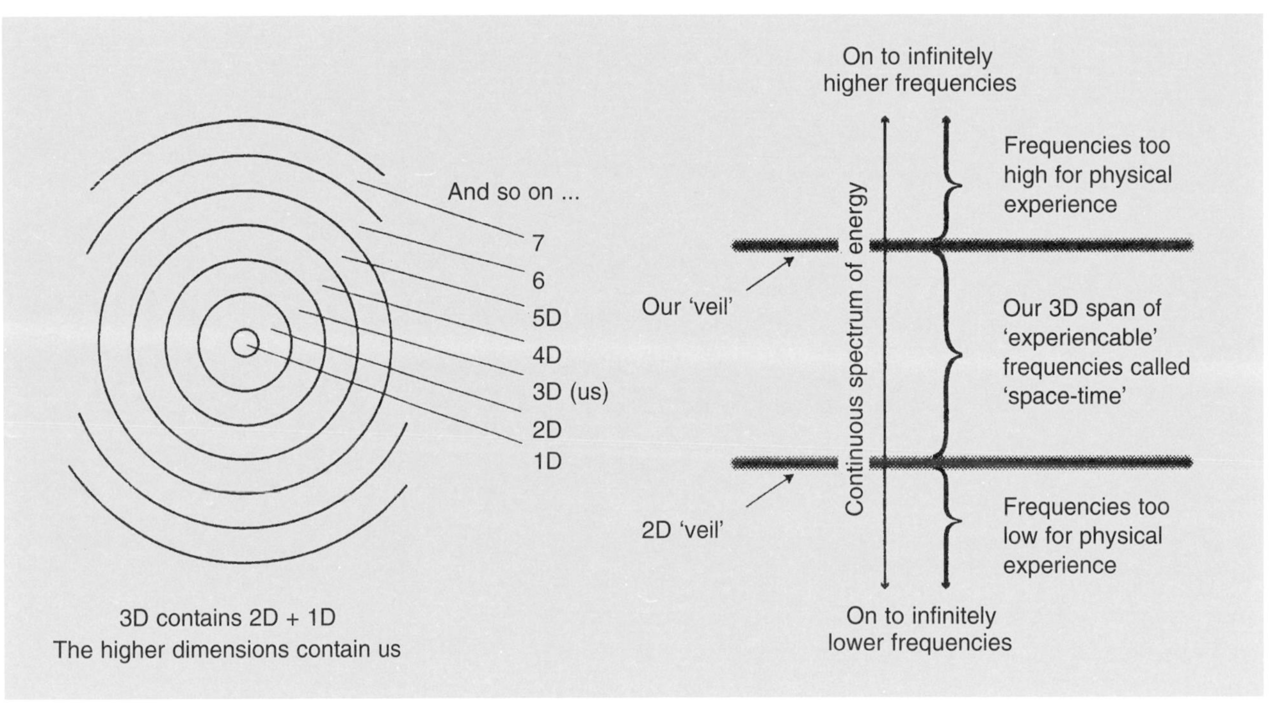

Fig.2.1. Different Dimensions or Levels of Existence.
Each dimension has a 'veil' at its upper limit which renders higher levels inaccessible. To a lesser extent someone of a 'lower' state of consciousness may be unaware of another in a 'higher state.'

external to the body, although, paradoxically, it is both within and without, and permeated by the higher one (see Fig. 2.1).[5]

Intuitive or inspired creativity, the level of expanded consciousness sometimes reached by inventors or by people of great vision, belongs to the fifth and sixth dimensions. It is apparent that Viktor Schauberger had the ability to tap into this reservoir of inspiration. All subtle dimensions are present on Earth, interpenetrating the third dimension, though we are not normally conscious of them.[6] The other animals or humans with raised consciousness have a wider range of perception. A close relationship with a dog, cat or horse often reveals instances where the animal is aware of a non-physical 'presence' which is beyond our own awareness or which may be a spirit presence. If we lower our consciousness, we feel less ability to control our own lives. If all our three components of consciousness are being fully used, then we can experience the full potential of being human, which is the gift of free will.

We shall not discuss in detail here the important energy shifts that are occurring on our planet at this time. In line with the idea that God, or the All-That-Is, seeks constant evolution or expansion of consciousness, ancient teaching has long predicted that the Earth and all its inhabitants would graduate from the third to the fourth dimension in these times. Human society is becoming increasingly polarized between the materialist-based (third dimension) power structures that are reluctant to release their control, and those who wish to participate in a fairer and more spiritually based society.[7]

Changing octaves

When Viktor Schauberger said, "We must think an octave higher," (if we are to get out of this mess), one tends to think he means being less taken in by the physical view of life, and become more aware of its subtle aspects. While that is true, he did propose an interesting way of illustrating the concept of how a particular kind of energy can be taken up one octave. On the face of it, the following may be considered contradictory, but a more interesting view is to see them as complementary or reciprocal energies an octave apart, one a development of the other (like thesis and antithesis), which, when combined are reconciled and become a unity:[8]

lower octave		*higher octave*	
Matter	*x*	*Spirit*	*= unity*
Egoism	x	Altruism	*(= unity)*
Analysis	x	Synthesis	*(= unity)*
Heat	x	Cold	*(= unity)*
Gravitation	x	Levitation	*(= unity)*
Electricity	x	Magnetism	*(= unity)*
Bioelectricism	x	Biomagnetism	*(= unity)*
Pressure	x	Suction	*(= unity)*
Expansion	x	Impansion	*(= unity)*
Centrifugence	x	Centripetence	*(= unity)*
Oxygen	x	Carbones	*(= unity)*
Yang	x	Yin	*(= unity)*

The second column, the 'antitheses,' being more refined, have the potential to contribute to creative evolution by being able to bridge the gap between the idea and manifestation. They are, if you like, endowed with special vibrational energies and powers.

Callum Coats, in translating some of these more difficult concepts from Viktor's German terms, coined his own to describe the different forms of subtle energies from the fourth and fifth dimensions, which collectively he called 'ethericities.' By these he meant the bioelectric, biomagnetic, catalytic, high-frequency, vibratory, super-potent elements of quasi-material qualities:

> These ethericities are further categorized as 'fructigens,' 'qualigens' and 'dynagens.' They respectively represent those subtle energies whose function is the enhancement of fruitfulness (fructigens), the generation of quality (qualigens) and the amplification of immaterial energy (dynagens). According to their function or location these may be female or male in nature. There are thus female fructigens and male dynagens, for example."[9]

We shall be using these terms from time to time where they are helpful.

3. The Attraction and Repulsion of Opposites

The Sun as a fertilizing entity

We all know that sexual reproduction requires insemination of the female by the male but, according to Viktor Schauberger, the Earth works on the same principle. From Nature's point of view, this starts with the Sun. Throughout nearly all of humanity's time on this planet, the Earth has been regarded a sacred being, the Great Mother. The Sun held an equally significant place in our forebears' worldview. Most of the ancient cultures regarded the Sun as the primary, masculine deity, fertilizing the Earth in order to create life. The eighteenth century thinker, Johann Wolfgang von Goethe referred to Earth's creative spirit as the 'Eternally Female' and the 'All-uplifting' (or levitating).

Viktor Schauberger uses explicit sexual terms to explain this vital natural process. He talks of the Sun impregnating Mother Earth in order to create the incalculable number of different life-forms that inhabit this planet. The Sun behaves very much as a living body. It is known to pulsate rhythmically, its surface expanding and contracting 3km (1.8 miles) every 160 minutes. Its life-giving energies warm the atmosphere and penetrate deep into the ground to inseminate the elements and substances of the Earth (the sleeping princess). The beneficial UVc rays[1] which the ozone layer allows through, have to decelerate in order to unite with the receptive and passive female energies rising inside the Earth; these slower energies have to accelerate, for fertilization can take place only if the two resonate with a sympathetic rate of vibration (see Chapter 4).

All of life, from the gross material to the ethereally subtle, evolves through the interaction of male and female, positive and negative, energies. Each polarity has a particular manner of expression, the downwardly-radiating solar energy meeting the Earth at right angles to the energies of the Earth ranged in a layer below the surface (see Fig. 3.1). Their properties and potentialities are opposite, but complementary, to each other. The manner in which these polarized energies

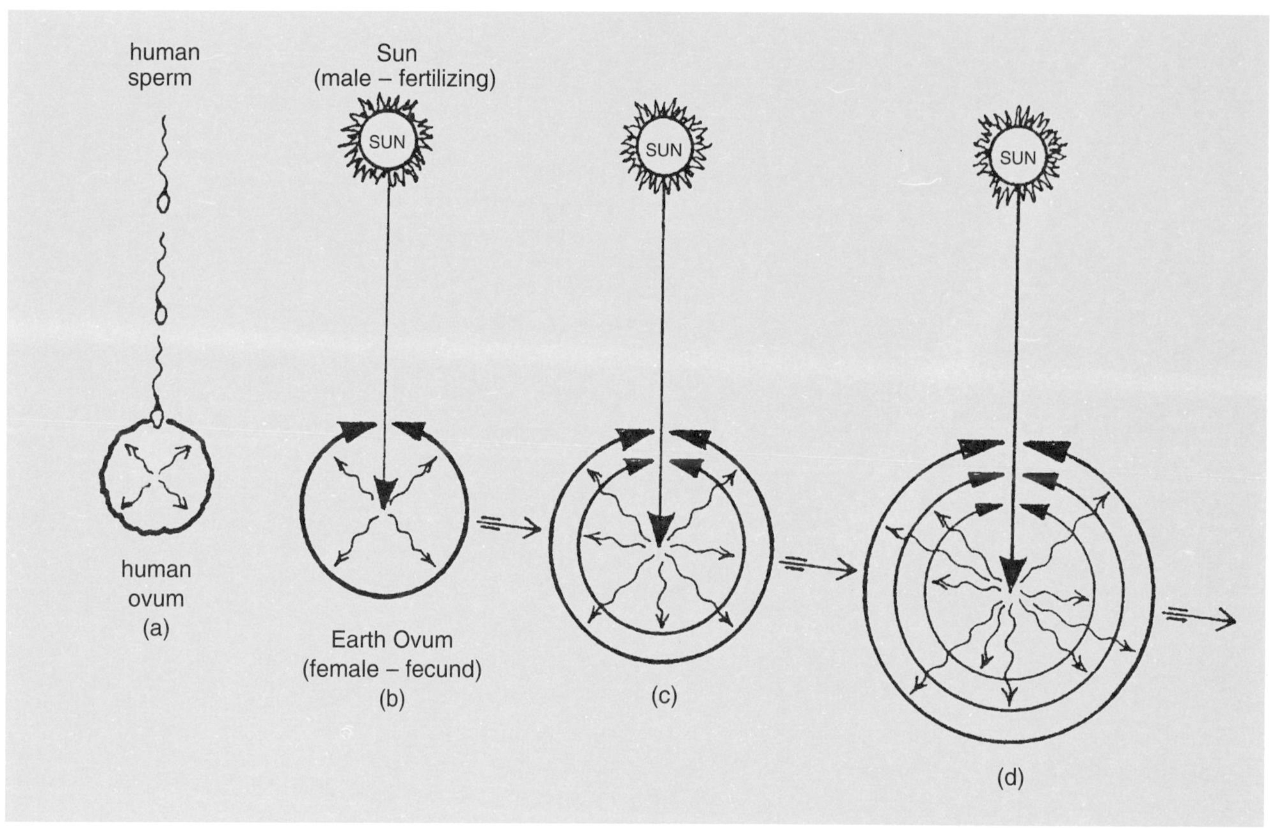

Fig.3.1. Cosmic Fertilization. *Schauberger saw the fertilization of Earth by the Sun as a similar process to human fertilization. The Earth responds to the Sun's energy by releasing propagating energies (the concentric circles) which become more developed and complex as evolution proceeds.*

interact alternate between attraction and repulsion, which sets up a pulsation which will vary according to the season.

In winter when the Sun's energy has the most blue and ultraviolet light and the Earth is passive, with low temperatures in the cold winter sunlight, the vegetation is dormant and much animal life hibernates. It is then that fertilization, reproduction and growth are at a minimum, but the solar energies continue to penetrate deep into the Earth to awaken the embryonic female energies lying far below the surface. This union produces the prolific growth of springtime.

In spring and summer however, when the Sun's radiation becomes relatively stronger, the balance between the ultraviolet and the infrared shifts towards the red end of the spectrum. This awakens the Earth, whose energy interacts with the Sun's high-frequency energy, producing a third kind of energy, which is dynamic growth. Viktor Schauberger saw this as the discharged precipitates of higher, bipolar subtle energy. In the summer months the solar energies fuse with their female opposites in the higher strata near the surface of the Earth. This repeated process of impregnation results in an almost continuous flow of fertile energies emanating from deep in the Earth to stimulate burgeoning growth.

Viktor grouped almost all the known elements and their compounds, with the exception of oxygen and hydrogen, under the general classification of 'female.' The exceptions were silver, zinc and silicon, which were considered to have paternally-oriented characteristics, while gold, copper and limestone were regarded as more maternal (these will be discussed in more detail in Chapter 17). Schauberger used the term 'carbones' for all these elements, (the extra 'e' meaning more than just 'carbon'), because of the prevalence of various sorts of carbonous matter in the multitude of living organisms created in the body of Mother Earth.

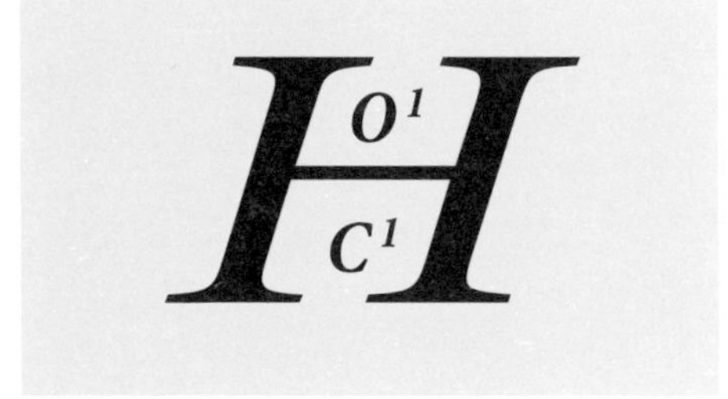

Fig.3.2. Hydrogen Symbol.
Hydrogen as the 'carrier' of both carbone and oxygen.

The Sun's energy, of course, is regarded as male, and Viktor saw oxygen as a lower form of solar energy. Together, the role of the Sun and its assistant oxygen is to fertilize these female, propagative energies, the Sun being responsible for all of life, and oxygen for organic growth and development. To hydrogen, Viktor gave a special role, as the carrier substance of both oxygen and carbone (see Fig. 3.2 above). From a detached view, far outside the atmosphere, our planet, composed of carbones and fertilized by oxygen, is indeed floating in the hydrogen gas ocean of space.

The words 'matter' and 'material,' both have their root in the Latin word *mater*, meaning mother, which supports the idea that physical substance is feminine in nature. Thus all the physical elements (except for oxygen and hydrogen) can be seen as the maternal progenitive constituents of 'Mother-Earth.' Viktor Schauberger visualized all physical structures and all new living entities coming into being through the union between these 'mother-substances' and the inseminating agent of oxygen.

Polarities

Viktor Schauberger used to call polarity Nature's engine. He once described the harmonious interplay of the attraction and repulsion of polarized atoms as "the dance of creation". Electricity depends on the positive and negative charge of electrons. Magnetism expresses the polarities of attraction and repulsion. Polarities also apply in biological terms, of course, where balance is achieved between contrasting qualities, and of course between different sexes.

Without the attraction and repulsion of atoms there would be no water, no plants, nor chemical compounds. The mutual attraction of 2 x H and 1 x O gives birth to the marvel of water.

We are more familiar with the terms 'positive' and 'negative' than 'male' and 'female' in scientific contexts; as, for example, with electricity. Of course, positive and negative in this sense are not judgmental terms, but opposite poles. Schauberger felt that to use the terms masculine and feminine was more in keeping with Nature, which he saw as a living organic system.

Opposites working towards balance

We tend to think of Nature as being chaotic. The reverse is true. Schauberger discovered that Nature operates according to very strict laws. One of the most important is that concerned with the balance between energy polarities, each of which has its particular manner of expression. Masculine and feminine together make up a complete human being; one cannot exist without the other, and each needs the other to be whole. You might think that to be in balance, masculine and feminine energies need to be about 50/50, as they nearly are with the distribution of the human sexes.

For the last three thousand or so human society has functioned in a predominantly masculine mode and is now quite out of balance. If you consider masculine energy to be represented by rationality, concern with the physical, forceful, expansive and individualistic; and the feminine by a tendency to be inclusive, intuitive, connecting and compassionate — then most will agree we need a swing of the pendulum towards the latter.

The natural law about balance is that it must be weighted towards the feminine for creative growth to proceed. Otherwise growth (in terms of higher quality) is arrested, and degeneration takes place. This applies to all the qualities, like:

matter and energy or spirit
chaos and order
yang and yin
positive and negative (not in judgmental terms, more electrical)
egoism and altruism
quantity and quality (a confusion of our present society)

And then in the more technical areas of life-building energies which we will cover in the relevant chapters:

gravitation and levitation
electricity and magnetism
oxygen and carbones
centrifugence and centripetence
negative temperature gradient and positive temperate gradient

What is the correct proportion by which the negative should dominate? Ancient Chinese society was very much taken up with these questions, and they believed the ratio of the correct balance was three-fifths to two-fifths (60%). Viktor Schauberger, who worked very intuitively, particularly on the temperature gradients in water, came up with two-thirds to one-third (66.7%). Callum Coats, who worked with Viktor's son Walter, a mathematician and physicist, related the proportion to the sacred geometric ratio of ϕ (*phi*) which is 1.618, which gives the negative share of 61.8%.

The interaction and combination of opposites is found throughout all natural processes. It is true of heat and cold. The crucial interplay of heat and cold is found in many life-forms. Some types of fruit and seeds cannot germinate properly unless they have been exposed to frost. Brussels sprouts are best after the first frost! Growth is dependent on the right combination of heat and cold.

There is, however, no such thing as stable equilibrium, which would bring immobility and uniformity with which evolution would be impossible. Development and evolution in the dynamic Universe depend on an inherent imbalance, since movement is always occurring somewhere between one extreme and the other.

Gravity and levity

Gravity is recognized as a powerful physical force in the Cosmos. However, Viktor Schauberger demonstrated that its opposite, levity, is tremendously important in Nature. That levity is not acknowledged by conventional science presumably has to do with its being one of these more subtle energies which are anathema to the reductionist mindset. Without levitation, fish would have great difficulty swimming upstream in a strong current, and we would not have majestic trees reaching for the heavens; only ground-hugging species.[2] Levitation force may indeed be related to these female subtle energies spiralling upwards to the Earth's surface in their desire for fertilization.

Levitation has much greater potential power than gravity, much as suction does over pressure. Schauberger used this to great effect in his implosion machines, as we shall see later. Levitation can best described as the life-force present in all healthy living things, particularly the more youthful, which gives a feeling of lightness and of relative weightlessness. It gradually weakens with age, so that the elderly become conscious of the weight of their bodies and the greater difficulty of movement. When this levitational force withdraws, so too does the life-force of the body.

4. Nature's Patterns and Shapes

The essence of the Gaia principle is that all life is interconnected. Nature is a conscious system in which all phenomena or happenings affect everything in their environment — the micro-environment for a small incident, or the whole world in the case of a major event. Life forms in Nature respond to each other by means of resonance; you might call it 'Gaia's glue.' When you say someone has 'good' or 'bad vibes,' you're talking the language of resonance; flowers attracting insects by their colour and scent, our response to certain kinds of music, the practice of *feng shui* in the home; monks chanting, bees humming.

Resonance is the language of communication and response. It is how energetic information is transferred from one object to another. It is also the mechanism of harmony. For example, the organs and cells in the human body vibrate each at its specific frequency, and in the healthy body they resonate in harmony like the different instruments of an orchestra. Water, as the principal constituent of and the bringer of life to all organisms, is the most powerful carrier of resonance.

Sound as resonance

Every musician knows that a tuning fork of the note C struck in a concert hall will make any number of C tuning forks respond in the same space. When you rub your finger round the rim of a wine glass, its note will sound. If a singer finds this note, the glass will resonate in sympathy, or even shatter if the vibration becomes too strong.

Sound is probably the most ancient form of resonance in the human experience. Jericho was reputedly destroyed by destructive sound resonances. There are accounts in oral traditions of how early societies, such as the ancient Egyptian, the Tibetan and the Inca employed the use of sound to levitate enormous blocks of stone used in their buildings. Music itself is a more than a paradigm of Nature's resonances. For millennia people have sung and played music to their crops, their lovers and their children. Schauberger describes how the Alpine farmers while stirring the fertilizing liquid would sing into it (see p. 230).

Callum Coats cites:

> Research carried out by Dr John Diamond in the field of behavioral kinesiology (BK), yields some interesting insights.[1] A member of the International Academy of Preventive Medicine, Dr Diamond found that while the deltoid muscle of a healthy adult male can normally resist a force of 40–45lbs, its strength is reduced to 10–15lbs through the negative effect of certain types of rock music, such as heavy metal and hard rock.[2]
>
> In contrast to a more natural rhythm, where the beat emulates that of the heart, with emphasis on the first beat, i.e. DA-da-da or 'LUB dup rest,' as he puts it, in the above type of music this emphasis is reversed, i.e. da-da-DA, which conflicts with the body's natural pulsation and in poetry is known as an "anapestic beat." As Dr.Diamond states: 'one of the characteristics of the anapestic beat is that it is stopped at the end of each bar or measure. Rock music that has this weakening effect appears to have this stopped quality; it is as if the music stops and then has to start again, and the listener subconsciously "comes to a halt" at the end of each measure. The anapestic beat is the opposite of the dactylic or waltz like beat, which is DA-da-da, and in which there is an even flow.'[3]

Dr Diamond further asserts that:

> these forms of music and unnatural rhythms cause switching in the brain's responses, which induces 'subtle perceptual difficulties' that may well manifest themselves in children as decreased performance in school, hyperactivity and restlessness; in adults as decreased work output, increased errors, general inefficiency, reduced decision-making capacity on the job, ... in short, the loss of energy, for no apparent reason.

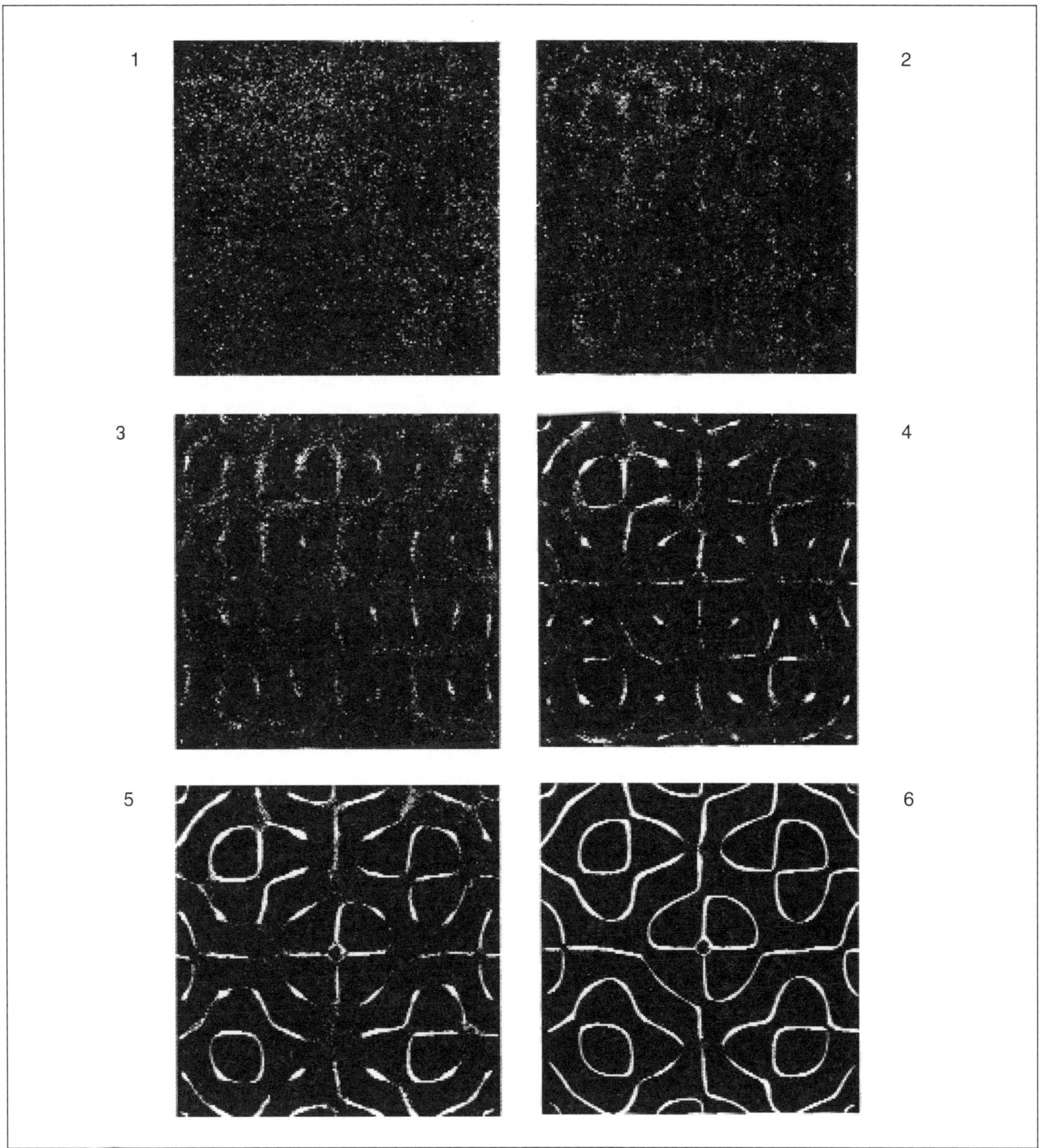

Fig.4.1. Sonorous Figure. *The photographs show a simple sonorous figure taking shape under the action of crystal oscillators. Steel plate 31 x 31 cm; thickness 0.5 mm; frequency 7560cps. The material scattered on the plate is calcined sand.*

Thus a given physical structure is created by an idea dependent on a particular frequency level or pattern of vibrations or resonances, higher vibrations producing higher forms and vice versa.

As we survey the world around us today this is precisely what appears to be happening — the quantitative thrust of our technology and ideology is pressing downwards towards uniformity, to a vibrationless state, which is equivalent to zero energy and quality (see Fig. 5.1 on p. 78). Thus species after species is disappearing simply because the prevailing creative energy pool available for qualitative evolution is absent. If we may imagine that all that can be preserved is what remains, we forget that Nature has her own urge to proceed with evolution.

What is required of us is to purge our technology's production of so much debased energy. This would create positive feedback into human consciousness, raising its level, which would produce an outflow of positive, creatively potentiated energy, creating a swing towards the negative or feminine in society (see Chapter 3, p.52).

An urgent swing from carbon-based energy production to renewable sources is vital if global warming is gradually to level off. Schauberger believed that this would help restore the energy balance towards Nature's need for dynamic evolution. But it is not the whole answer; only a radical change of consciousness so that we recognize our sacred role as part of Nature and begin to follow her laws can bring about a new way ahead for Nature and the planet.

Resonance is about qualities

As we saw in Chapter 2, all matter, though it may look solid and stationary, is based on sub-atomic particles that are always in motion.[4] The velocity of this motion determines its vibratory rate; this and the type and size of the object contribute to its vibrational frequency. A piece of wood, and each of the organs in our bodies have different resonant frequencies; planet Earth has its own — a frequency of 7.83Hz (Hertz). Every thing, both animate and apparently inanimate has its own vibrational or resonant frequency that can be enhanced by sympathetic vibrations, or harmed by destructive.

There is increasing evidence of the harmful effects on human health from the ceaseless bombardment of the body's very sensitive, electrically charged cells by the veritable salad of electromagnetic emissions from high-tension cables, radio, television, radar, microwave transmitters, etc.

A very tragic example of this was publicized by the media in the summer of 2001.[5] The navies of several countries, notably the US and Britain, have developed sonar technology for hunting submarines. This involves using massive blasts of sound up to 230 decibels which have been blamed for several mass killings and strandings of marine mammals, notably in the Bahamas in 2000 when at least seventeen Cuvier's beaked whales are known to have died.

Post mortem examination showed that sonar killed them through resonance, a process in which air bubbles in water can amplify sound waves by up to 25 times. When whales dive the air is forced out of their lungs into the tiny air spaces around the brain. Harmful resonance in these air spaces is believed to cause massive tissue damage and hemorrhaging, so that injuries can occur at much lower sound levels and over a much larger area than is presently acknowledged.

The rules that the US navy scientists follow are based on old-fashioned physical science which puts the safe noise level below 180 decibels, and the safe distance below 2.2 km (1.4 miles). There is now evidence that resonance effects could injure whales up to 100 km (62 miles) away.

Plants have perception and memory

Cleve Backster was a former CIA interrogator who trained police in the use of the polygraph, or lie detector. One of their techniques was the use of 'threat to wellbeing' to evoke emotionality in suspects. In a spontaneous experiment, he attached the electrodes of the instrument to a plant. In considering what a plant would regard as a threat, he thought of applying a burning match to a leaf. Without even moving, only his thought alone triggered a strong response in the plant.[6]

Subsequent experiments, which were then widely repeated by different researchers, showed that plants are able to communicate or 'resonate' their shocked or pleasurable experiences to one another. Backster describes how he tried to block whatever signals were being passed between plants with a variety of complex screens, without success, suggesting that their signals are outside our electromagnetic spectrum. One of the hazards of this research is that unless the researcher is truly aware of his/her own emotional states, these can confuse the results. Perhaps every scientist who wishes to produce 'objective' results should go on a course to make him/her more aware of their prejudices! There is probably no such thing as truly objective research. (The same could be said for anyone whose work brings them into a role influential with others.)

Backster's best known experiment excluded the human factor. Live brine shrimps were dumped in boiling water automatically at pre-determined intervals, near the plants which reacted 'emotionally' each time the massacre took place. Not only do plants respond as if they had a nervous system, but they also exhibit a capacity for memory. As we shall see later, water also has this memory facility. With specially adapted equipment, 'emotional' reactions have also been monitored from amoebas, blood samples and cell cultures. Experimenting with fertilized eggs, it was found that when one egg was broken others, even in the next room, responded with shock.

Societies with ancient roots still celebrate this knowledge, as in the kosher quietening rituals, prior to the sacrifice of animals, or in the blessing of crops before they are harvested. This is more than consideration for the sacrifice, for it also recognizes that the food thereby retains higher vibrations and is more beneficial for human consumption.

Cymatics

One of the first to convert vibration into visible form was an eighteenth century German physicist, Ernst Chladni, who found he could influence patterns of sand scattered on a steel disc by playing different notes on a violin. This was developed last century by Hans Jenny of Zurich, using sophisticated equipment with liquids, plastics, metal filings and powders.[7] He then vibrated the discs at ascending pitch, and found that the harmonic patterns that appeared at different pitches formed a variety of organic shapes: spirals of jellyfish turrets, concentric rings of tree growth, tortoiseshell patterns or zebra stripes, pentagonal stars of sea-urchins, hexagonal cells of honeycombs, etc. The higher the frequency, the more complex the pattern. Jenny also produced a stunning film which shows that raising the pitch of sound caused a static pattern to change into a moving one.

All of these were, of course, the same geometric and vortical forms which underlie the ordering of physical matter; thus 'inorganic' matter vibrated simply with sound produces 'organic' shapes. But what is intriguing is that the sand collects on the 'dead' areas of the plate, for the 'life' of the pattern is vibrating on the background that is free of sand. The paradox is that the visible expression of energy is the inverse of the actual vibratory pattern, which is invisible. Organic growth and development require harmony. Resonance is the process by which harmony is brought to lower systems which then provide a firm basis upon which higher structures may be built.

One is reminded that the early Christian Gnostics insisted that the physical world is but a shadow or shell of a supreme ordering energy that exists in another dimension. Schauberger also saw the physical form like a discarded mantle or energetic detritus, the creative energy of the fifth dimension having been spent. Callum Coats saw the resonant pattern associated with a life form as the seed bearing the image or idea of what is to be created. He argued that all physical manifestation develops as the product of focused energy from the 'Will-to-create' or original 'Source.'

Patterns and shapes

Patterns are to do with order; with design and structure. Nothing can come into being without a design or template. The patterns in Nature are governed by laws that oral tradition tells were the gift of the gods (perhaps a rationalization of a chicken-and-egg situation!). Holistic or spiritual science sees Nature as a mirror of the original creative impulse in the Universe, a manifestation of the Universal Mind, or The-All-That-Is.

Our science, since the Renaissance, has been searching for immutable Laws that help to explain how the natural world works. Because the territory it observes is limited to the physical, conventional science rejects the idea of a cosmic order that affects the Earth and its inhabitants at a subtle energetic level, which frustrated Schauberger. He demonstrated that a new science that has more in common with ancient wisdom does show how the world is subservient to cosmic laws, creating 'correspondences' between the two orders.

Until comparatively recent times, scientists and philosophers recognized the creative energy of Nature as sacred. They saw the way in which Nature's patterns and its complex interdependences were so often expressed in very specific shapes and numbers as proof of God at work. So they called these correspondences sacred numbers and sacred geometry. It is certainly difficult to explain away the complex mathematical and symbolic patterns in Nature as purely accidental or fortuitous (see below, p.66).

Patterns in motion

In the beginning was the vortex[8]

All life is motion. Natural movement is not in straight lines, but in spirals, or in spiraling vortices. Spirals are the actual shape of fluid energy evolving order from chaos. Viktor Schauberger saw them as the natural movement of life, from the structure of galaxies down to the atom. The spiral is the most common vehicle for 'correspondences' — as above, so below.

The spiral can develop in a number of different ways: as a vortex, moving upwards or downwards, round in a circle, or doubling back on itself. Whenever there is movement, spirals form, visibly with water; but gases and even electrical fields express themselves in spirals or doughnuts. Sinews, tissues, blood and bones and so many formations in organic life are spiral in form.[9]

Rhythms within the solar system

The relationship between Earth and Moon can be very subtle. Professor Frank Brown of Northwestern University has shown how the 'biological clocks' that initiate cyclical activities like rat-running, and colour change in fiddler crabs are subject to lunar rhythms. His better known experiment involved the shipment in hermetically sealed containers of oysters from the sea shore at New Haven, Connecticut to Evanston, Illinois, 2000 miles inland. Within a couple of weeks they had adjusted the conspicuous rhythm of opening and closing their shells to the lunar tides that would have existed at Evanston had it been on a sea coast.

The terrestrial environment is teeming with electromagnetic phenomena and their secondary effects, which are demonstrably related to greater events in outer space. Dr Harold Burr of Yale University kept extensive records of the voltage changes measured in holes bored in the trunks of trees. When both ends of a wire were inserted into two holes vertically a yard apart, an electrical current could be detected moving either up or down, at different voltages, in regular cycles that were not related to the Moon's phases, but to some other unidentified non-terrestrial source. His records showed that all trees, even hundreds of miles apart, would simultaneously experience the same changes of the voltage and direction of the current. It is as if the whole family of trees responds to the same electrical rhythm, like a cosmic breathing.[10]

It seems that there are universal laws, not yet fully understood, which guide an organism's growth into predetermined patterns. As the vehicle for creative energy, the spiral is clearly involved in the organic growth of plants and embryos. Buds contain all the concentrated energy of the future plant, and their mathematical analysis can yield clues as to how this formative energy is expressed. Rudolf Steiner, the founder of Anthroposophy, initiated these studies, which have been developed in great detail by the projective mathematician Lawrence Edwards.[11]

Edwards discovered that tree buds expand and contract in a curious rhythm, specific to the species. He applied Steiner's theory that a species often has a particular connection to a planet. Steiner suggested correspondences between particular trees and flowers and certain planets, for example, the oak with Mars, and the beech with Saturn. The results clearly showed that these bud pulsations are linked to the cycles of particular planets. The Moon on its own had little effect, but when amplified by an alignment with Saturn (for the beech) and to Mars (in the case of the oak), showed unmistakable fortnightly rhythms. There was one beech tree studied that did not show these phenomena. It was found to be growing a few yards from an electricity supply substation!

The confrontation of two geometric systems

Schauberger was at odds with scientific rationalism. He described our prevailing Euclidean geometric system as 'techno-academic'. It is essentially a controlled, closed system whose elements are the point, the straight line, the circle and the ellipse. This system dominates the contemporary worldview and mindset and is incompatible with Nature.

In more traditional communities, the hard, straight lines of structures were often softened with decorative embellishments, such as are still found on the eaves or rooflines in some Alpine villages. In the last century, ornamentation has been stripped away in architectural design and we are left with buildings that present a naked angularity and sterile uniformity (*cf* agricultural monoculture).

Until modern times the Chinese rejected the Euclidean model. Their building designs were informed by geomantic principles that recognized the straight line as the path of the dragon, the personification of destructive energy. This energy could be tamed by making it flow into curves and spirals. The Chinese understood in those days that straight lines fostered disruptive behaviour. Perhaps it is time to consider what a deadening effect the boxes we inhabit may have on our thoughts and emotions; of how our dependence on the straight line may cause us to behave.

Nature's system is non-Euclidean, open and dynamic; its elements are open spirals forms, shell, egg and vortical forms. This facilitates a fluid and adaptable environment, one in which forms are able to evolve into more complex and creative arrangements. Other creatures, whose sensitivity is nourished by the subtle energies of open forms, make use of roundness and curves in their nests, burrows, and shells. In order to arrest the downward spiral of our culture, we must take note of systems that encourage creative change (see Fig. 5.1, p. 78). Schauberger wished that we could remember that we were created as part of the organic processes of Nature, rather than the mechanical processes that we have adopted.

Sacred geometry

Viktor Schauberger saw patterns and rhythms as the heartbeat of the Universe, and was fascinated by the traditional use of the language of number and form to codify how they are repeated and in what form. It is hard for us, schooled in a rationalist worldview which separates form from the natural order to see that they are part of one whole. The ancients regarded mathematics and geometry as the tools to understand patterns in Nature and in the Universe. The religious leaders of old, who were also the scientists and mathematicians, did not make our mistake of putting different phenomena in separate compartments. To them, the world of matter and reason and the world of spirit and the awareness of God were all one. In the context of myth and symbol, they used numbers and forms in a way that would satisfy the spiritual sense of meaning and the scientific need for structure and reason. Out of this process arose the traditions of numerology and sacred geometry.

In all the ancient cultures, the square symbolized the Earth of matter and rationalization, and the circle the encompassing world of spirit and feeling. How to bring them into balance was called 'squaring the circle' and was the pursuit both of architecture and philosophy. The sum of the sides of the square was equal to the circumference of the circle, so they come into harmony by enclosing the same area. This is sometimes used as a metaphor for the balanced personality. So 'circling the square' indicates someone whose rationality is greater than his/her sense of feeling.

As with other problems in sacred geometry, though it is not possible to draw this relationship by simple measurement, because it is part of the natural order, that is where the solution is to be found — in fact in the relationship of the size of the Moon to the size of the Earth.[12] You draw a square around the circle of the Earth (each side of which will equal the Earth's diameter). Then you draw the Moon on the same scale, sitting on top of the Earth. A circle with its centre as the centre of the Earth, and its circumference passing through the centre of the Moon will have a circumference equal to the sum of the sides of the square enclosing the Earth.

This figure (Fig. 4.2) also contains the 3–4–5 Pythagorean triangle which connects the corners of the Earth and Moon squares. It was from such relationships that the 'Pythagorean canon of proportions' was created. The basics of musical harmony depend on intervals created by these divine proportions. There were canons of architecture, of painting and of musical harmony taught in the medieval mystery schools, and partly revived in the Renaissance.

Fig. 4.2. Squaring the Circle.
Sacred geometry is based on observations of cosmic relationship. The Great Pyramid's base straddles the Earth's equatorial diameter; its apex is at the centre of the Moon, which is in true proportion to the Earth, and held to the square by a Pythagorean 3–4–5 right-angled triangle.

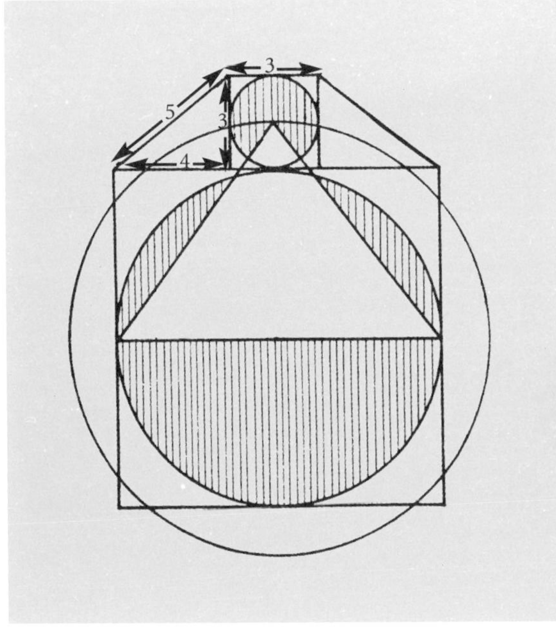

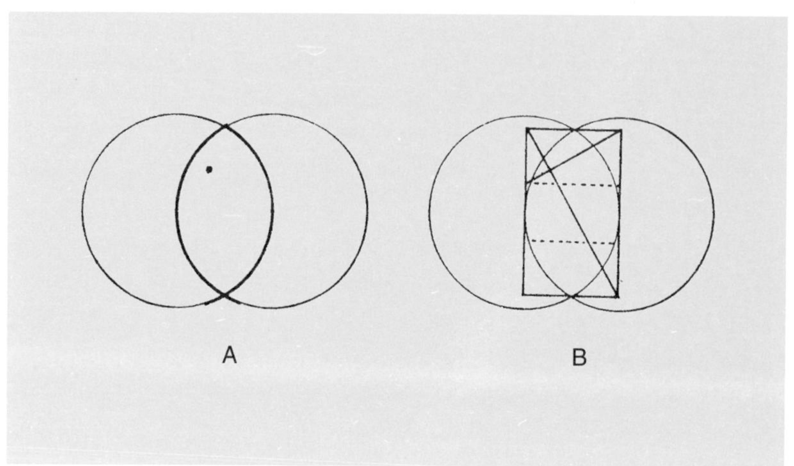

Fig.4.3. Vesica Piscis.
'The Vessel of the Fish' is the simplest and most informative geometrical symbol, being the orifice of two interpenetrating circles which inspired the master masons of the medieval cathedrals. Many Christian symbols, including the fish and the bishop's mitre, have been derived from the vesica. On the left is the fish, whose eye corresponds, on the right, to the geometric 'eye' of the $\sqrt{3}$ rectangle enclosing the vesica.

The golden mean

The search for perfect proportion, a shape for containment that is aesthetically pleasing, led to the discovery of the 'Golden Mean' or $\sqrt{3}$ rectangle. The square is too mechanical, a long rectangle too awkward. The shape that 'seems' to be just right is a square rectangle with the proportions 1:1.618. This turns out to be the magical proportion favoured by Nature in her designs. A series of these, reducing in size, form a perfect spiral, like the nautilus shell (Fig. 4.4).

Spiral forms often display a similar 'sacred' proportion of 1:1.618; numbers in the Fibonacci series, for example, which maintains the Golden mean proportions indefinitely, and dictates the beautiful spirals in a sunflower head, Nature's ingenious way of packing the maximum number of seeds into the head.[13] An intriguing form that arises in Nature, either on its own, or as part of a more complex form, is the *vesica piscis* (Fig. 4.3). It is the feminine principle of generation from which spring all other geometrical forms, from triangles, squares, polygons, to Golden mean rectangles, which abound in sacred architecture.

All the traditional arts and sciences were based on the same cosmic truths expressed in number, and the sacred numbers were the ratios in a revealed world order, drawn from the experience of mystics and confirmed by precise measurements of the solar system. Sacred buildings from Stonehenge to the Temple of Solomon, ancient Egyptian paintings, the works of Michelangelo, all have their magical effects and power over human consciousness attributed to the use of these divine proportions.

The Middle Ages were a time when the physical and the spiritual were completely intertwined, but our histories, based on the rational 'Enlightenment' worldview, regard those centuries as a time of ignorance and deprivation. In fact they were seething with creativity and inspiration: thus the Gothic cathedrals which relied more on an understanding of correct proportion than on reasoned engineering skills. Medieval musicians were fascinated that if you divided an open string by whole numbers, you can get notes that are in exact proportions.[14] They rediscovered the miracles of harmony, and easily accepted them as Divine. This may be the reason for the extraordinary beauty of medieval chants.

The magic of the egg form

We noted in Chapter 1 that Viktor Schauberger was one of a breed of innovative natural scientists who are able to immerse themselves so deeply in direct perception of the natural world that concepts or theories spontaneously emerge. But his intuition also would bring up ideas directly. An example of this was his discovery that Nature

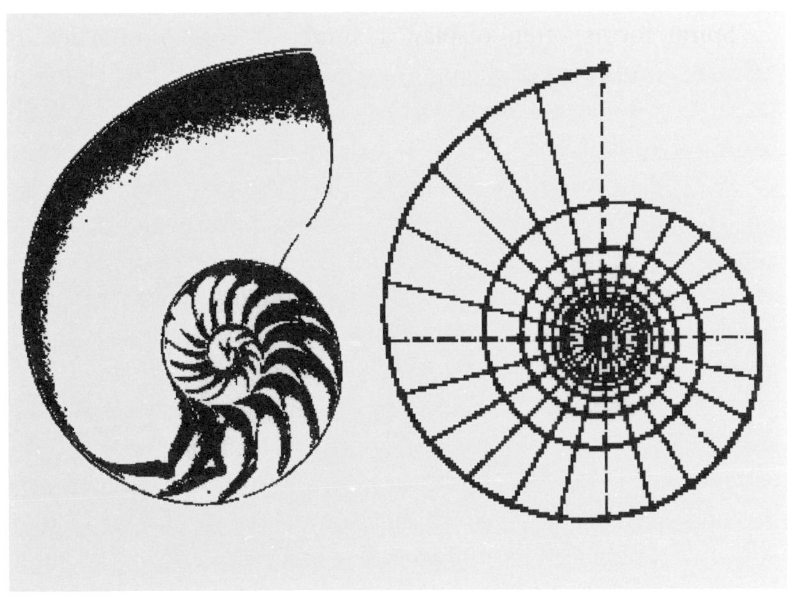

Fig.4.4. Snail Shell & Hyperbolic Spiral. *The spiral of the snail compared to a similarly-shaped hyperbolic spiral (right), a non-Euclidean open system whose constantly changing curvature is based on very precise geometry.*

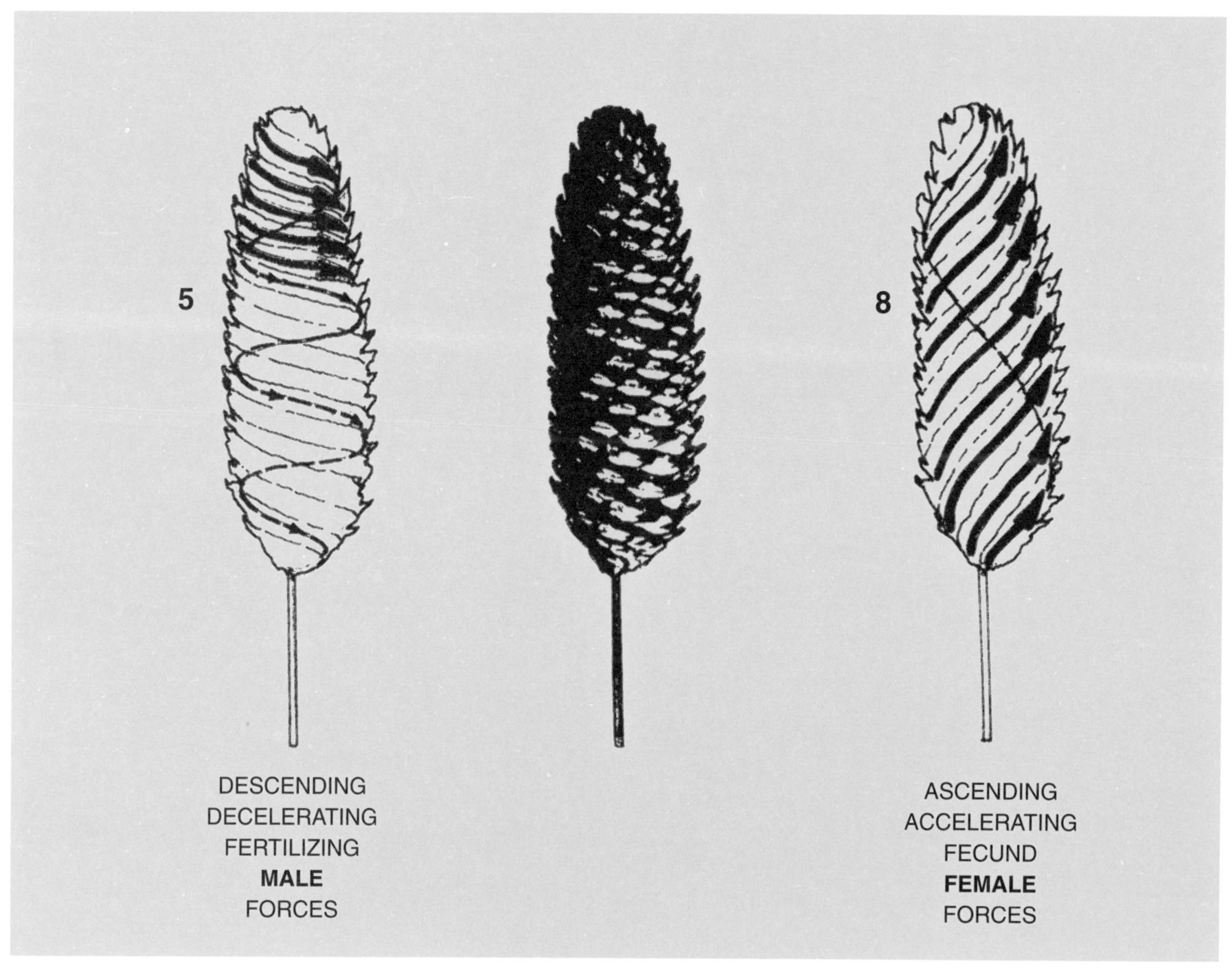

Fig.4.5. Pine Cone Symmetry. *The left hand cone shows the five decelerating, positive mail spirals of energy descending to meet the eight accelerating, rising negative female spirals. Where they cross each other, a union of the two forces produces a seed of new life. This illustrates how two antithetical, but oppositely charged forces can interact harmonically and be in balance.*

uses egg-shapes to generate creative energies. The egg-shape became an important ingredient of his inventions. The egg is the only closed shape that will naturally generate vortical movement. We shall see in Chapter 17 how Schauberger used egg-shaped compost piles to generate what he called 'fructigenic' energies, to stimulate plant growth.

The egg-shape is found, especially in the leading edge of growth, in many organisms. The structure of the pine cone is also a good example of the egg-shape, though an elongated one. Its form is developed according to another strict geometric formula. When you examine the structure, you will see that the seed 'wings' form two opposing spirals. Moving from left to right (anti-clockwise) the descending (male) spirals complete three revolutions in the wavelength of the cone; the eight ascending (female) spirals, rising to meet the male, are slower moving, completing only one revolution in the cone's overall length. Where the male and female spirals intersect, a seed is born.

This relationship (proportion) of 5:8 is the signature of the 'Golden Section,' known also by the Greek letter *phi* (ϕ), which resolves into the ratio 1:1.618033988. *Phi* — and *pi* (π), the transcendental number that describes the circumference of the circle, are called 'divine proportions.' Many of Nature's forms depend on *phi* for their generation, as it is one of the vehicles for transforming energy into form. By varying the length of the radii from the centre growth point (the radius length being determined by *phi*), a large variety of natural spirals and leaf shapes can be created.

PART TWO

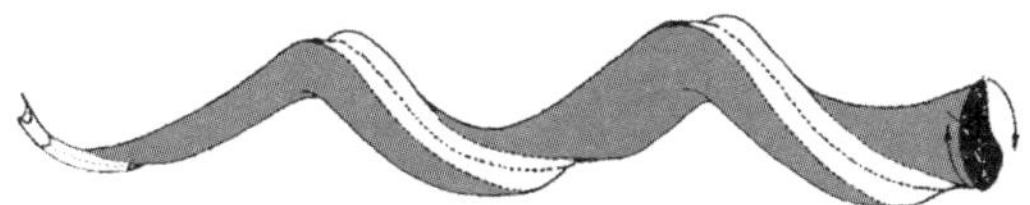

How the World Works

5. Energy Production

The inefficiency of modern technology

Why are the accepted methods of producing energy so inefficient? Far more energy in terms of fuel must be applied than is produced, in most cases more than twice. This has up to now not been of concern, as fossil fuels have been regarded as unlimited and free for the taking, and still are by most, though there is more discussion now of sustainability. The main argument for reducing their use is that their consumption produces CO_2, the principal source of global warming.[1] A power source is now regarded as unsustainable unless, as for example with solar panels, it is renewable; it does not take from the Earth without giving back.

To compare the efficiency of modern technology with that of the human body is illuminating. Walter Schauberger (Viktor's son) calculated that a typical car on a journey of 1000 km (621 miles) consumes as much energy as a human being uses in a whole year. In an 11 hour journey, the car has consumed one human being's annual oxygen requirement. To replenish the oxygen consumed by the world's motor vehicles annually requires healthy forest covering 28% of the world's land area, far more forest than our present, and dwindling, forest cover.[2] There is alarming evidence that the amount of free oxygen in our atmosphere is actually reducing. This comes from an analysis of air captured in bubbles in ancient glaciers in Antarctica as well as in amber.

Using the famous Hasenöhrl-Einstein equation $E=mc^2$, Walter Schauberger calculated that the amount of energy stored in 1 gram of material substance (e.g. flesh, wood, water) amounts to 25 million kWh.[3] The challenge is how to unlock this source of energy. Viktor Schauberger once said: "More energy is encapsulated in every drop of good spring water than an average power station is able to produce".[4]

Schauberger observed that Nature's methods of producing energy were far more efficient, which led him to design implosion machines for natural energy production in the belief that they would solve the crisis of modern technology.

Entropy and ectropy

James Lovelock proposed in his Gaia hypothesis that Nature (for his mathematical model he used the name "Daisyworld") regulates the Earth's energy balance through natural feedback mechanisms to suit the evolution of life forms. All energy used by living and non-living systems eventually degrades to irrecoverable waste heat, or disorder. All our physical processes lead to entropy. Nature made use of this to create the greenhouse effect, by which increasingly complex life forms were introduced into the biosphere as the climate was gradually modified.[5]

Entropy or disorder has been recycled by the Earth's greenhouse effect for millions of years. Every time we walk a pace forward, respiratory processes in the body burn a little ordered carbohydrate to power the muscles of our legs, and some disordered waste heat has been lost without trace from the surface of the body. Every time a simple bacterium moves a milli-millimetre it releases a few micro-calories of disordered heat waste. But every time a jet plane cuts its way through the stratosphere it leaves behind a massive amount of irrecoverable heat that disperses into the planetary heat sink in total disorder. It is all a question of degree. We are now increasing entropy to an unsustainable degree that is decimating life on the planet.

The Earth environment provides an extremely narrow temperature range compared to the extremes found in the Universe. Growth and development of life forms require moderate temperature conditions, as large or abrupt changes are harmful to most organisms. Our warped technology has made us used to very high temperatures; we produce power through combustion and hot fission. Most of our manufacturing processes require excessive heat and high pressure. We create chemical compounds using the coercion of heat and pressure. Technical man can indeed produce a high degree of order in one place, but in so doing he creates a much greater amount of disorder elsewhere.

Scientific 'laws'

Scientific laws are fairly reliable general statements about particular events *under specific circumstances*. The Second Law of Thermodynamics, for example, which states that all closed systems must generate into chaos without input of energy to maintain the ordered state, is thought to be inviolable. Schauberger, by demonstrating that energy could arise spontaneously in his 'perpetual motion' machines, or that frictionless movement could be achieved, disproved this axiom.

Due to the remarkable feedback systems of the atmosphere and the biosphere, temperatures on Earth are kept within the narrow band of those required for abundant life, especially of higher life forms. Gaia research has shown that it is life itself which has fine-tuned that thermostat, so that more complex life forms are able to develop. Some species live within small microclimates, so that on one tree you can find several kinds of finch, each having its own niche.

Humanity is considered to be the most adaptable of species, able to survive in a range of about −10°C (14°F) to +40°C (104°F). While that is true for the species, it is not true for individuals, unless you believe that individual physical health and spiritual wellbeing are stronger than they have ever been. One of the requirements of Nature is that, in order to be whole, we have to be in tune with our environment. It takes many generations of adaptation to a specific environment for people to develop fine physical qualities and sensitive psychic faculties. Similarly it takes generations to adapt safely to a change in the environment (for instance, as a result of global warming or microwave radiation). In the past two hundred years our bodies have been challenged to adapt to higher temperatures and in the last sixty to stressful microwave energy.

Compare this to the efforts modern humans take to accommodate a life divorced from Nature, to jet travel life and unnatural food, and one subject to enormous electromagnetic stress. We take mountains of pills to counteract physical and emotional imbalances or go to psychotherapists to assuage our spiritual starvation. While he does not suggest returning to primitive life-styles, Schauberger assures us that, while our lives are now completely out of balance, by following Nature's clues we can regain both equilibrium and sanity.

Energy pollution

We usually think of pollution in physical terms, like a room full of tobacco smoke, or a factory's chemical effluent poisoning a stream. This is the boundary for conventional science. Thus when people raise fears about the safety of microwave ovens, radar transmission towers, mobile phones, the official response from scientists is inevitably, "there's no evidence that they are any danger to health". Naturally, cynical collusion between government and industry only strengthens this misguided view in order to discourage public protest or lawsuits.

Viktor Schauberger brought a further dimension to the concept of energy pollution. He understood that the creative process of Nature is consistently to refine, to diversify and produce higher forms of organic systems — to use a metaphor from human experience — to raise consciousness (consciousness as integration of higher levels of connectedness). He distinguished three forms in which subtle energies perform these upwardly evolutionary functions, which in the last chapter we called *dynagens, fructigens* and *qualigens.*

They are produced, as we shall see in the chapters that follow, through the specific forms of motion and temperature that Nature designed for the purpose of evolution. If I were in a court of law, it is these complex processes that I would cite as evidence for meaning, purpose and above all, intelligence in Nature. Schauberger described these 'enlightened' control systems thirty years before Jim Lovelock and his colleagues proposed the Gaia theory of intelligent self-sustainability in Nature, and in the area of evolutionary energies, went far ahead of them.

The blocking of these creative energies by the emanations from modern technological processes Schauberger saw as the most dangerous form of pollution. Their heat, pressure and, above all, chaotic effects actually destroy the more delicate energies of Nature's constructive developmental processes. Thus, chemicals invading a stream not only make it dirty and smelly, but they also destroy the complex structure of the water, so that it can no longer behave like healthy water, but literally dies (see Chapter 11).

This form of pollution has an evolutionary as well as a health effect on people. Schauberger suggested that this explained the well-documented degeneration of intelligence and the increase of violence in industrial communities. Dr Weston Price, studying fourteen isolated indigenous communities around the world in the early 1930s noted this in the effect that changing from their slowly evolved local diet to a western-type diet had on these people (for food is energy medicine!).[6]

We don't know how much energy pollution from anti-Nature technology affects the environment in general. Logically it should be most prevalent near power stations, large factories and the like. However, when rivers, which are the arteries of the blood of the Earth (see Chapter 11), and normally transmit energy to the surrounding countryside, are turned into "lifeless corpses" (as Schauberger used to say), what effect will this cadaverous energy have on the environment? Clearly, if humanity is to reverse the downward devolutionary spiral, our first priority must be to change over to Nature's energy systems.

The choice before us

Humanity lived a relatively natural and sustainable lifestyle until fairly recent times. The growth of industry and its massive demand for energy resources has introduced increasing degrees of instability. Going back over 2000 years, but much more clearly in the last 350 years, it has been possible to chart a different kind of development which has brought with it a deterioration of the natural environment, increasing disorder and inefficiency.

Callum Coats shows this divergence of the two systems in the accompanying chart (Fig. 5.1). In the last 150 years with rapid industrialization, a scientifically based technology developed, and the divergence shown by the lower curve has become dramatic, with dire consequences for the environment.

By contrast, the curve rising up toward 'ectropy' shows how natural evolution builds more complex systems with more evolved species on the foundation of earlier ones. This is how biodiversity increases. The appearance of new species requires a surplus of evolutionary energies deriving from the improved conditions of interdependence. It is as though the growth in natural capital from the sound economy of evolution produces interest or surplus energy from which new life forms may be formed. Nature's system is so economical that little is wasted. The many seeds, nuts and fruits which sustain all the currently existing life forms, can be seen as the surplus on Nature's interest.

The mineral resources of the Earth, which are Nature's base capital, should never be used. As we shall see in Chapter 17, Schauberger illustrates how they are essential building blocks in the production of formative energies. The indigenous people understood their

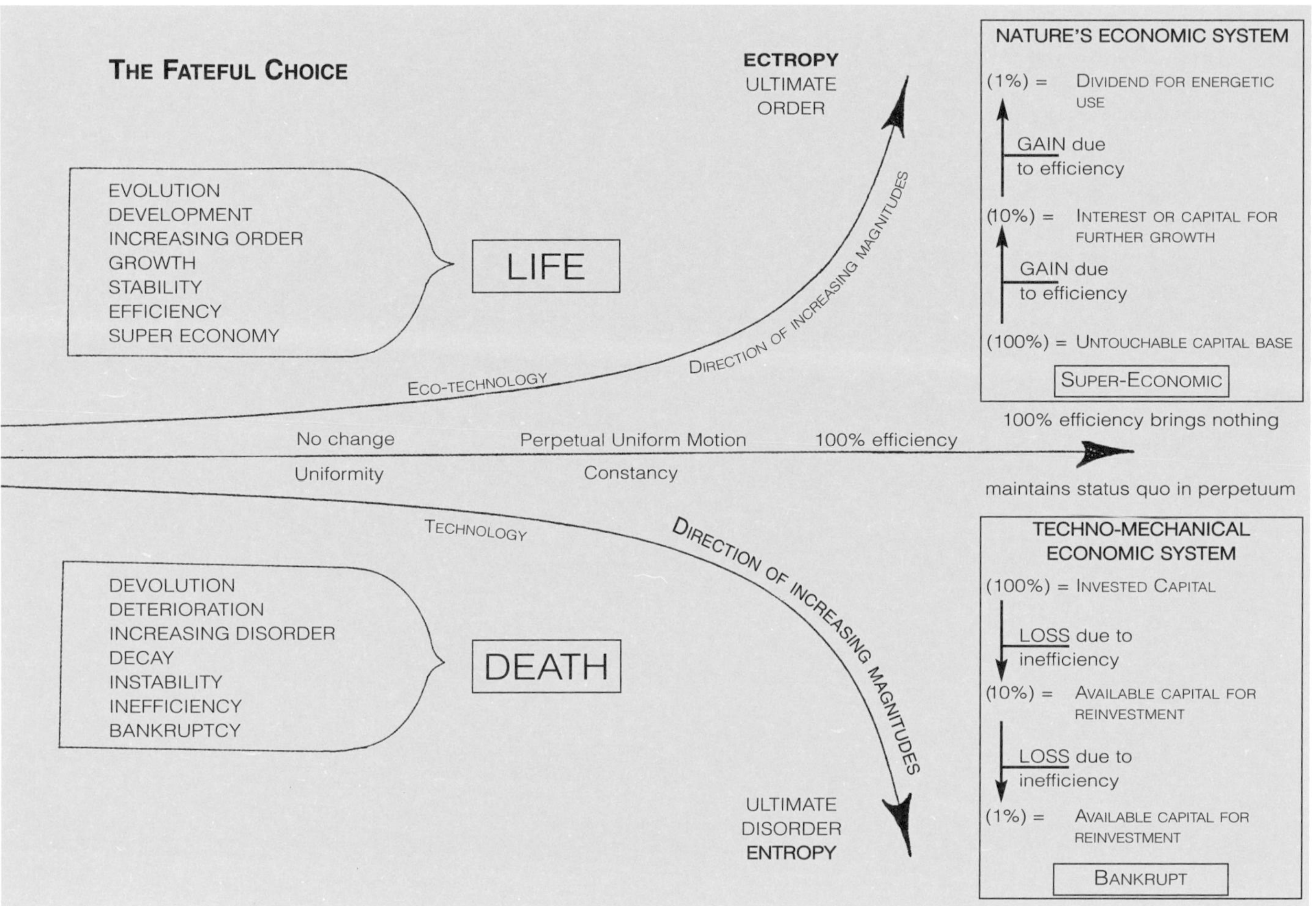

Fig.5.1. The Fateful Choice.

importance. Mineral-rich lands are for them energy-enhanced areas that they regard as sacred.

Nature has to increase her capital by say 10%, to allow for growth, movement, and evolution of new life forms. To live sustainably is to live off Nature's surpluses (such as the careful harvesting of trees under properly controlled mixed forest management). The increasing diversity of evolving Nature brings more stability and the ability to withstand temporary setbacks (Fig. 5.1).

The centre line in Fig. 5.1 represents 100% efficiency. This may seem the best direction, but it is not the answer. It is undynamic, like circular motion. Its uniform condition means it never increases or decreases. Above all, the purpose of Nature is to seek movement, change and evolution; she despises stasis and uniformity.

The lower curve represents the path on which we are at this

time. The use of energy is improvident and wasteful, replacing diversity with mass production for quick return, which Nature cannot tolerate. Where once rich forest flourished, with a wide diversity of interdependent species of trees and animals, there exist now only monocultures. This requires enormous, hedgeless fields where only one crop is grown, dependent on fertilizers that slowly destroy the living humus; they become monotonous environmental wastelands. Gone are the high yielding, organically nourished fields surrounded by windbreaking hedgerows teeming with birds, small animals and wildflowers. The frequently reported notices of endangered or newly extinct species bear witness to this ebbing biodiversity.

What Schauberger calls the "techno-mechanical economic system" produces a downward curve, accelerating as unnatural systems of energy are applied more widely. Pollution apart, these systems are clearly inefficient. In the 1970s, Walter Schauberger discussed industrial efficiency with Dr Fritz Kortegast, head of research and development at Mercedes-Benz in Stuttgart, who confirmed that at that time the propulsive energy produced by their most sophisticated engines was only 13% of the total energy introduced, the balance consumed as dissipated heat and pollution. A business this inefficient would soon fail.

The truth is that our techno-mechanical economic system is created by vested interests that consume energy through the massive exploitation of non-renewable resources. It must be clear that the ultimately such unsustainable technology can produce only economic collapse, social chaos and environmental deterioration. The disorder and decay that we are witnessing come from our dependence on an energy system that is self-destructive. In this system, an investment of $100 produces $13, which in turn would produce only $1.69.[7]

Energy defines quality

Convinced that we are the pinnacle of life on the Earth, we humans are actually destroying the very basis of creativity on the planet. It is the diversity of Nature that supports our place in the biosphere. The ongoing extraction of oil, coal and other minerals, deforestation, overfishing, and the continual loss of animal and plant species threaten our very existence. It is well accepted that only inferior kinds of fish can live in poor quality water. It is no different for people. By allowing the natural resources of the environment to depreciate, the quality of human potential inevitably suffers.

Conventional science does not understand the importance of quality. For the reductionist scientist water is water, or a genetically engineered crop is the 'substantial equivalent' of a conventional crop. No two things can be identical in Nature whose processes depend on constant change and transformation. While quantitative science states that 1 + 1 makes 2, no two natural systems can ever be equated.

Monocultures and mass production mean repetition. They repeat an energetic or experiential process that has already happened, in which no new development, no advance, however slight, is possible. Identical repetition goes against evolution, because it wastes energy. The development of a new natural process or system demands change and variety.

George Gurdjieff, the Caucasian mystic and teacher, used to say that the ordinary person operates like a blind machine with no awareness or consciousness. Viktor Schauberger saw contemporary humans as superficial creatures that look, but never see. Our seeing is limited to recognition, not deep examination. We mistake outward appearance for totality, effect for cause. What we actually see are the external shells of manifestation, what is left by the formative energy. We don't see the energy that created the organism.

The creative energy-vortex

Callum Coats illustrates the process of the creation of matter in the diagram (Fig. 5.2). As we have seen, creative energy moves spirally in the form of a vortex. The creative process takes place as the energy containing the blueprint of what is being created moves in whatever way it needs to in order to create the system it wishes. It draws down matter as a mirror image of the idea or blueprint. This is why the physical is said to be the shell of the organic reality.

What we have described is the formative energy. There is also the sustaining energy, the *Ch'i* in Chinese terms, which moves in the same way. This is the way a healthy river moves; and the blood in our capillaries, external manifestations of an energy path. We

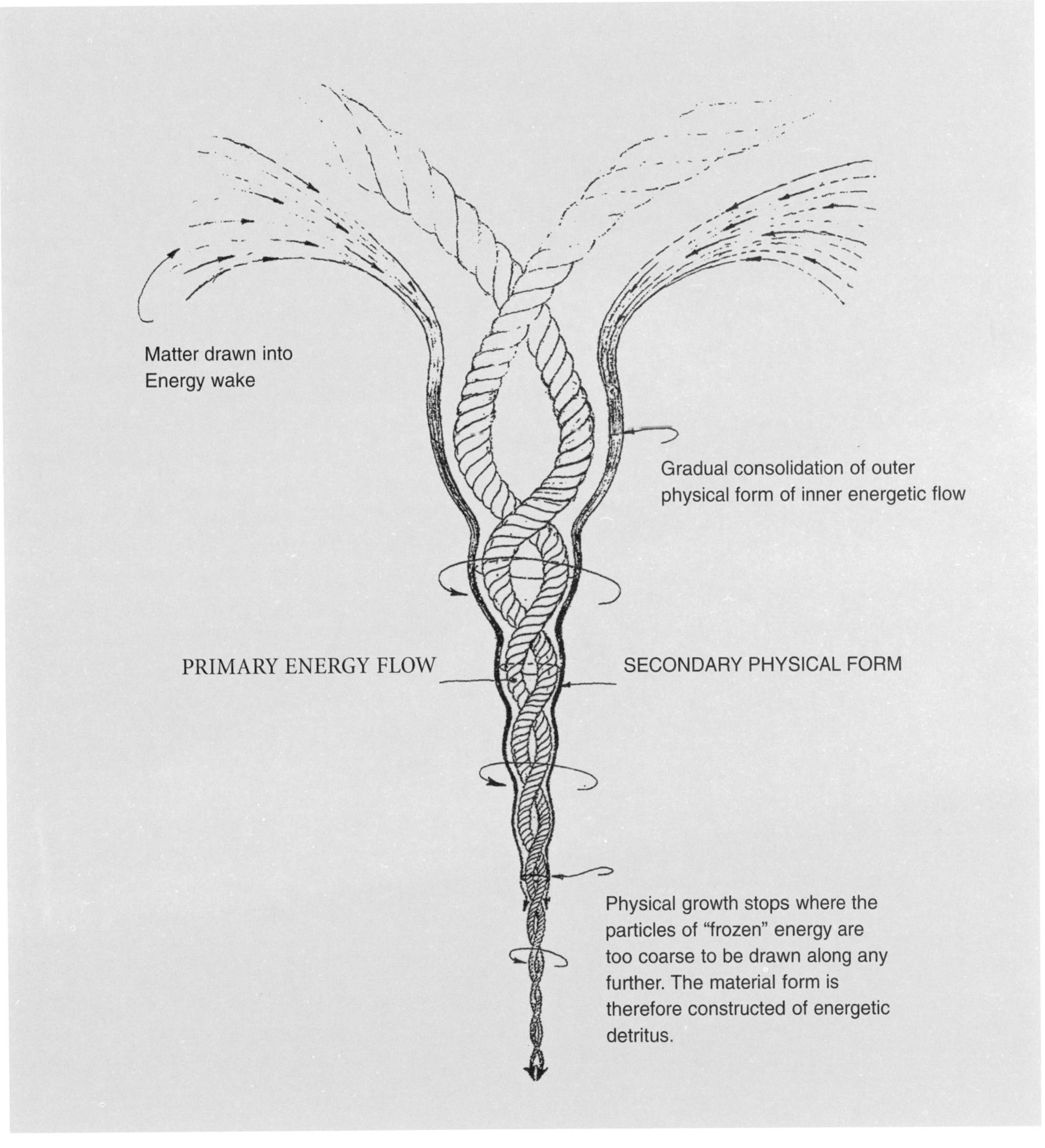

Fig.5.2. Energy and Form.
In the beginning was energy; it is primary — the cause; it creates the form in which it wishes to move; the form is the mirror of the energy — the secondary effect.

see the blood, but we don't see the energy that pushes it. What is visible in blood is the matter that is too coarse to be taken to the final destination of the energy. Energy manifests how it wants to move in the most efficient way. It is as if, when we build a house, we build it to suit our lifestyle, one in which it is easy to move around.

All natural systems are mirrors of their pattern of energy, or of the 'idea' that sought to create them in the first place. When the system is in place, the energy from which it originated is rejected as matter being too coarse to be carried further in the energy stream. Viktor Schauberger used to describe the Earth as a huge dung-heap, saying that all living things were the result of waste matter ejected by the creative energies moving in a certain way, and which were unable to continue transporting the material further.

Put simply, it is only those energies that remain immaterial that contribute to an increase in life-force, while the remaining energetic material is expelled as waste, just like daily human defecation. There are subtle nonmaterial energies in the food we eat, which are used to produce thought processes and metabolic functions. The human body is like a energy path containing a complex vortex which transforms the energy of matter into intellectual and physical actions. It is therefore axiomatic that the quality of our functions is dependent on the quality of the energy that we ingest. Viktor Schauberger campaigned for high quality nutrition and water.

So, physical manifestation depends on the movement of energy. All of Nature's creations that we observe are the outward shell of the formative energy path. Schauberger used to say that a tree will grow only to the height to which the energies can draw up the physical mass, although the tree's main energy body lies above it.

He demonstrated that the vortex is the natural form of movement for energy. The accompanying photograph (Fig. 5.3) well illustrates the spiraling form that water prefers. Each of the twists is slightly smaller than the one above. Viktor's son, Walter, calculated the mathematics and proportions of this structure.[8]

Callum Coats used the action of our weather to demonstrate the importance of the vortex in creating material substance. The spiraling air masses possess very little density, very slow rotational velocities and a large radius of influence. When these air masses converge, they gain in speed with the reduction in their radius of rotation.

Fig.5.3. A Natural Vortex.

At their extreme development, these air masses take on the more physical form of a tornado or waterspout. With their source in the lower density air mass subjected to solar radiation, as they descend with increasing velocity they become denser and more physical. The core of some tornados becomes so dense they can bend railway lines.

Viktor Schauberger found it hard to understand why science has not ascribed any fundamental importance to the natural movement of energy and Nature's systems of spiral movement, which are so clear, from the scale of a galaxy to that of a DNA molecule. Perhaps this is because it has been too immersed in the Euclidean elements of mechanics with little knowledge or conception of organics. We have never taken the time to understand enough Nature's dynamics to be able to copy them.

A famous professor of logic once pointed out:

> We must conclude, I think, that there is no room for telepathy in a materialistic universe. Telepathy is something that ought not to happen at all, if the materialist theory were true. But it does happen. So there must be something seriously wrong with the materialist theory, however numerous and imposing the normal facts which support it may be.[9]

Goethe too said of scientists, "Whatever you cannot calculate you do not think is real."

6. Motion — the Key to Balance

What we are doing is wrong and contrary to Nature. Nature moves in other ways. She primarily employs drawing (i.e. sucking), energies, since these are indispensable to Nature for the growth and maintenance of life. Nature uses pressure energies and explosive forces only for reducing quality and destruction. The work of atomic physicists is also upside down. They would be more correct if they started with simple nuclear fusion. They should set about the cold transformation of hydrogen into helium, as Nature has done over the millions of years of Creation. Today's technology has a tiger by the tail, because it splits the heaviest atoms with the greatest development of heat and an enormous expenditure of energy.[1]

We use the wrong form of motion

The way earth, water and air are moved determines whether pathogenic or healthy life-forms come into being. New life can arise from burnt (carbonized) bacterial cultures, but if it is wrongly moved and processed then its parasitic nature soon becomes evident. However, if this culture is placed in soil that has been spared humanity's misguided interference, then its life-force blossoms again immediately.[2]

Motion and energy are inextricably interlinked. Movement is an expression of energy, and together with temperature, these are the cornerstones of Schauberger's Eco-technology. Through his careful observations and experiments he became aware of the difference between Nature's way of working and the prevailing human technology. He realized that the principles under which conventional technology operates must be basically unsound to have produced such appalling consequences for water, for soil and indeed for all of life.

Most of us are aware of the effects of chemicals in the body and on the soil, of the dangers of radioactive waste and biotechnology. But Schauberger was also concerned with something much more basically wrong with our technology. Being above all a practical man, he observed the appalling squandering of resources; why are the internal combustion and steam engines on which our civilization depend not even 50% efficient? The energy that is not turned into power or motion is wasted and heats up the atmosphere, adding to the greenhouse effect. From his observations of Nature came the answer, which is probably the most important of Schauberger's discoveries — that we use the wrong form of motion.

Our machines and technological processes channel agents such as air, water and other liquids and gases into the type of motion that Nature uses only to decompose and dissolve matter. As a consequence, the air, water and other substances are devitalized and debilitated, affecting their surroundings. The energy produced by our technology is harmful because, by its very nature, it causes deterioration in the environment through strengthening those energies that break down structures and degrade quality, while at the same time suppressing those that increase quality and thus help plants and animals to be healthy.

Biodynamic and organic gardeners have commented that they value Viktor Schauberger's advice on how to treat materials that Nature breaks down for recycling, for these insights have been lacking for this form of cultivation (see Chapter 17 for more on this topic).

Through its dependence on the decomposing mode of motion our technology is dangerously affecting the vital biodiversity and balance of our ecosystems, the stability of our societies, and is one of the main causes of human-generated global warming. The form of motion on which we depend for building and development is the one that Nature uses to destabilize and break down. Nature uses another form of motion for creating and rebuilding. It is hardly surprising then, that our technology is self-destructive and unsustainable.

Our mechanical, technological systems of motion are based on explosive, outward pushing energies which always meet resistance, producing heat and friction. This form of movement goes out at a tangent, producing the fastest movement at the periphery (as in a wheel), a form of motion that is disintegrative, noisy and inefficient, because so much of the energy is dissipated. The effect is to break apart, to fragment. This is the way we generate our power; from the inside to the outside. It is called *centrifugal* movement, and is a process that Nature will use only to break down before reassembly into some other form takes place (see Fig. 1.2, p.33).

By contrast, Nature uses the opposite, *centripetal*, form of motion, moving from the outside to the inside with increasing velocity, which acts to cool, to condense, to structure; like water going down a plughole. When we talk of something imploding on itself, there is not the resistance or dissipation of energy that is found in the explosive process. The reverse takes place, cooling and condensing. Schauberger called this 'constructive' movement.

The centrifugal form of movement should not be called 'destructive,' because the word has such a negative connotation, and it has its rightful purpose in Nature; instead he called it 'deconstructive.' Viktor Schauberger demonstrated with his remarkable implosion machines that replicated the in-winding motion of Nature, that this was the way to create energy for human needs in the future.

As Schauberger's discovery has such enormous implications for the future of human culture, why has it not been openly debated in scientific circles? The reasons are two-fold. Firstly, Schauberger, being *persona non grata* with the German postwar establishment, was not granted the oxygen of publicity. Secondly, he was talked of in postwar Germany as a Nazi collaborator, by association rather than fact, as his work for the Nazi regime was carried out under duress. Though both the Russians and the Americans secretly confiscated his research papers, the Cold War days kept his name in the shadows. His discoveries have been enthusiastically embraced by the alternative culture, but as yet have not become more widely known.

The 'original' motion

Viktor Schauberger was always comparing terrestrial laws of motion to the patterns of movement in the Heavens. He firmly believed that there existed a "form originating" motion that was responsible for the evolutionary dynamics of the Earth and the Cosmos, generally referring to it as the "original" motion. The whole Universe is continually in motion. This movement is in spirals, many spirals within spirals. Galaxies take a spiral form. As we saw in Chapter 4, forms in Nature very often follow the law "As Above, so Below," implying that there is a Universal language of form and motion. Liquids and gases prefer to move in spirals; likewise energy. Dowsers find energy spirals in the ground. Energy in the human body seems to do the same.

Fig. 6.1. Spiral Galaxy superimposed by Hyperbolic Spiral.[3]

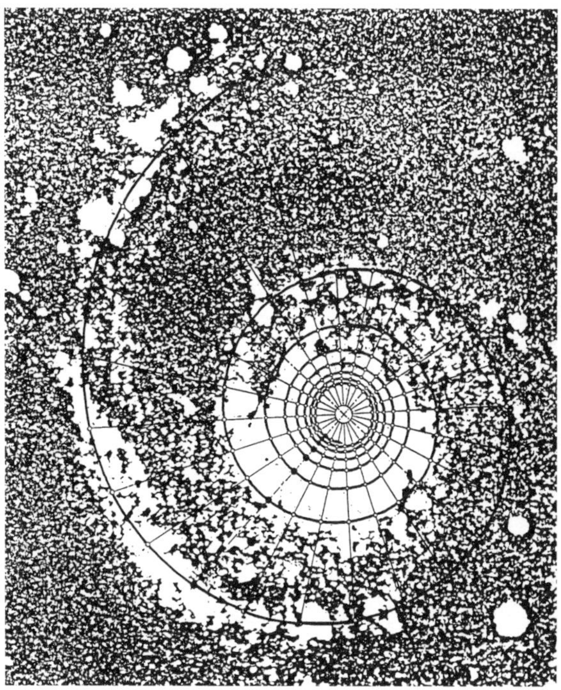

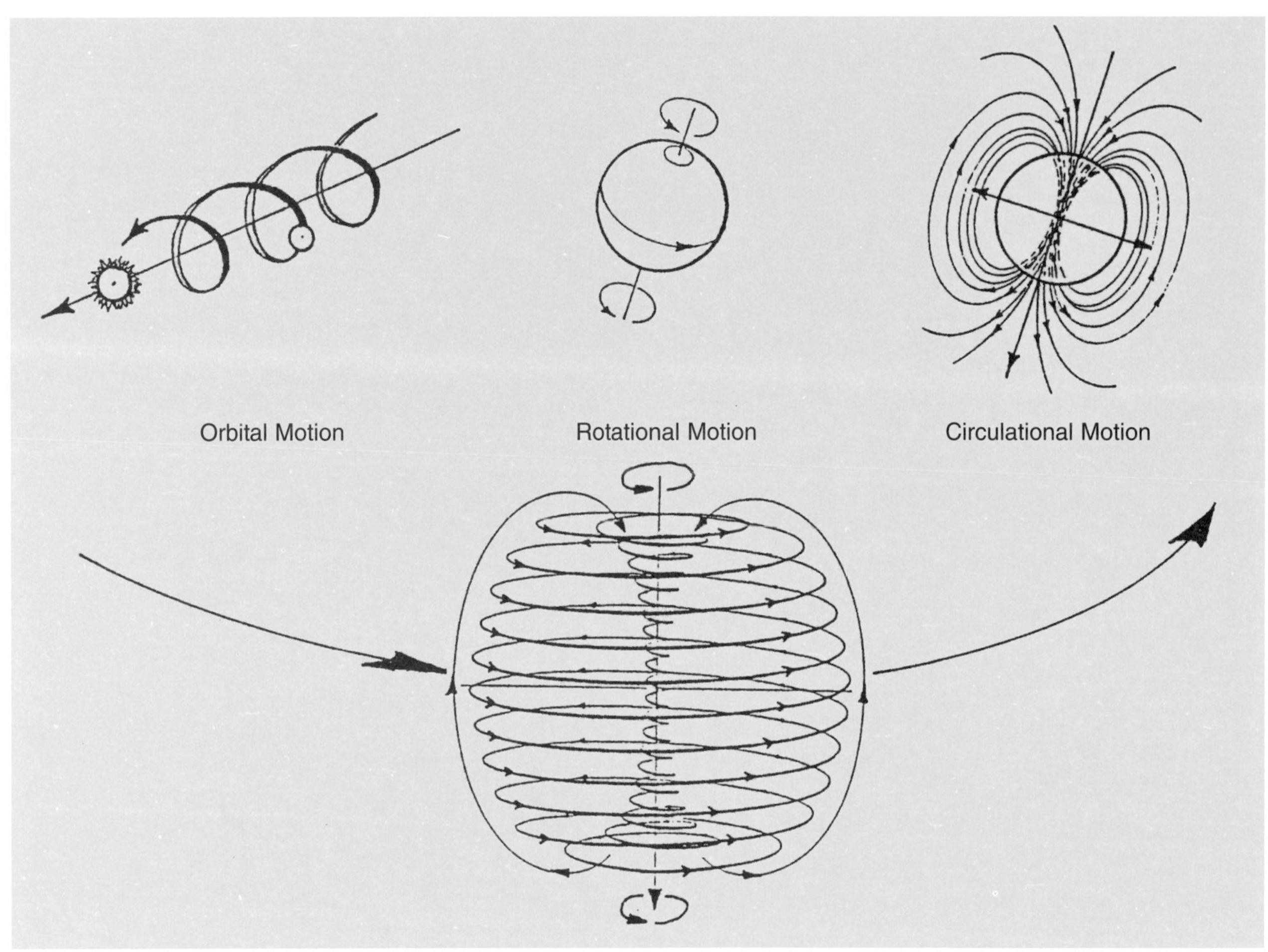

Fig.6.2. Three basic forms of motion. *When combined into one, these make up the dynamic, creative, formative spiral-vortical movement.*[5]

As Callum Coats recounts:

> There are many examples in ordinary language which recall this spiral movement. When we ex-(s)pire, we leave this our 'mortal coil.' When we are in-spire-d, we feel drawn to higher ideals. Our spir(e)it is raised when we are sucked into the upward spiral. Similarly through re-spir(e)-ation the ionization balance of the body, which varies according to the time of day, is adjusted by the proportional ionization of the air indrawn through the nostrils, which due to opposite directions of rotation, is negatively ionized by the left nostril and positively by the right nostril. Sneezing, therefore, may perhaps be a compensating process, through which high opposing charges resulting from over-ionization are reduced to zero.

Interestingly, the German word — *Wirbelsäule* — for the spinal column, the fundamental supporting structure of the human body, literally means a 'spiral' column. Similarly each of the vertebrae is referred to as a whirlpool or vortex. Clearly the Germans have long had a completely different view of the central structure of our bodies. Whereas we see it as a stiff, more or less rigid, physical structure, they understand it more as an energy path. This has obvious associations with the Hindu concept of Kundalini, the name given to the two serpents that metaphorically dwell at the base of the spine, whose rising energizes that spiritualize the various higher chakras (energy vortices) of the physical body and whose entwinement on Mercury's staff (the caduceus) empowers him as Messenger of the Gods. Nature too, provides us with countless examples of dynamic spiral growth and movement in the form of galaxies, cyclones, whirlpools and tornadoes, of which we, in our blindness and arrogance, fail to take note in our pursuit of mechanical perfection.[4]

Types of motion

All natural dynamic motion consists of one or more of three basic types of movement — orbital, rotational and circulatory (see Fig. 6.3). When these are put together they produce a complex form we call spiral-vortical motion which Nature uses to build, structure and purify.

Viktor distinguished two forms of spiral-vortical motion — *radial→axial* (or centripetal) and *axial→radial* (or centrifugal) motion. In Fig. 1.2, axial→radial motion is shown initially as a movement around a centre, changing to a tangential movement as it moves outward. There is no motion at the centre but, with increasing distance from the centre, the speed of movement and the degree of disintegration also increase. The wooden wagon-wheels of yore had an iron band around them for this reason. The 'tie-er' (tyre or tire) held the wheel together.

The form of movement employed by our technology produces excess energy in the form of heat or noise. Initially, with no movement at the centre, velocity and resistance increase with the outward 'explosion.' This axial→radial centrifugal form of motion can be described as divergent, decelerating, dissipating, structure-loosening, disintegrating, destructive and friction-inducing.

While the explosive dispersion of energy creates noise, its creative concentration of energy, is silent. As Viktor often insisted, "Everything that is natural is silent, simple and cheap". A natural forest can be a haven of silence. The millions of chemical and atomic movements and interactions taking place are energetic processes, an extraordinary concentration of quiet creative energy. In contrast, its destruction brings the horrendous racket of chainsaws, heavy machinery and crashing trees. Our mechanical forms of movement are almost always axial→radial and heat- and friction-inducing. Nature's dynamic processes, on the other hand, use the opposite form of movement, the slowest at the periphery and the fastest at the centre. The movements of a cyclone or a tornado are a good example, flowing from the outside inwards with increasing velocity, which acts to cool, to condense, to structure. The centre of a cyclone is not hot; it is cool.

Radial→axial (centripetal) motion can be defined as convergent, contracting, consolidating, creative, integrating, formative, friction reducing.[6] The dynamics of evolution must therefore follow this centripetal path, for if the opposite were the case, all would have come to a stop almost before it started.

Force is the employment of energy to do work, and can be measured as acceleration. It is important to distinguish between two forms of acceleration, for one form breaks apart and the other consolidates. In the deconstructive form the radius of rotation is expanding and the form of acceleration is pressure- and friction-

Fig.6.3: The Planetary Vortex.
The movements of the inner planets, shown dynamically over a period of one full Saturn cycle of 29.46 years, actually describe a vortex, with each planet describing its own spiral path about the Sun.

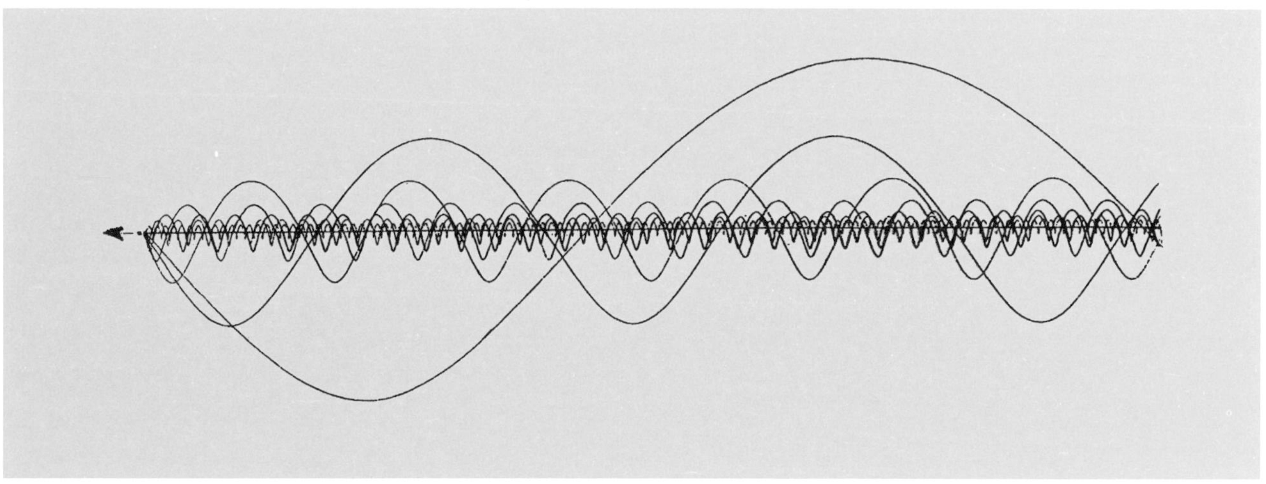

intensifying (centrifugal acceleration); the constructive when the radius of rotation is reducing, creating a form of acceleration that is suction-increasing and friction-reducing (centripetal acceleration).

More power must be applied to maintain the same velocity or to increase speed with centrifugal acceleration. With centripetal acceleration, the velocity and energy increase automatically. Viktor called this 'formative force', the constructive energies from which all life is created.

7. The Atmosphere and Electricity

It is thought that, when the Earth was young, after it had cooled from a molten mass of condensing gases and a crust had formed, it was entirely covered in water. In those early days there was great heat loss and the Earth was cooler. The lower part of the initial atmosphere was composed of water vapour evaporated from the vast ocean, with a contribution of other gases emanating from volcanic eruptions. Because of its high specific heat[1] and its capacity to retain heat, the water vapour gradually absorbed the heat of the Sun, thus raising the average temperature. Heat losses were kept to a minimum at night because water absorbs infrared heat. It was these qualities of water that allowed the greenhouse effect to take hold. Otherwise the Earth would have remained cold, lifeless and barren.

Of all liquids, water has the greatest ability to store heat. It absorbs heat slowly, releasing it slowly. Water vapour was thus an ideal medium for conserving heat on the Earth's surface, enabling life to gain hold and, once it was established, water became the medium for complex life forms to develop.

What makes water different from all other liquids is its so-called 'anomaly point' or 'point of anomalous expansion,' which will be discussed in more detail in Chapter 9. Contrary to the behaviour of other liquids, the volume of water does not decrease continually with increasing cold; below a temperature of +4°C (39°F) it starts to expand again, and on freezing expands still further.

Pure water will freeze only at a temperature of around –40°C (–40°F) or in clouds at about –10°C (14°F), which again is fairly important, as we shall discover later. Compared to absolute zero (–273.15°C), supposedly the lowest temperature found in the Universe, the temperature of 0°C (32°F), or freezing point, is relatively warm. The normal human living environment, between approximately –10°C (14°F) and +40°C (104°F), is not a large range.

At a height of about 22 km (14 miles) above the Earth's surface, water vapour becomes so thin and unsubstantial that it is dissociated into its constituent atoms of oxygen and hydrogen through the action of strong ultraviolet radiation. As it is the heavier element, the oxygen then sinks back to Earth, while the lighter hydrogen atoms rise eventually to reunite with the hydrogen of space.

The widowed single atom oxygen atoms are now exposed to high levels of ionizing radiation which causes them to combine with molecular oxygen (O_2) to form an allotropic form of oxygen, O_3 or ozone, which absorbs dangerous ultraviolet radiation, a process vital for shielding life on Earth.

Earth's atmosphere

The atmosphere is a relatively thin veneer surrounding the Earth, containing the gases essential to life. Its total thickness is about 400 km (248 miles), which represents about 0.3% of the Earth's diameter. It has four principal zones, through which the temperature swings alternately from a falling mode to a rising mode: [2]

During each of these temperature transitions, the anomaly point of 4°C (+39°F) is passed, so that in each zone there is first a band of negative temperature gradient, followed by a band of positive temperature gradient (see Chapter 5). The three lower zones each have a water layer close to these anomaly points, cumulus and cirrus clouds (troposphere), nacreous clouds (stratosphere) and noctilucent clouds (mesosphere) as shown on Fig. 7.1 which would resist the transfer of an electric charge. Callum Coats has suggested that this could result in the creation of a natural biocondenser, a condenser being a device with which an electric charge can be accumulated and stored.

Table 1: The four principal zones of the Earth's atmosphere.

	height (km/miles)	temperature	
Troposphere:	13/0 to 8	+15°C *(59°F)* to –60°C *(–76°F)*	area of weather activity
+4°C (39°F) layer	3.5/2		and the greenhouse effect
Stratosphere:	13/8 to 50/31	–60°C *(–76°F)* to +10°C *(50°F)*	contains ozone layer
+4°C (39°F) layer	40/25		and very high clouds
Mesosphere:	50/31 to 80/50	+10°C *(50°F)* to –100°C *(–148°F)*	rapidly falling temperature
+4°C (39°F) layer	65/40		and pressure
Ionosphere:	80/50 to 400/248	–100°C *(–148°F)* to +600°C*(+1100°F)*	absorbs Sun's shortwave
+4°C (39°F) layer	100/62		radiation

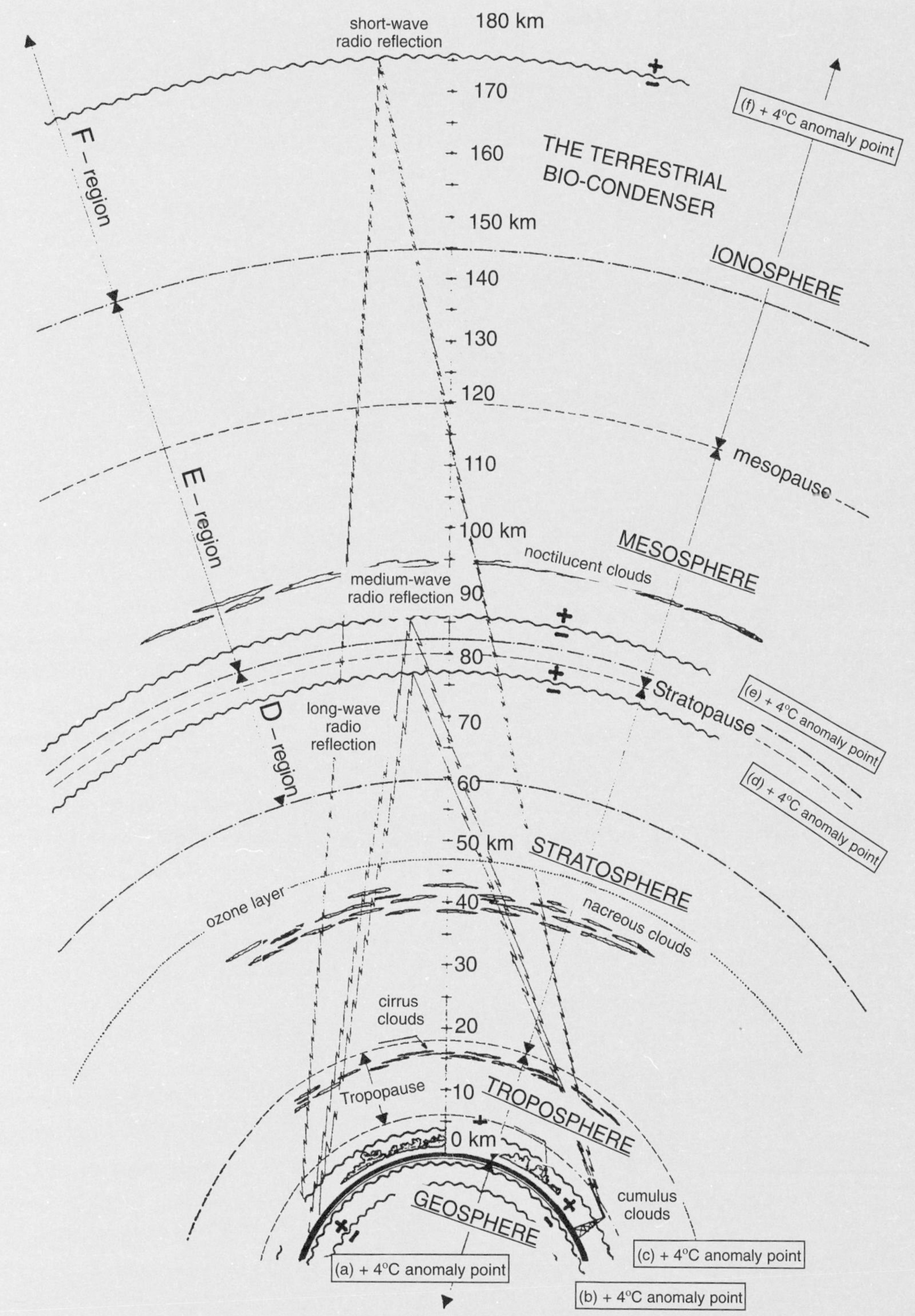

Fig.7.1. Section through Earth's atmosphere, showing temperature fluctuations.
Callum Coats postulates a series of concentric rings where the temperature reaches water's anomaly point of +4°C, which Schauberger identified as water's state of greatest potential, together creating an accumulator of energy to facilitate the emergence of life.

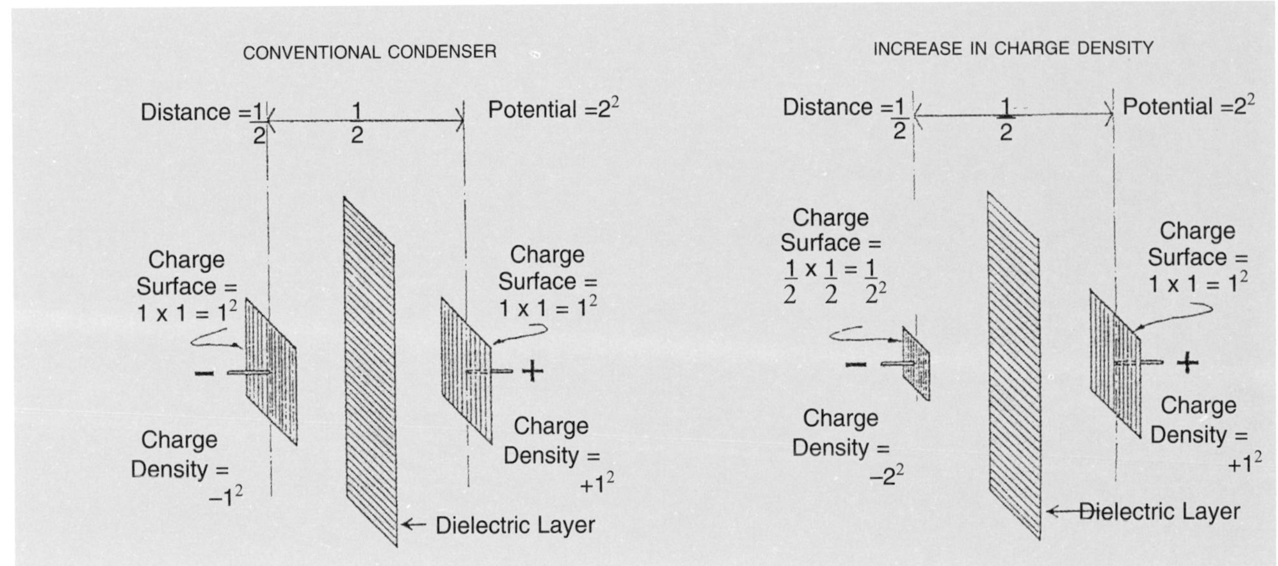

Figs.7.2 & 3. Increase in potential and charge density.
In a condenser for accumulating electrical charge, the energy potential increases by either reducing the area of one plate, or by bringing it closer to the dielectric layer (separating plate).

Electricity

Electricity is the result of magnet polarities put into motion. In electricity the process depends on the polarity of electrons in the atom. At the physical level electricity is familiar in thunderstorm activity and the electrical current supplied to our homes through cables. There is a much more refined form of electricity more properly called bioelectricity which is produced by living organisms. It is much less studied or even recognized, being an octave higher, but Schauberger found that this is crucial to all natural processes.

For electrical activity to be possible, the charges of different polarity must be either joined by a conducting path or separated by an insulator or dielectric. Figs 7.2 and 7.3 illustrate two situations in a normal electrical condenser or capacitor for accumulating an electrical charge. By reducing the surface area of one plate, the charge density on that side of the dielectric is increased, in the ratio of its area to the larger plate. So if it is a quarter the area of the larger plate, its charge density will be four times that of the larger plate. What is called the potential is the amount of energy with which the two opposite charges try to balance out the difference. The energy potential increases as the distance between the plates is decreased.[3] If the area of one plate is reduced at the same time as it is moved closer to the dielectric, the potential is increased exponentially.

The terrestrial biocondenser

While Fig. 7.2 illustrates the principle of a normal electrical condenser, Fig. 7.5 shows the typical situation at layers of the atmosphere where the air temperature is close to the anomaly point of +4°C (39°F). The pure water layer takes the place of the dielectric layer. Generally speaking the positively charged surface is influenced by the positive temperature gradient, and the negatively charged surface by the negative gradient. If the charge of the positive plate is raised, that of the negative plate will rise automatically to the same level, the charges being distributed evenly on the plates' surfaces.

If we now rearrange these plates in the form of concentric cylinders as shown in Fig. 7.4, to simulate the proposed pattern of the +4°C (39°F) condensers in the atmospheric zones, you will see that the surface area of the inner cylindrical plates reduces from the outside inwards and the charge and potential increase automatically. The greater the number of nested plates therefore, the more intense the energy potential.

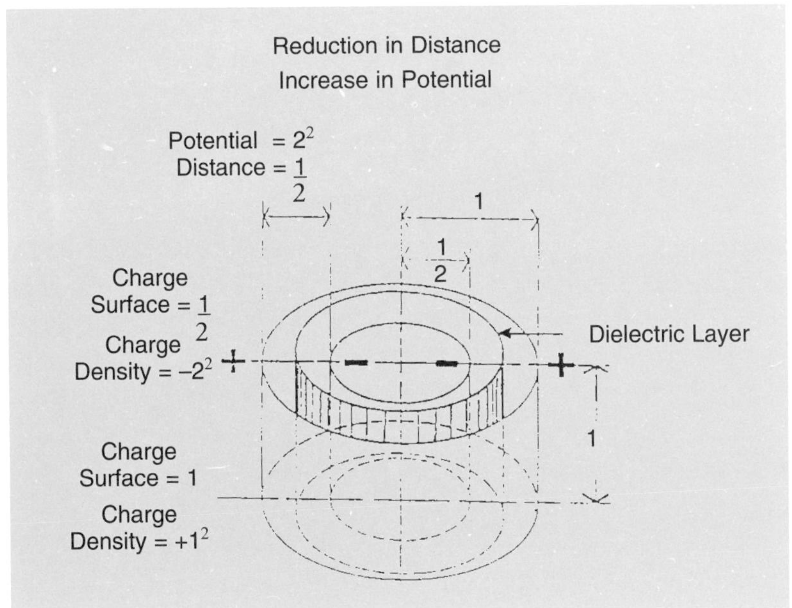

Fig. 7.4. Reduction in distance, increase in potential.
The dielectric layers act like non-conductive membranes or insulators, separating positive and negative charges.

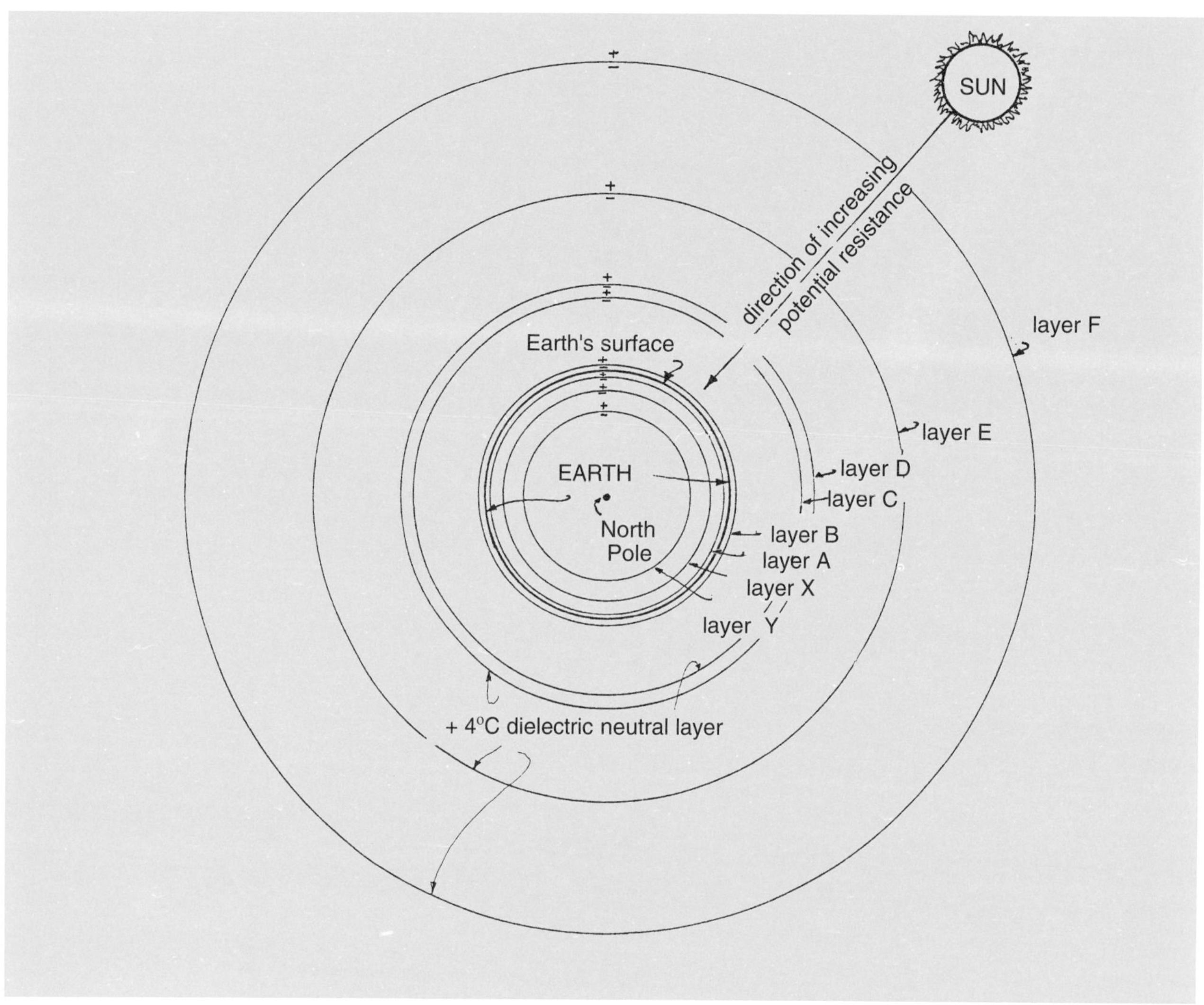

Fig.7.5. Terrestrial bio-condenser. *A schematic proposed by Callum Coats, illustrating how the Sun's electromagnetic energy is amplified by the diminishing radius of each dielectric layer formed by water strata at a temperature of +4°C.*

Fig. 7.5, drawn roughly to scale, shows how we can see that each succeeding layer from the outside inwards, like an onion, has a smaller surface area owing to their concentricity. In other words, these layers form a condenser with concentric spherical plates. This demonstrates how, on encountering each successive, concentric, spherical +4°C (39°F) dielectric layer, the energy potential coming from the Sun is gradually magnified. As the Sun's energy penetrates the atmosphere, it becomes increasingly concentrated as it approaches the Earth's surface, due to these enveloping layers of +4°C (39°F) water. (Remember that pure water does not freeze at temperatures above −40°C /−40°F.)

Earth as an accumulator of energy

Viewed from a more cosmic perspective these strata are extremely close together, producing a very high potential of energy. Callum Coats proposes an ingenious concept of the Earth as an accumulator of energy gradually building up an electromagnetic charge (Fig.7.5). This accumulation of energy would naturally enhance the emergence of life because, without differences in electrical charge, gender, potential or a suitable energy field, life is impossible.

Viktor Schauberger was concerned to identify which natural processes and functions might promote the concentration of the energetic matrix within which physical life can evolve. He favoured an energy matrix being created by the 'original' motion of the Earth as it rotates about its own axis and circulates its biomagnetic and bioelectrical energies through itself during its 365.26 day, orbital waltz around the Sun.

It seems reasonable to propose that these variously charged layers in the atmosphere are a product of the Earth's rotation. The +4°C (39°F) layers form charge-resisting strata which may contribute to the reflection of radio waves, though the conventional explanation for their reflection is the different ionization levels, water vapour being present at different densities in the different layers.[4] The development of electricity can be demonstrated by very simple experiments, in which energy in the form of an electric charge is generated by falling water.[5]

These experiments demonstrate that through an increase of water vapour, a saturation level is reached where individual water molecules can form raindrops that generate an electric charge as they fall. This charge is released at a certain point as lightning. Ozone is created by the intense ionization caused by an electrical discharge, and is often carried up by the powerful rising currents of a thunderstorm, to reinforce the ozone layer, which screens life from excessive ultraviolet radiation.

Photographs taken from Earth-orbiting satellites show how frequent are lightning discharges, occurring at about 100 per minute. If they average 15,000,000kw per strike, the annual total would be a prodigious 13,000,000,000kw/hrs per year.[6] Lightning discharges can reach 9 km (6 miles), and sheet lightning up to 100 km (62 miles). There is some evidence in recent years of a decline in thunderstorm activity.[7]

If this were the case, the implications for the protective ozone layer would be serious. Water particles have to be very fine in order to spin fast enough to produce an electrical discharge (the water atom is an electrical dipole). One of the features of more stormy weather is to produce a larger water drop that cannot spin fast enough to produce a significant electrical charge.

Electricism and magnetism

Viktor Schauberger coined the term "electricism" for the *effect* that electricity has on life, which is destructive, dismantling, disintegrative and debilitating. Magnetism is the energy that circulates through and around the Earth on its polar axis. Electricism and magnetism are apparently contradictory (or dialectic partners, see p. 47). Together they form the electromagnetic whole, magnetism being the more cohering and life-affirming (female) of the two. Its higher state, biomagnetism, which is associated with living organisms and whose qualities are uplifting and upbuilding, is an energy responsible for the combining of elements in the creative process of building new life forms on a higher, more refined octave (e.g. the fourth dimension). Bioelectricism, on the other hand, is associated with the deconstructive aspect of organic life.

As we saw in Chapter 3, bioelectricism and biomagnetism are complementary, but operate differently in contrasting functions, representing extremes of bielectromagnetic quality. As in all formative and life-building processes, both bioelectricism and biomagnetism are part of the action, but normally balance each other. However, in order for creative processes to be successful, biomagnetism must predominate.

The Van Allen belts, encircling the Earth roughly over the area between the tropics of Cancer and Capricorn, form the radial expansive (centrifugal) electric (bioelectric) function of the Earth dynamo. The axial magnetic (biomagnetic) contractive (centripetal) function is performed by the magnetic lines of force passing through the centre of the Earth from the South to the North Pole and sweeping around the Earth globe from North to South. Between these two component forces, a pulsation, which is the hallmark of all living things, is created as electrical and magnetic moments alternately attain their maxima. According to Viktor Schauberger, these oscillations take place at such a high frequency that we cannot perceive them, and view them as a state of rest.

Storms, water vapour and climate

The amount of water evaporated annually from the oceans has been calculated to total about 333,000km^3.[8] By comparison, the amount from rivers, lakes and land surfaces is more like in 62,000km^3, or 18.6% of the world's annual rainfall (395,000km^3). This has in the past been derived mostly from forests. However, the enormous deforestation of the last fifty years, particularly for agriculture and beef production, has led to a much higher evaporation rate from the Sun-exposed land surfaces.

This leads to a higher volume of water vapour in the atmosphere, which in turn increases the greenhouse effect, leading to higher temperatures which produce a further increase in evaporation from the oceans.[9] There is one feedback mechanism which alleviates the increase in surface temperature; this is the increase in cloud cover as a result of the increased water vapour, increasing the reflection of the Sun's energy back into space (the albedo effect).

While this additional water vapour will increase the general atmospheric temperatures, much of it will drift towards the poles due to the movement of the upper air streams, there to fall as snow, adding to the volume of water fixed almost permanently as ice. This abnormal water vapour content increases the amount of cloud cover, increasing the albedo effect by which the Sun's energy is reflected back into space from the clouds' surface.[10]

The catastrophic rainfall in some areas like Bangladesh and Mozambique and the severe drought conditions of central Africa and northern China are the result of this serious disturbance of the Earth's water balance. Man's destruction of the forest starts a chain reaction that precipitates the cumulative effects of an increasingly disrupted world climate.

PART THREE

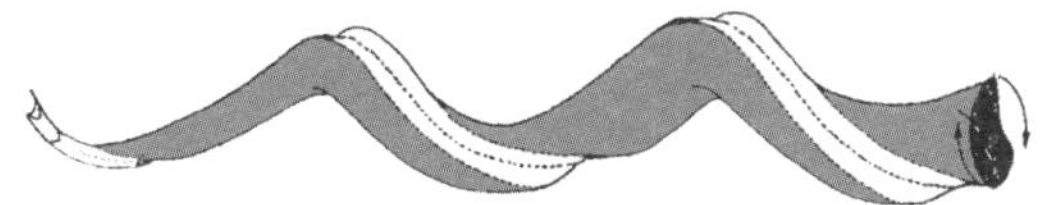

Water — the Source of Life

8. The Nature of Water

The Upholder of the Cycles, which supports the whole of Life, is WATER. In every drop of water dwells a Deity, whom we all serve; there also dwells Life, the Soul of the 'First' substance — Water — whose boundaries and banks are the capillaries that guide it and in which it circulates.

Viktor Schauberger [1]

Our Earth is the planet of water. Seventy percent of the world's surface is covered by water. Our bodies are seventy-five percent water. It is essential to all life. Yet, our present science understands little of its real nature. We have no respect for water; we use it for transporting inappropriate substances, usually waste and pollutants. We destroy its complex structures by driving it through turbines, pipes or straightened riverbanks. We treat it as a commodity. Viktor Schauberger called it a living organism, "the blood of the Earth," and insisted that in its various forms, as blood, sap or water, it is the basis of all life.

Viktor Schauberger was known as "The Water Wizard" because he made profound discoveries about its nature. His principal preoccupation was with water as the key to all life, and its vital relationship to the forest. He saw water as the foundation of all life-processes and the channel that nourishes and energizes all life. He also recognized it as a living entity, whose main function is to accumulate and transform the energies originating from the Earth and the Sun. The source of all our problems, according to Schauberger, is our failure to regard water as an organism; we arrest its creative processes and when it becomes our enemy it can do enormous damage.

As a young man, searching for inspiration in his beloved forest, Viktor was sitting quietly by the bank of a pristine stream when he unexpectedly found that his consciousness entered the water. It connected with an intelligence in the water that spoke to him. It told him what movements it needed to make in order to stay healthy, and under what conditions. It was from this mystical experience that he built up his awareness of how healthy water is essential for the creation and maintenance of all life. Water needs to flow in a particular dynamic way, and must not become overheated. Movement and temperature are the key criteria for water, and therefore for all life.

Still water is passive; it is amorphous and apparently lifeless. As soon as it begins to move, it is filled with surfaces that define little structures, convoluted in form, and with magical vortical shapes. The nature of water is to move. When it is active it comes alive; in movement it fulfils its potential, which is to bring life.

When it is immature, water takes, absorbing minerals with a voracious appetite, to give back the much needed nourishment to its environment only when mature as a mountain spring. Water has a memory; when we think we have 'purified' water of the chemicals and hormones we have mindlessly thrown in, in order to make it drinkable, the energy of these contaminants remain, polluting our energy bodies in the same way that chemicals affect our physical bodies. Because of its nature, water sacrifices itself entirely to the environment, for good or for bad.

People mocked Viktor when he insisted that water behaves like a living organism. When it has reached maturity water displays amazing properties. He showed how, when it is vibrant and healthy, it pulsates, twists and spirals in a very specific way that maintains its vitality and purity, enabling it to fulfil its function for all organisms as an energy channel and a conveyor of nutrients and waste.

If we watch water streaming down an inclining road after a shower of rain, or a rivulet on the sloping beach sand towards the sea, we will notice how it pushes down in a jerky rhythm, as pulsations. That is because water is alive — it actually does pulsate, just as blood pulsates through the veins and arteries of the body. But the most miraculous fact about water is that it has the power of self-purification, and can restore its generative properties in the same way that other living things can heal themselves.

In all symbolic traditions, water is linked with the emotions. It is the emotions that open us out to life, that make us sensitive, receptive and compassionate. Artists love water for its inspiration; it has the ability to stimulate awareness and imagination. I am fortunate to live by a stream; the murmur of a little waterfall by my gate has the quality of calming my emotions. The sounds of water are very evocative; the 'plop' of a drop on a pool surface echoes in the cave;

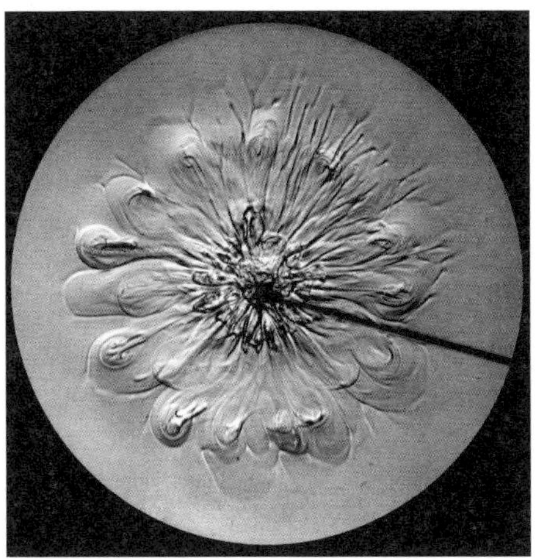
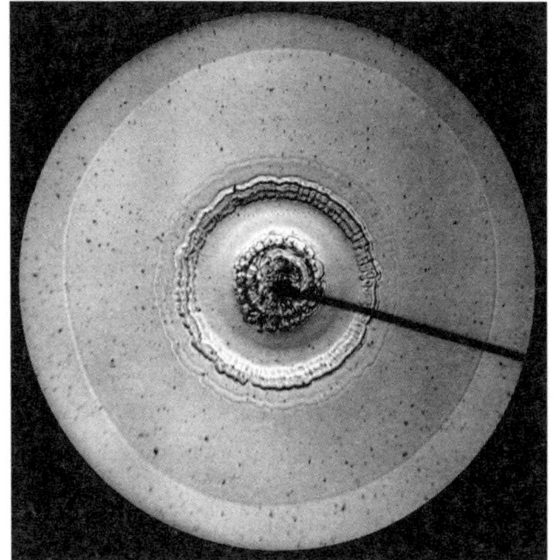
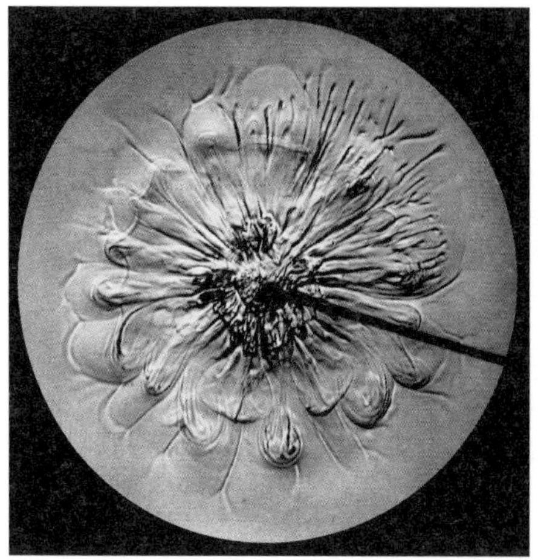

the rhythmic crescendo and fall of the waves hitting the rocks, or the swish and suck of the waves on the beach.

Fig.8.1. These 'drop' pictures show the structure of water.
The first is of living spring water with its structure complete; the second downstream after domestic sewage and industrial effluents, with a trace of rudimentary development, but no formative capacity; a third taken from further down the stream will show how it has, through its natural spiralling movement, rebuilt the water's structure.

Current wisdom accepts that water is important because it is the most common substance on the Earth's surface, and that it is the main physical constituent of all living organisms. But conventional science regards water only as inorganic, with no life of its own.

The memory of water

Water's reputation as a powerful solvent derives from its electromagnetic qualities. The positive hydrogen atoms in the water molecule attract to themselves negative ions from the substance they are in contact with, while the oxygen atom with a double negative charge joins up with positive ions, so that balance is maintained. In this way water breaks down and dissolves substances into their constituent parts, taking oxygen, nitrogen and carbon dioxide from the air, and calcium, potassium, sodium and manganese, etc, from the rocks. Water continually collects substances from one source, depositing them, usually as building blocks for new growth, somewhere else.

When water is flowing as its nature dictates, energetically in spirals and vortices, it creates the structure necessary for it to carry constructive information. These are microclusters of vibrating energy centres, constantly receiving and transmuting energy from every contact the water body makes. Despite water's fluidity and its ability constantly to change its state, the molecules, if conditions permit, generally organize themselves into structures. The vortical movement creates the microclusters and also a complex laminar structure that generates energy from the interaction of their plane surfaces against each. These structures can be observed with a suitable microscope. The more powerful the vortical action, the greater the storage capacity of information (like adding memory to your computer). Thus water put through Viktor Schauberger's implosion (powerfully vorticized) process (see Chapter 18) has the ability to enhance the energy of organisms with which it comes in contact. The clusters have the ability to store vibrational impressions or imprints. If these are beneficial, they may be able to restore healthy resonance in the human body, as through homeopathy. On the other hand if they are the imprints of toxins or pollutants in the drinking water, they may be carriers of disharmony and disease (see p. 119).

Viktor demonstrated that water as an organism has a life cycle from birth, through maturation to death. When it is treated with disrespect or ignorant handling, instead of bringing life and vitality, it becomes anti-life, facilitating pathogenic processes in the organisms it inhabits, which initiate physical decay and eventually bring death. One of Schauberger's more controversial discoveries was that water that has been structurally damaged takes on negative energy that precipitates deterioration in the human being, affecting our actual moral, mental and spiritual wellbeing.

The creation of water

Where does water come from? No one really knows. It is one of Nature's mysteries. Its source cannot be the upper atmosphere for, as we saw in Chapter 7, the water molecule is actually broken down at high altitudes. The only other source must be the Earth herself. Fascinating research done by the American Stephan Riess in 1934 showed that enormous quantities of virgin water could be obtained from crystalline rocks. A combination of geothermal heat and a process known as triboluminescence, a glow which electrons in the rocks discharge as a result of friction or violent pressure, can actually release the oxygen and hydrogen gases in certain ore-bearing rocks. This process, called cold oxidation, can form virgin water.[2]

Riess was able to tap straight into formations of hard desert rock of the right composition and produce as much as 3,000 gallons per minute. Unfortunately, his efforts to provide needy areas with copious quantities of high quality, fresh water were thwarted by Californian politicians with vested interests, and he was persecuted relentlessly. His experiments should now be replicated.

Water is conventionally described as H_2O, having two hydrogen atoms, each carrying a positive external charge, and one oxygen atom carrying two negative external charges. It has, however, been analysed to contain 18 different compounds and 15 separate types of ions.[3] Both seawater and our bodies contain 84 elements in the same proportion. There is 4% salt in our blood; in the oceans it is also 4%.

Water is not a straightforward substance with its own identity, for it takes on the qualities of the medium in which it moves, or the organism in which it resides. It has the unusual ability of being able to combine with more elements and compounds than any other molecule and is sometimes described as the universal solvent. Viktor called it an 'emulsion' when it is supercharged with these creative, 'fructigenic' energies. The more diverse the make-up of constituents dissolved or suspended in water, the more complex the emulsion and the broader the range of its properties. (Carbon, its so-called inorganic counterpart, has a similar capacity that no other elements possess.) Water is found in three physical states: solid as ice, liquid as water and gaseous as water vapour. It also comes in many guises and forms: it is saline and fresh, it is blood and it is sap.

The anomaly point of water

The density of water is crucial to its behaviour. It is at its densest and has its greatest energy content at a temperature of +4°C (39°F). This is the so-called 'anomaly point,' which has a major influence on its quality. Viktor called the temperature of +4°C (39°F) the state of indifference of water, meaning that when in its highest natural condition of health, vitality and life-giving potential, water is at an internal state of energetic equilibrium and in a thermally and spatially neutral condition. Above a temperature of +4°C (39°F), water expands. Below this temperature it also begins to expand and become lighter in weight. Because of this ice floats and is able to protect the fish in the water below from extremes of cold.

It was very convenient for Nature to arrange that mammals and other creatures should depend on blood. In the body, the temperature of the blood (composed 90% of water) is almost exactly the same as the temperature of water at its point of lowest specific heat of +37°C (+98.4°F). This means that our bodies are able to tolerate a wide range of ambient temperatures, for a great amount of heat or cold is required to change the temperature of water. But it also holds on to heat well; good for body temperature and for domestic heating systems.

We are familiar with the principle that the normal temperature of blood in the human body is +37°C (+98.4°F). A very small change in that temperature indicates sickness. It is the same with water and with sap. Schauberger demonstrated this to the world-renowned hydraulicist, Professor Philipp Forchheimer by putting some hot water into a mountain stream. The marginal rise in temperature downstream caused the complex structure of the water filaments to break down, so that a trout that they had observed holding its station in the torrent was unable to stay, and was swept downstream. Forchheimer was dumbfounded, because conventional science does not recognize the importance of small temperature differences.

If science were able to see water as possessing as well as giving life, it would be a giant step towards the rehabilitation of water in human society. Schauberger wrote:

> Were water actually what hydrologists deem it to be — a chemically inert substance — then a long time ago there would already have been no water and no life in this Earth. I regard water as the blood of the Earth. Its internal process, while not identical to that of our blood, is nonetheless very similar. It is this process that gives water its movement.[4]

The symbol H_2O represents pure or distilled water. Schauberger called it 'juvenile' water, because it has no developed character or qualities. It is raw and hungry. Like a baby, it grasps at everything within reach. If you drink only this juvenile water, it will weaken and eventually kill you because it leaches out the minerals and trace elements from your body. Water is mature when it is suitably enriched with raw material, what we call 'impurities,' on which other organisms depend for their energy and life.

The qualities of different waters

Although good water is tasteless, without colour or smell, it quenches our thirst like nothing else. In order to be healthy, we need to drink, according to some authorities, 1–2 litres (5–9 pints) of good quality water a day.[5] Some types of water are more suitable for drinking than others. In Chapter 12 we shall consider some of the choices we have of improving the quality of the available water before we drink it. High quality water should contain elements of both geospheric (female) and atmospheric (male).

Distilled Water

Considered physically and chemically to be the purest form of water. Its nature is to extract or attract to itself all the substances it needs to become mature itself, and therefore absorbs everything within reach. Such water is really quite dangerous if drunk continuously long-term. The 'Kneipp cure' uses distilled water for its short-term therapeutic effect, where it acts to purge the body of excessive deposits of particular substances.

Rainwater

If it has not been affected by industrial pollution (acid rain), rainwater is the purest naturally available water. Slightly richer through the absorption of atmospheric gases, it is still unsuitable for drinking in the long term. When drunk as melted snow-water, it also gives rise to certain deficiencies and if no other water is available it can on occasion result in goitre, the enlargement of the thyroid gland.

Juvenile Water

Juvenile water is immature water from deep underground sources, like geysers. It has not mellowed sufficiently on its passage through the ground. It has not developed a mature structure and contains some minerals (geospheric elements), but few gases (atmospheric elements), so as drinking water it is not very high grade *(cf* most spa waters which arise from mineral rich depths*)*.

Surface Water

Water from dams and reservoirs contain some minerals and salts absorbed through contact with the soil and the atmosphere. Its quality deteriorates through exposure to the Sun, to excessive warming and to chemicals and other pollutants. Although most urban communities now depend on this source, generally speaking it is not good quality water.

Groundwater

Groundwater has a higher quality due to a larger amount of dissolved carbons and other trace salts. This is water emanating from lower levels, seeping out at the surface after passage along an impervious rock surface. Often this is now polluted by the chemicals of industrial agriculture.

Spring Water

True spring water has a large amount of dissolved carbons and minerals. Its high quality is often shown by its shimmering, vibrant bluish colour. The product of infiltrating rainwater (full complement of atmospheric gases) and geospheric water (full complement of minerals, salts and trace elements), this is the best water for drinking, and it often retains this quality in the upper reaches of a mountain stream. Commercially bottled 'springwater' is unfortunately not always of the best quality — many are not from true springs — even if it is bottled in glass rather than the plastic which impairs its quality.

Other Groundwater

Artesian water is obtained from boreholes and is of unpredictable quality. It may be saline, brackish, or fresh. Water from wells can vary from good to poor, depending on how deep is the well and what stratum of water is tapped, and they can be polluted by nitrates and herbicides.

How the river protects itself

Schauberger saw water as being conceived in the cool, dark cradle of the virgin forest. As it slowly rises from the depths, water matures. It absorbs minerals and trace elements on its upward path. Only when it is ripe will it emerge as a spring. A true spring, (compared to a seepage spring), has a water temperature of about +4°C (39°F). In the cool, scattered light of the forest water begins its long journey down the valley as a lively, sparkling and gurgling stream.

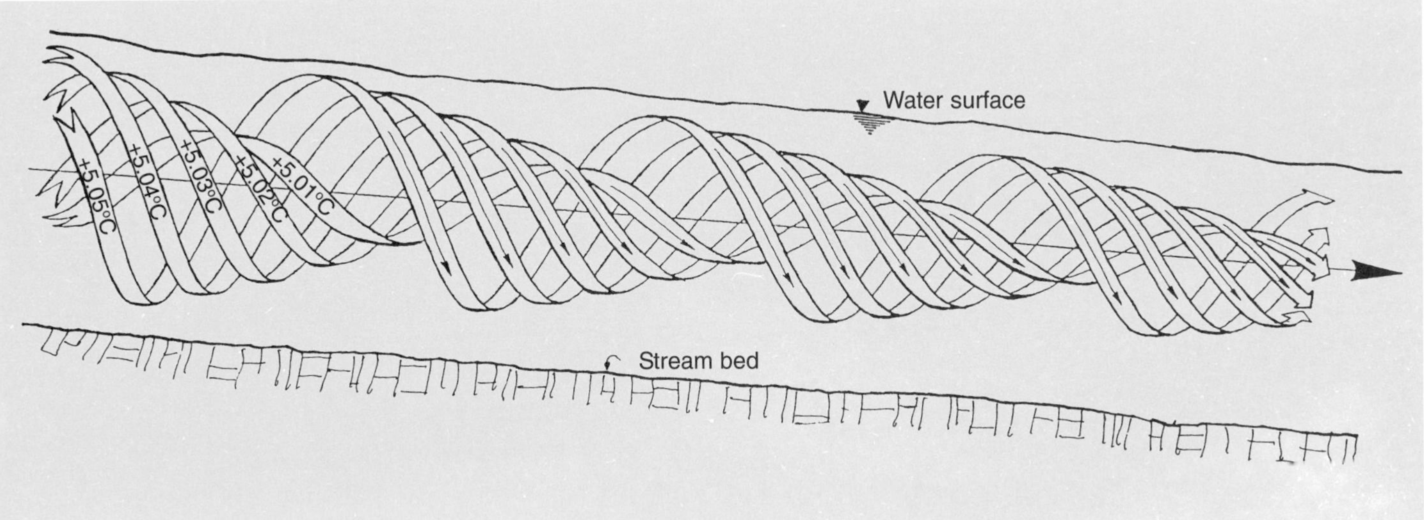

Fig.8.2. A longitudinal vortex showing laminar flow about the central axis.
The coldest water filaments are always closest to the central axis of flow. Thermal stratification occurs even with minimal differences in water temperature. The central core water displays the least turbulence and accelerates ahead, drawing the rest of the water-body in its wake.

Water, when it is alive, creates this spiralling, convoluting motion to retain its coolness and maintain its vital inner energies and health. It is thus able to convey the necessary minerals, trace elements and other subtle energies to the surrounding environment. Have you noticed how refreshing and enlivening it is to sit by a healthy bubbling stream?

Naturally flowing water seeks to protect itself from the damaging direct light of the Sun. The reason that you find trees and shrubs growing on the banks of streams is not from people planting them, but because the energies from the flowing stream facilitated their growth there, to shade the water. When a stream is able to maintain its energies, it will rarely overflow its banks. In its natural motion, the faster it flows, the greater its carrying capacity and scouring ability and the more it deepens its bed (Fig. 8.2).

Schauberger discovered the reason for this — that in-winding, longitudinal spiral vortices form down the central axis of the current, moving alternately clockwise and anti-clockwise. The nature of inwardly-spiralling vortical movement is to cool. So these complex water movements constantly cool and re-cool the water, maintaining it at a healthy temperature, leading to a faster, more laminar, spiral flow, ejecting or transforming undesirable substances.

As the stream gets bigger, it is less able to protect itself from light and heat, and it begins to lose its vitality and health, and with this its ability to energize the environment through which it passes.

Ultimately becoming a broad river, the increasing silt content makes the water flow more sluggishly and become more opaque. This, however, protects the lower strata from the heat of the Sun. They remain cooler, retaining the spiral, vortical motion which is able to shift sediment of larger grain-size (pebbles, gravel, etc.) from the centre of the watercourse, and keep down the risk of flooding. This motion also discourages the generation of harmful bacteria and the water remains disease-free.

Viktor Schauberger wrote in 1933 in his book, *Our Senseless Toil,* how he was able to put to practical use his discoveries about water:

> It is possible to regulate watercourses over any given distance without embankment works; to transport timber and other materials, even when heavier than water, for example ore, stones, etc., down the centre of such watercourses; to raise the height of the water table in the surrounding countryside and to endow the water with all those elements necessary for the prevailing vegetation. [6]

The temperature gradient

One of Viktor Schauberger's most important discoveries was to do with temperature. He showed how small variations of temperature are as crucial to the healthy movement of water and sap as they are for the human blood. He clarified this by identifying temperature change in its relationship to the anomaly point of water +4°C (39.2°F). When the temperature departs from this anomaly point, either up or down, it is said to have a negative gradient. When it approaches the anomaly point, from either direction, or when the groundwater is colder than the air temperature, it has a positive gradient. Heat always moves towards cold.

In the natural process of synthesis and decomposition in all waters, trees and other living organisms, both the rising and falling temperature gradients are active. Each form of gradient has its special function in Nature's great production; the positive (cooling) temperature gradient must play the principal role if evolution is to unfold creatively.

This important factor affects all the features of a river, such as flow velocity, tractive force (shear force), sediment load, turbidity, and viscosity, and everything to do with water management generally, like its storage and transport through pipes (see Chapter 12). It is because modern hydrologists do not recognize the temperature gradient that they are unable to prevent rivers flooding or to deliver better quality water to our homes.

In Nature, the positive gradient is used for creating and building life forms, the negative for breaking down as part of recycling. Biodiversity and evolution, in order continually to develop more complex life systems, require the finer energies that a predominating positive temperature gradient will provide. These two temperature gradients co-exist in the same environment because they have complementary roles. The problem with our civilization is that we have allowed the negative to become dominant, so we have disappearance of species, and the prevalence of coarser energies that result from a degenerating environment.

The quality of any process in Nature depends on the relative influence of the positive and negative temperature gradients. The way the two forms of temperature interact is of crucial importance, for this affects not only the movement of water, but sap in plants and the flow of blood in our veins. It also determines the configuration, structure and quality of the channels, ducts and vessels surrounding and guiding them, as we shall see later.

Schauberger called the stronger temperature behaviours 'essences,' for they have a critical effect in creating life forms. For example, if the positive temperature gradient is very powerful, then the reciprocally weaker negative temperature gradient will help the manifesting of a high quality substance in material form. On the other hand, if the negative temperature gradient is dominant, what manifests is a material substance of poor quality. For evolution and growth to proceed with increasing quality, vitality and health, which form is uppermost and at what level is significant.

Flowing water behaves according to whichever temperature gradient is active. The positive temperature gradient builds up living systems by cooling, concentrating, and energizing as it approaches +4°C (39°F). The key to this process of healthy growth and development is that the ionized substances are drawn together into intimate and productive contact, and the contained oxygen becomes passive and is easily bound by the cool carbones,[7] the building blocks of life. The increasing warming of the negative temperature gradient however, reduces the cohering energy and loosens the structure of an organism and the forms start disintegrating. The oxygen becomes increasingly aggressive and instead of helping to build structures, pulls them apart, encouraging pathogenic disease.

If only our science would recognize the importance of temperature in natural processes and we could rapidly implement changes throughout our technologies, the effect on our environment would be immediate. Our current environmental crises are not limited to increasing global warming through entropic heat pollution. If our technologies were more eco-friendly, there would quickly be a magnifying effect of balancing in the environment, a positive feedback effect, because Nature is always seeking balance. We seem to think that working with Nature is like trying to be honest in our lives (a nice thing to do). In fact Nature's need for balance is so powerful that once we began seriously to work with true ecological integrity, we would be amazed how our efforts would be reciprocated and amplified by Nature.

Schauberger demonstrated, not only that living water possesses extraordinary healing properties, but that it is possible, by designing machines which follow Nature's dynamic processes, to produce this living water from lifeless water.

> In this way it is possible to produce quality drinking water for humans, beasts and for plants artificially, but in the way that it occurs in Nature; to render timber and other such materials non-flammable and rot resistant; to raise water in a vertical pipe without pumping devices; to produce any amount of electricity and radiant energy almost without cost; to raise soil quality and to heal cancer, tuberculosis and nervous disorders.
>
> ...The practical implementation of this... would without doubt require a complete reorientation of all areas of science and technology. By applying these new found laws, I have already built some large structures for log-rafting and river regulation, which have functioned faultlessly for a decade, and which today still baffle the water hydraulics experts.[8]

9. The Hydrological Cycle

In the same way that blood flows through the arteries and veins of the human body, so does water through the lithosphere of the Earth. The cyclical movement of water from subterranean regions to the atmosphere and back again is called 'the hydrological or water cycle.' Today this complete circulation of water is usually interrupted by human intervention, being limited to the atmosphere and the Earth's surface. Viktor called this the half hydrological cycle, the shortcomings of which contribute significantly to our present climate change.

The full hydrological cycle

The diagram below (Fig. 9.1) shows the full hydrological cycle. At the left hand side the upward, anti-clockwise spirals indicate the evaporation of water from the sea. This rises, condenses and falls as rain. Some sinks into the earth and some drains away over the ground surface, depending on whether the ground is forested and what type of temperature gradient is active. In areas of natural forest where a positive temperature gradient normally prevails about 85% of rainfall is retained, 15% by the vegetation and humus and about 70% sinking to the groundwater aquifer and underground stream recharge.

This underground recharge is important, because water that is linked to the subterranean water system acquires the negative energy charge of the Earth. In a natural forest, the mature trees with deep roots bring up this negatively charged water, along with vital minerals and trace elements from the deeper soils. As we shall see in Chapter 14, trees act as biocondensers, harmonizing the positive energy from the Sun with the negative energy of the Earth. As a result, the evapo-transpiration from the leaves of the trees is a balanced, creative energy. This is shown in the diagram as a different direction of spiral from the evaporation from the oceans, to indicate its superior quality. The forest, as a more dynamic living system, creates transpiration that carries the energy (nonmaterial) imprint of all the resonances of the complex biosystem, including the subterranean

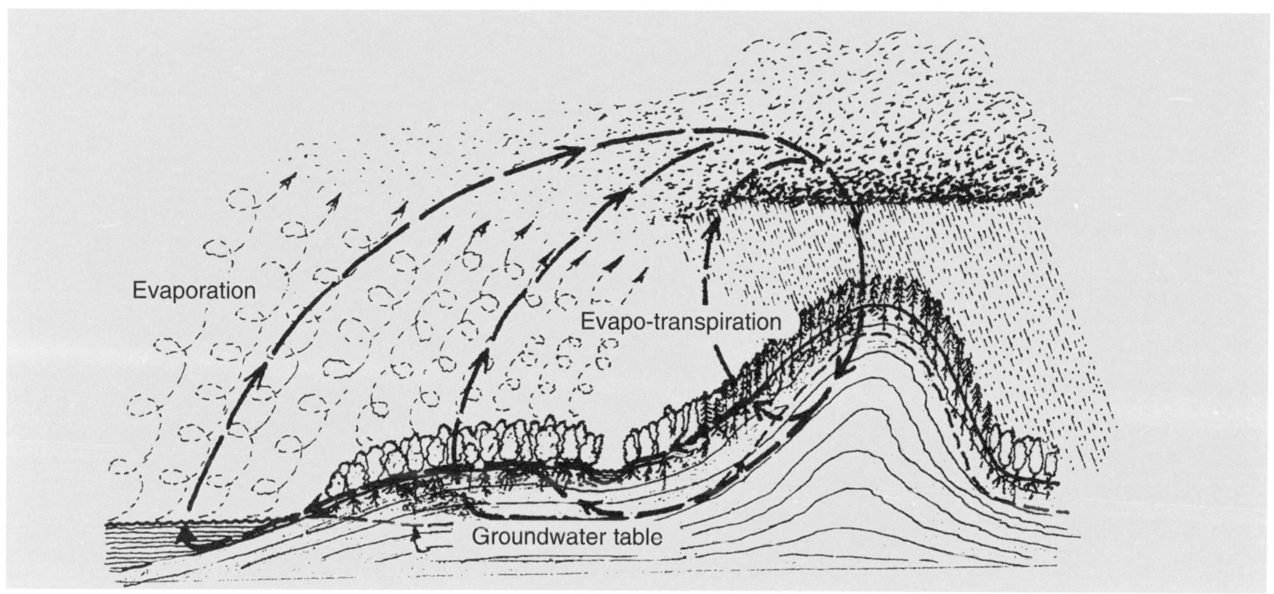

Fig.9.1. The Full Hydrological Cycle.

The FULL CYCLE of water, is characterized by the following phases:

- *Evaporation from oceans and evapo-transpiration from vegetation;*
- *Rising water vapour;*
- *Cooling and condensing;*
- *Formation of clouds;*
- *Precipitation as rain;*
- *Infiltrates the ground under positive temperature gradient;*
- *Recharge of groundwater and aquifers;*
- *Maintenance and regulation of height of groundwater;*
- *Formation of +4°C centre-layer of the groundwater;*
- *Creation of underground retention basins;*
- *Passage through the +4°C centre-layer of the groundwater;*
- *Purification at this temperature;*
- *Further sinking into the subterranean aquifers due to its own weight*
- *Transition to a vaporous state due to the influence of the Earth's hot interior*
- *Rising again towards the ground surface with the simultaneous uptake of nutrients;*
- *Cooling of the water and deposition of nutrients;*
- *Draining away over the ground surface;*
- *Evaporating and forming clouds;*
- *Falling again as rain — and so on.*

elements. Rainfall generated from the forest will carry this beneficial influence. The ocean, although it is recharged by undersea volcanic eruptions and exposure to the atmosphere, mainly consumes all it produces and therefore lacks these dynamic qualities.

This is best explained in terms of homeopathic theory, in which the greater the dilution of a substance, the more powerful its energetic effect. One of the most important discoveries by Professor Jacques Benveniste is that water (even in the form of vapour) carries information.[1] The implication of this is that our tap water may contain the energies that are recycled from human sources, but also that water can be imbued with a healing energy that can be used to treat other water. Some of the domestic water treatment systems now available use this principle.

In the full cycle, water evaporates from the forest and the oceans. The rising water vapour cools with altitude, condenses, forms clouds, with the help of dimethyl sulphide emitted from the leaf protoplasms and from marine algae, combines into larger drops and falls as rain. With full forest cover the temperature of the land surface is cooler than the falling rain, which readily soaks into the ground because of the positive temperature gradient. In other words, the temperature decreases from the atmosphere, through the earth towards the central layer of the water-saturated ground where the temperature is +4°C (39°F). As it falls on the cooler ground, the warmer rain is easily absorbed; it replenishes the groundwater, developing subterranean aquifers. Vegetation depends on groundwater being recharged by rainwater entering under a positive temperature gradient (Fig. 9.1).

The temperature range that life on Earth has adapted to lies roughly between –10°C (14°F) and +40°C (104°F). It is the balanced greenhouse effect that maintains this range. As global temperatures rise with global warming, the stress on all life forms is immense, because they do not have time to adapt to the new conditions.

Water vapour is the principal greenhouse gas. The reduction in evapo-transpiration from the dynamic forests substantially affects the quality of the water vapour and its distribution in the atmosphere. The water vapour created by the natural forest has been balanced by fertile energies from the Earth that bring with it the power to stimulate and heal. Water vapour from the oceans has more of the raw untamed energy of the Sun, and global warming increases the evaporation from the oceans. Without the forest's water, there is a greater contrast between areas with abundant water vapour and those with almost none. This greatly disrupts weather patterns, with an increase in violent storms, hurricanes and serious flooding near coasts, while the areas away from coastal winds suffer droughts and freezing night temperatures.

The half hydrological cycle

Without forest cover, the ground surface overheats, causing a negative temperature gradient in the soil. This means that the cooler rain cannot penetrate into the warmer ground, and fast surface runoff in areas of heavy rainfall causes catastrophic floods. The cause of the floods in recent years, in Columbia, Mozambique, Assam and Bangladesh was the deforestation on high ground.

This disruption of the natural water cycle Schauberger called the half hydrological cycle, which is now prevalent almost worldwide. Notice the difference between Fig. 9.2 below and Fig. 9.1 on p. 118. The drawing below shows that, in the absence of tree cover, the water table has sunk. Once the forest has been removed, the exposed ground heats up rapidly, all the more so if dry, and to much higher temperatures.

This type of evaporation, now lacking the evapo-transpiration from living things, has more destructive energies. If the rainfall is excessive, then flooding inevitably occurs. In many hot countries denuded of vegetation, dry valleys and creeks can be suddenly engulfed by a wall of water as terrifying flash-floods sweep away everything in their path.

In the absence of trees and ground cover to absorb it, the rainwater spreads widely over the surface of the ground, resulting in massive abnormal re-evaporation. The increase in water vapour in the atmosphere soon causes increased precipitation. What happens is that one flood causes another, while in inland areas, droughts become more frequent. The only answer to this vicious cycle is a massive international campaign to plant trees, particularly in the warmer latitudes.

The most serious result of the half cycle is that there is no replenishment of the groundwater. With the sinking of the groundwater level, the supply of nutrients to the vegetation is cut off. The water that is evaporated into the atmosphere is virtually lifeless, lacking in the energy and the qualities that groundwater acquires. Viktor Schauberger called this a 'biological short-circuit.' The essential soil moisture, trace elements and other nutrients that the tree roots normally raise to the benefit of other plants sink below reach as the groundwater sinks. This is the cause of desertification, now becoming prevalent in many tropical areas. The groundwater disappears, probably for ever, into the womb of the Earth where it came from.

The limited circulation of the half water cycle increases the intensity of thunderstorms. These can raise the water vapour to levels far higher than normal. At altitudes of 40–80 kilometres it is exposed to much stronger ultraviolet and high-energy gamma radiation, which break up the water-molecule, separating the hydrogen and oxygen

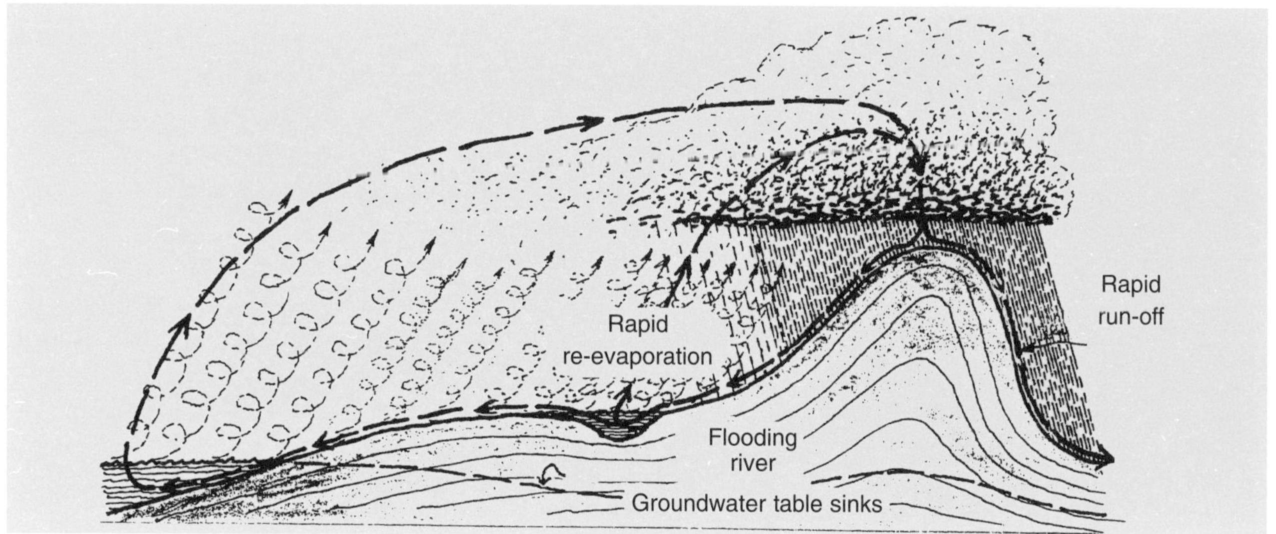

Fig.9.2. The Half Hydrological Cycle.

The HALF CYCLE in contrast, has the following features:

- *Evaporation from oceans;*
- *Rising water vapour;*
- *Cooling and condensing;*
- *Formation of clouds;*
- *Precipitation as rain;*
- *No infiltration due to negative temperature gradient;*
- *Rapid runoff over the ground surface;*
- *No groundwater recharge;*
- *Sinking water table — in the long term;*
- *Cessation of natural supply of nutrients to vegetation;*
- *Under certain conditions, major flooding can occur;*
- *Excessively fast re-evaporation;*
- *Oversaturation of atmosphere with water vapour;*
- *Rapid reprecipitation as storm rain.*

Fig. 9.3a &b. Positive and Negative temperature gradients:
Fig. 9.3a illustrates a positive temperature gradient — ground cooler shaded by trees — rainwater warmer than the ground surface will soak in easily, recharging the groundwater. But where the surface is unprotected (Fig. 9.3b) it heats up, does not allow the rainwater to penetrate (negative temperature gradient), causing the water table to be forced upwards, with the dissolved salts, which remain near the surface, possibly causing problems of salination.

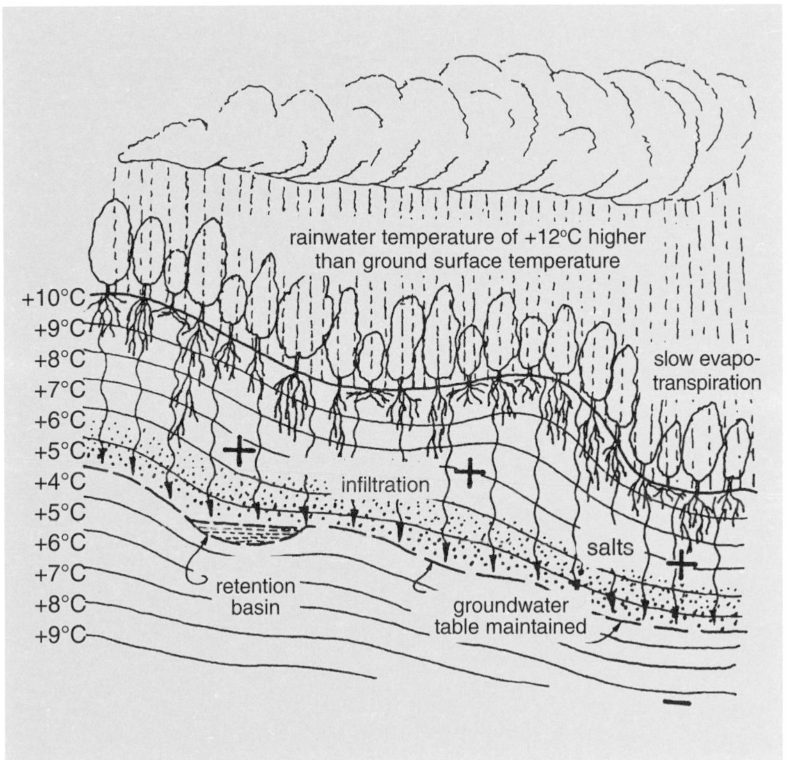

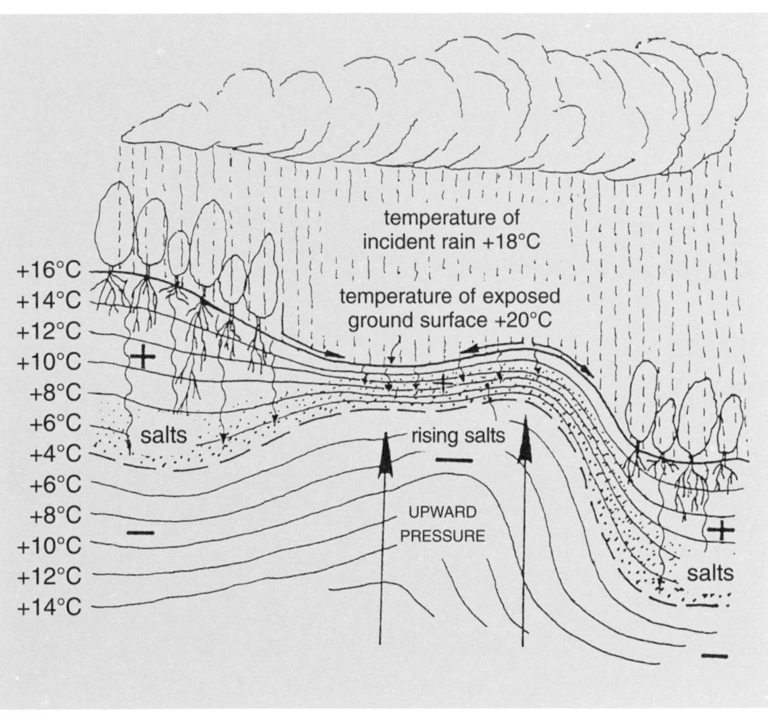

atoms. The hydrogen then rises because of its lower specific weight, and the oxygen sinks. That water becomes permanently lost. The effect of global warming is complex. The atmosphere first warms up due to the greater amount of water vapour, some of this increase of heat being offset by the loss of water atoms at high altitudes.

Temperature gradients and nutrient supply

As we have seen, unless vegetation keeps the ground surface cooler than the falling rain, the water will not easily penetrate the soil. The direction of the temperature gradient indicates the direction of movement. Energy or nutrient transfer is always from heat to cold. So a positive temperature gradient is also essential for nutrients to be able to rise up to the roots of the plants (see Fig. 9.3).[2]

If the surface is well forested, the rainwater is warmer than the soil, and penetrates to the lower strata, replenishing the groundwater body and the aquifers. The salts remain at a level where they cannot pollute the upper strata where they would harm those plants which are salt-sensitive. The groundwater hugs the configuration of the ground surface. Fig. 9.3 shows how the salts in the ground rise near the surface, particularly on a hilltop, when part of the forest is cut down, leaving the ground exposed to sunlight.

Schauberger demonstrated that when light and air are absent well below the surface of the ground, the minerals and salts are precipitated near the temperature horizon of +4°C (39°F). Warm ground will encourage evaporation of the moisture near the surface, so that the minerals and salts are deposited near the surface, lowering the fertility of the soil. If all the trees are removed (Fig. 9.4), there will be no penetration of rainwater; the water table initially rises, due to the now uncompensated upward pressure from below described in the following chapter, bringing up all the salts, but will eventually sink or disappear altogether without the replenishment of rainwater. Fertility can be restored in time only through reforestation, bringing about the reestablishment of a positive temperature gradient.

Replanting must be done initially with salt-loving trees and other primitive plants, as only they would survive under such conditions. Later, due to the cooling of the ground by the shading of the pioneer trees, the rainwater can penetrate the ground, taking the salts with it. Over time, as the soil climate improves the pioneer

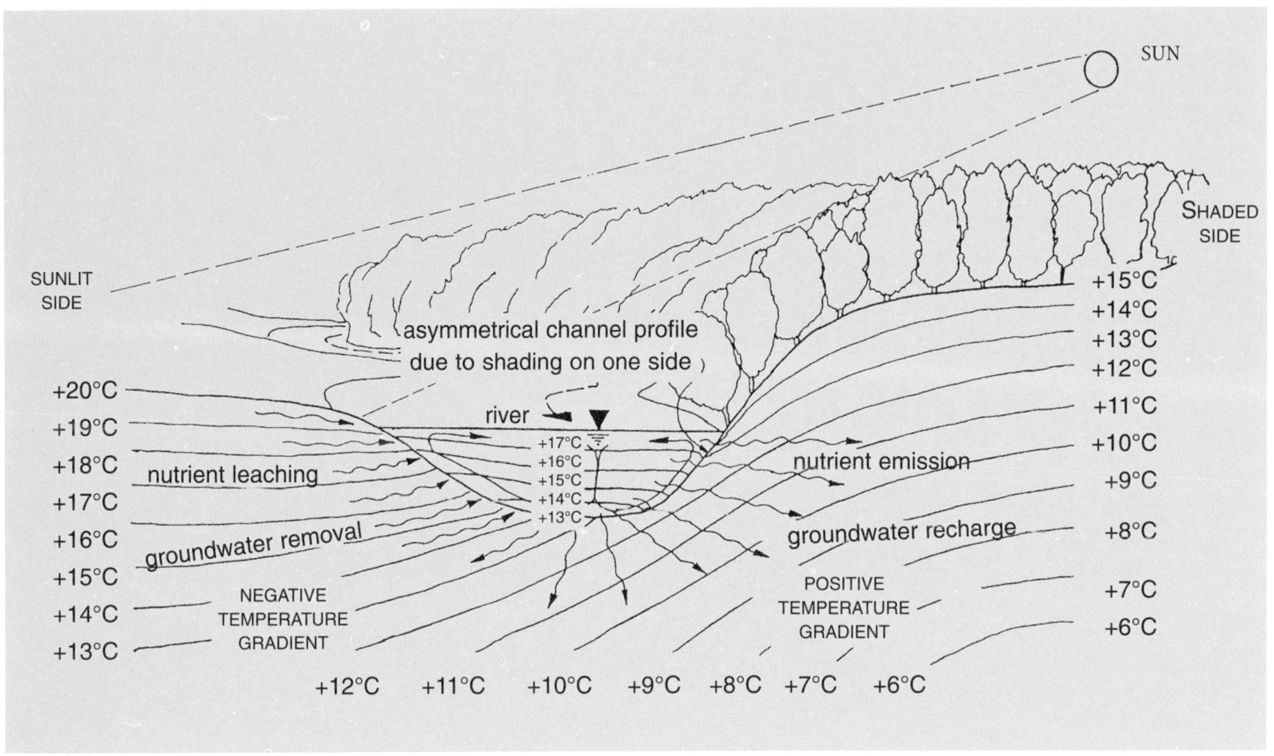

Fig.9.4. Asymmetric River Development. *The orientation of a river relative to the Sun's position affects the nutrient supply. Where the river flows east>west or west>east, the side nearest the Sun tends to be more shaded and the water cooler; a positive temperature gradient develops, allowing the cooler ground to absorb mineral-rich water from the river, and the soil becomes more fertile. On the side exposed to the Sun, the reverse occurs, with a negative temperature gradient forcing groundwater, with its minerals to leach into the river.*

trees die off, because the improved soil conditions don't suit them. Other species of tree can replace them and the dynamic balance of Nature is restored.

Irrigation in hot climates aggravates the problem because, as the ground temperatures cool during the night, the irrigating water can penetrate the upper salt-containing strata. With the increase in temperature during the day, the infiltrated irrigation water with its acquired salts are drawn up, and upon exposure to light and heat are deposited on the soil surface. The seriousness of the problem will vary with latitude, height and season.

All healthy rivers will carry nutrients in suspension that will be absorbed by the vegetation on the river banks if the soil is cooler than the river water. This improves soil fertility and recharges the groundwater. But, if the soil is warmer than the river, due to the absence of protective cover, a negative temperature gradient will cause the nutrients to leach from the soil into the river, which will eventually make the soil sterile and unproductive. The longer a river flows through irrigated, sunlit farmlands, the more it becomes contaminated with salts, artificial fertilizers and pesticides, making it unhealthy in the lower reaches as a source of water.

In the diagram (Fig. 9.4) opposite, the river water temperature varies from +17°C (63°F) at the surface to +13°C (55°F) at the bottom. Where the ground under the wooded area on one side of the river is cooler than the river water, a positive temperature gradient exists from river to ground. On the opposite side, in the absence of trees, the ground is warmer and attracts a negative gradient from river to ground. The diagram shows nutrients being removed from the warmer bank and deposited on the opposite, cooler bank.

Where the tree cover cools the river, it flows faster with a laminar structure, removing sediment and deepening its bed.

The rivers are the arteries of Gaia. If they are not allowed to operate as natural conveyors of energy and nutrients to the land through which they flow, the fertility of the land gravely suffers. If we were really to take care of our rivers, protecting their banks from overheating, and allowing them to flow sinuously as they will, rather than make them follow straight lines, we would be taking important steps to give back to Nature her own power.

10. The Formation of Springs

Before the installation of public water networks, springs were the most valued or sometimes the only sources of drinking water, and they still are in many parts of the world. Settlements would establish around a spring that delivered high quality water. Possibly because of the connection between living water and good health, some established a reputation for curative powers. Viktor Schauberger insisted that the high quality water produced by his springwater machine had healing qualities.

The veneration of springs

Springs have long been associated with folk medicine, ritual and religion, frequently being reported as places of power in the landscape. Usually, springs thus endowed are called 'holy wells,' which is confusing, because the word derives from the Anglo-Saxon for spring — *wella,* (hence the expression to 'well up') not for its modern use as a shaft excavated to reach the underground water table. The tradition of venerated springs is found in all cultures and major religions, including the earliest known to us. The most common association is the bestowal of supernatural qualities, but more specifically as the abode of spirits or deities, or being linked with holy figures or saints. In Britain, in most cases the saints named had no connection with the site, but their qualities may be associated with those the previous pagans had ascribed.

The waters of most sacred springs are credited with healing powers, and with cures accomplished by bathing or drinking. In British lore the most common affliction claimed to be healed by springs is infertility, followed by eye complaints. However some springs are regarded as so powerful — as at Lourdes in France, or Bath in England — that they are reputed to heal many diseases. Offerings were made to the pools served by the springs, either as part of the locally established ritual, or as a 'trade' for a wish to be granted. Many 'wells' were 'dressed,' or decorated with flowers, paintings, statues or strips of cloth, a tradition found all over Europe and Asia, in Africa and Central America.

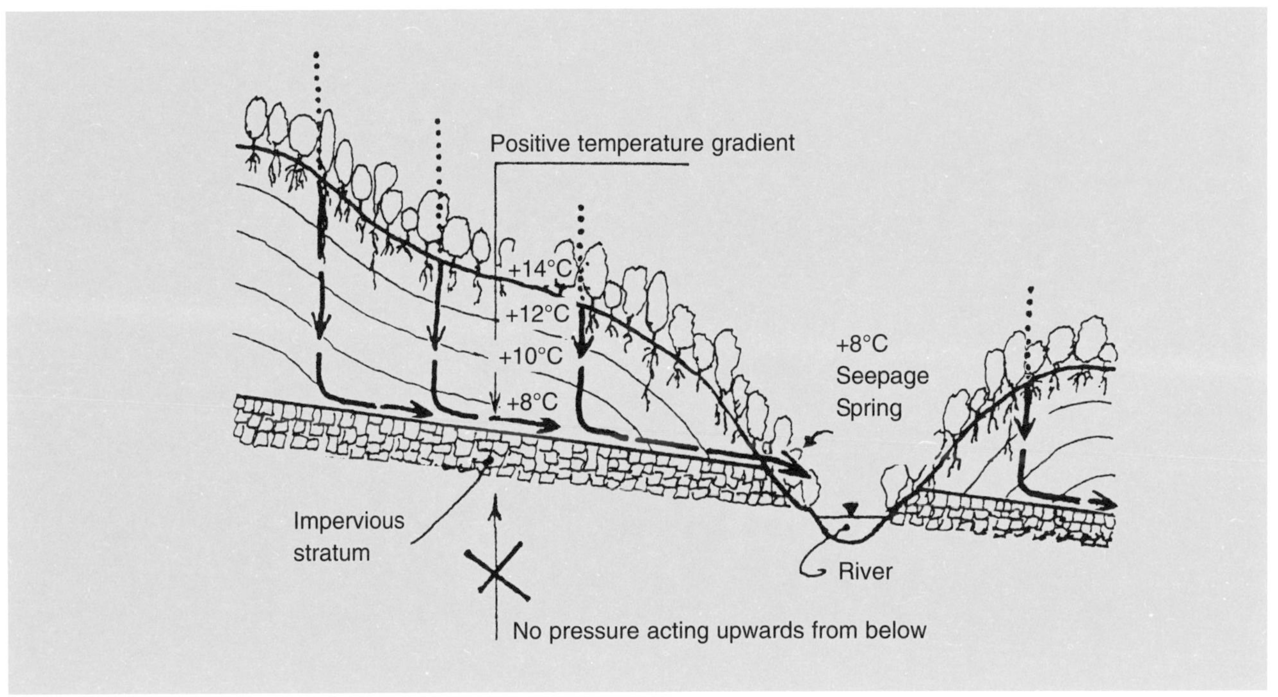

Fig.10.1. Seepage Spring.
Seepage springs occur when water infiltrating the ground (positive temperature gradient) encountering an impervious layer, seeps down this slope emerging where it meets the ground surface. The amount of the infiltrations determines the outflow rate and its temperature that of the surrounding area, seldom very cold.

Natural springs would be valued also because the quality and reliability of the water flow in times of drought might make the difference between life and death. It is not hard to see why people invested these sites with magical powers, or seeing them as inhabited by a living spirit who was the guardian of the waters. It is likely that many of our forebears would empathize with Viktor Schauberger's vision of water as 'the blood of the Earth' when they saw the pure, cold, nourishing liquid issuing mysteriously from the womb of the Earth.

Rivers frequently have their source at a spring.[1] The source of a great holy river is regarded as particularly sacred. Many churches and monastic institutions are associated with springs, the churches using the water for baptism. The monasteries pioneered the capping of the springs to deliver the water through wooden or stone 'conduits.' These proved to be the salvation of growing urban populations in England who, after the dissolution of the monasteries in the sixteenth century, would take 'feathers,' or branch pipes, off these monastic conduits. Like the springs from which they derived, in some localities these conduits were often venerated and adorned with flowers and gilded branches.

When the rationalism of the Enlightenment replaced the superstitions of an earlier age, some explanation had to found for the curative powers of certain famous springs. This led, in the 18th century, to the birth of the spa culture, and doctors would examine any deposits left behind when they had boiled away the water, in order to identify this and that mineral as the true elixir that would give legitimacy to their spa water. During the Protestant Reformation in England, and then with the decline of rural populations, many sacred springs fell into disuse, being rediscovered by Irish immigrants in the nineteenth century, whose Celtic-based Catholicism still had strong pagan roots.

Today, with the revival of ancient rural traditions, many sacred springs are being restored in Britain and in Continental Europe.

Seepage springs

What is generally understood as a spring is actually not a true spring, but a seepage spring which is the overflowing of surplus water from soil and rock strata that have a limited depth (Fig. 10.1). Rainwater which is warmer than the ground (a positive temperature gradient), soaks in and descends until it reaches an impervious layer like clay, which channels it out as a stream to the surface again, lower down. It acts by gravity. The temperature of the water will be that of the strata from which it emerges, probably between +6°C (43°F) to +9°C (48°F). This water will contain some trace elements, minerals and dissolved salts but, generally speaking, not in such a broad spectrum as true springs. The seepage spring responds quickly to variations in precipitation, frequently drying up in a hot summer, and flowing strongly after heavy rain.

True springs

A true spring originates from much deeper strata (Fig. 10.2). Water collects in ancient aquifers and retaining basins over many years, and the water emerging to the surface might be hundreds of years old; or even thousands in the case of the famous therapeutic hot springs. Because of their age, these spa waters are extraordinarily rich in well-balanced minerals. The rich waters of the Hunza Valley in Pakistan, or the Caucasus mountains, which are credited for the longevity of the local people, also originate in true

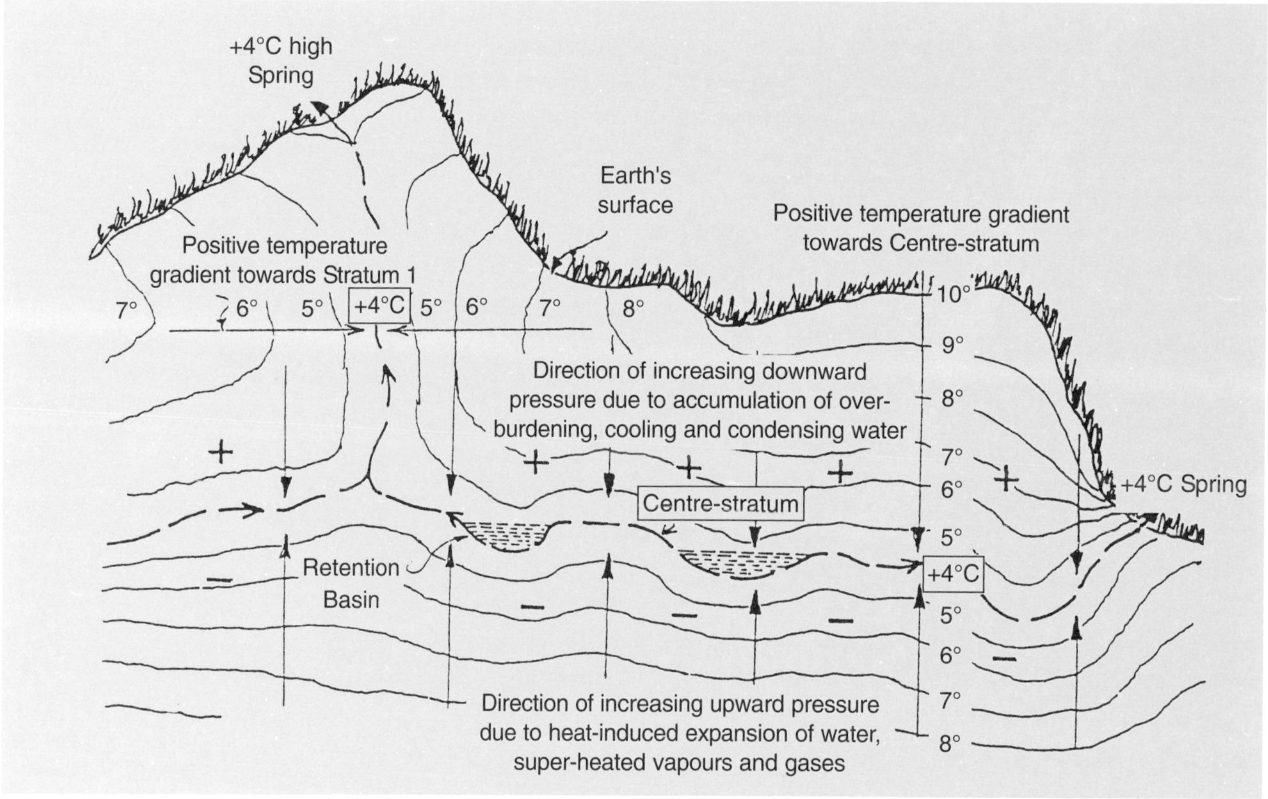

Fig.10.2. True Springs and High Altitude Springs.
These depend on the existence of the 39°F (+4°C) denser water level which is called the centre stratum. This gets squeezed between the weight of water in the rocks above, and the water strata below. At 39°F (+4°C) it will compress no more, and has to move vertically or laterally, eventually emerging as a spring. This is why they are normally very cold and may appear on mountain tops.

springs. The difference here is that, emerging in the high mountains, these waters are then augmented by rich glacial waters, and by minerals from the action of the aggressive mountain streams eroding the surface rocks.

The rainwater penetrates the ground surface under the influence of a positive temperature gradient, in a way similar to that of a seepage spring. But it is drawn down much more deeply, helped by the increasing pressure, so that it condenses and cools to around +4°C (39°F). Being immature water, it will absorb what it can, so it removes salts from the upper layers of the ground, depositing them later as the water condenses and cools with depth. This makes the upper layers more fertile, and the salts are now available to deep-rooted trees that have the ability to metabolize them, converting them to nutrients for more shallow-rooted plants.

The downwards-percolating rainwater increases the pressure on the groundwater body, pressing the lowest layer into rocks that are affected by geothermal heat. These are caused to expand, compressing the layers above. But the +4°C (39°F) stratum water is already at its densest and virtually incompressible at this temperature, so all it can do is to push out laterally, providing the springs with their flow. This action explains how springs can emerge from high mountain peaks at such cold temperatures, where there would be insufficient local collection for a gravity seepage.

Rain absorbs oxygen in its fall through the atmosphere. After it enters the ground and percolates through the soil, plant roots and organisms reduce its oxygen content. So when it eventually emerges as a true spring, the water is often oxygen-deficient, though rich in carbonic acid. It is dangerous to drink this water directly from the spring, for being hungry for oxygen, the water can steal it from susceptible organs, like the stomach, causing great discomfort. If breathed directly, the carbonic acid can damage the lungs. Known to mountain folk as 'damp-worm,' and by miners as 'choke-damp' respectively, both can be fatal. However, within ten metres of the source, the water has usually, through its active movement, absorbed sufficient oxygen to be quite safe to drink.

How springwater rises

Viktor Schauberger designed an experiment to demonstrate how groundwater rises during the day and recedes at night. The equipment consists of a glass U-tube with open ends, one of which has contact with the air only by two very fine capillary tubes, the other end being open. Each arm is sealed off from the other by some saltwater-saturated sand at the bottom of the U-tube. High grade springwater with low oxygen content, and having had no contact with strong light, is inserted into each arm. The U-tube is placed in a soil-filled bucket, containing ice at the bottom to create an artificial environment of +4°C (39°F) temperature.

When the bucket is put out in the Sun, a positive temperature gradient is set up and, because there is greater contact with the outside atmosphere, the water level can rise on the open end of the U-tube. At night, when the temperature gradient decreases, the water level rises on the side with the capillary tubes, falling on the open side, and rising on the partially blocked side. (This

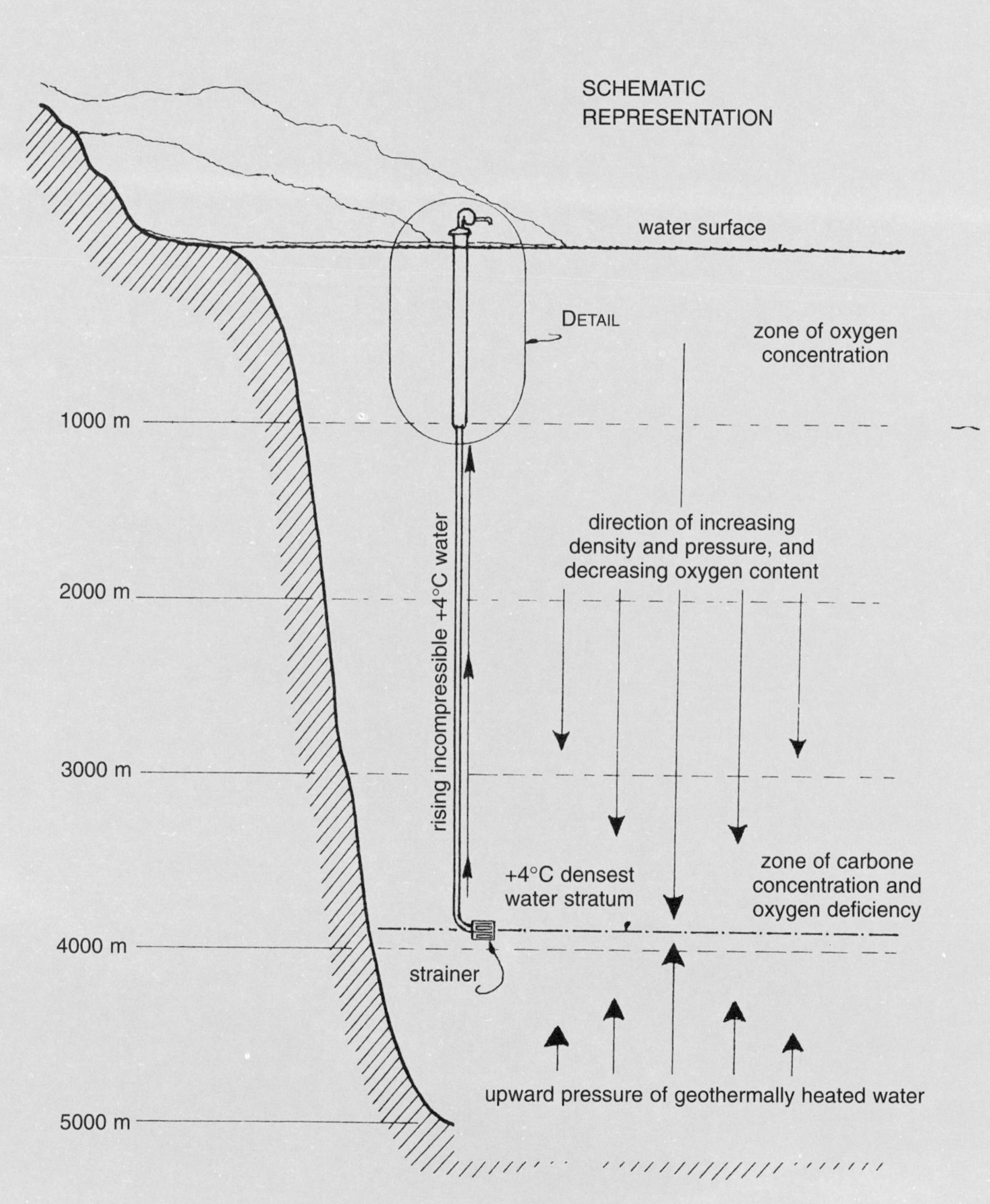
SCHEMATIC
REPRESENTATION
water surface
DETAIL
zone of oxygen
concentration
1000 m
direction of increasing
density and pressure, and
decreasing oxygen content
rising incompressible +4°C water
2000 m
3000 m
+4°C densest
water stratum
zone of carbone
concentration and
oxygen deficiency
4000 m
strainer
upward pressure of geothermally heated water
5000 m

experiment is illustrated on p. 202 (Fig. 15.3), the experiment originally being designed to show how sap rises and falls in a tree.)

Producing energy from the ocean

Viktor Schauberger alluded to the simplicity of emulating the dynamics of true springs for generating energy, although he gave no details. Having gained some insight into Schauberger's thinking, Callum Coats described how this might be done, publishing the process, so that no commercial company would be able to patent the idea.

Describing the formation of true springs, we spoke of the deep groundwater having had its oxygen content removed by needy roots and organisms on its journey through the soil, but having instead a concentration of the female fructigenic carbones. At its most dense at the +4°C (39°F) deep stratum, it is squeezed and can be lifted up to the highest mountain tops.

The water of the ocean deeps is in a similar condition of density at the +4°C (39°F) deep stratum, but also under high pressure because of the enormous weight of water above it. A long pipe would be lowered from the surface of the ocean to allow this oxygen-hungry water to rise in order to drive electric generators at the surface.

This would not be a viable system, however, without some essential additions that Schauberger added to increase the power of the rising abyssal water (Fig. 10.3). The pipe would be of double-spiral design, with vortex-inducing vanes similar to those used in the Stuttgart experiment (see Chapter 14). The bottom end of the pipe would have a tangentially-arranged vortex inducer, as well as a strainer to keep out marine creatures.

At a water level nearer to the surface, atmospheric air would enter through a one-way filter in order to introduce oxygen to the hungry abyssal water. (The filter would accept the smaller oxygen molecule, but exclude the larger water molecule.) On absorbing the oxygen, the rising water warms and rapidly expands with sufficient power to drive the generators, which would not be of the conventional design that destroys the water's structure, but with centripetal impellers that improve the quality of the water.[2]

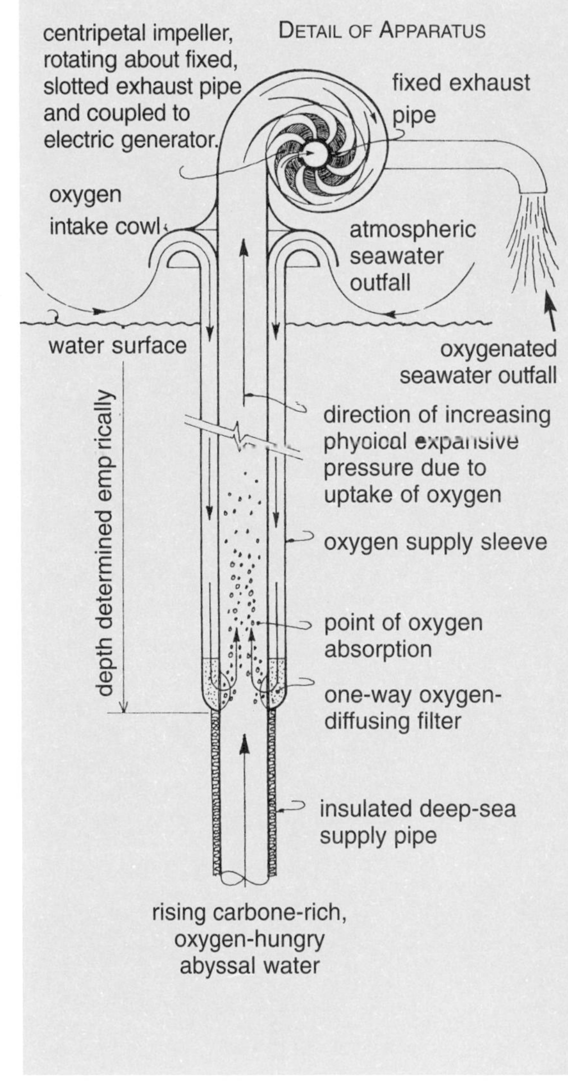

Fig.10.3 (opposite). Free Energy from the Deep Ocean.
Callum Coats' development of Viktor Schauberger's idea.
Fig. 10.4 (above). Detail of apparatus in figure opposite.

11. Rivers and How they Flow

If we understood the importance of water both for the environment and for life, we would nurture and protect our rivers, which are the great arteries of the Earth. Healthy streams and rivers are water at its most active, powerful and playful. In our ignorance of how water needs to move, we restrict rivers with embankments and other unnatural constructions. We treat rivers as sewers for waste, and we extract the energy and spirit from their form.

For scores of thousands of years, since people started to settle on the land, our forebears were aware that their prosperity depended on the river. Soils are quickly depleted of their nutrients by agriculture, particularly if intensive. Remineralization by regular flooding of the river was vital to obtaining good crops. This allowed the great civilizations to grow and flourish, in Mesopotamia, the valleys of the Nile, the Yellow River and the Indus, to name a few.

Today's technocrats have a need to control this apparently chaotic behaviour of the natural river, by steering the flow, sometimes behind high banks, and disregarding the ecosystem, to the great loss of fertility of the surrounding fields. Modern artificial fertilization (NPK — nitrogen, phosphorus and potassium) cannot take the place of Nature's remineralization; in fact it often causes great problems through creating imbalances and pollution.

Stages of a river

A river has three stages of life. Its youthful stage energizes the water as the steep landscape puts it through vigorous tumbling, spinning and intense vortical movements. The immature cold water is hungry, taking up minerals as it scours the rock, cutting gullies and steepening the sides of the valley, more especially when it is in spate. It is oxygenated in rapids and waterfalls. It is put through exercises that it will use well when it matures.

When the stream leaves the steep country, the flow slows, and some of the heavier rock matter it carried in suspension is deposited, to be picked up again when the flow accelerates. The water is now mature, having absorbed minerals and generative energies, and if it is prevented from excessive warming by trees on its banks, it recharges the groundwater of the surrounding countryside. The richness of movement of the young stream is carried into the body of the meandering river. The water is creating its own form which in turn regulates its flow.

Entering the plains the river, in its natural way, would meander across the flat country, and when a bend twists back on itself, a shortcut will be created at flood time, leaving behind an oxbow crescent lake. It is in the plains country mostly that people try to manipulate the river, heavy with silt, by straight embankments to stop the river spreading where it wants to. These natural floods are not particularly destructive, and remineralize the soil which becomes much more productive. But technical man believes he can control Nature. The old river is now typically forced to perch sometimes 50 feet above the surrounding countryside. If the river should burst its artificial banks at this stage, the flooding is catastrophic. Lacking its normal twisting movement and positive temperature gradient which keep the silt in suspension, it is deposited, blocking the channel. Its natural path thus obstructed, it becomes angry and unpredictable. There are now very few major rivers which are allowed to flow naturally.

Temperature and the movement of water

Viktor Schauberger made inspired studies of the natural flow in rivers. He found that the temperature gradient in moving water plays a very decisive role both in the way it moves and in the structure of the water masses within the river.

> To regulate a waterway by means of the riverbank itself is verily to fight cause with effect ... It cannot and should not be the task of the river engineer to correct Nature by violating her. Rather, in all watercourses requiring regulation his job should be to study the natural harmony of the river, and to emulate the examples that Nature provides in the way of healthy streams ... Every violation, however, rebounds on the perpetrator ... As water flows down a natural gradient, it does so according to a sublime inner law whose power our hydraulic experts are quite unable to comprehend ... The more the engineer, ignorant of the nature of water, tries to channel water by

the shortest and straightest route to the sea, the more the flow of water weighs into the bends, the longer its path and the more destructive and the worse the water will become.[1]

The variations in the temperature of the water-body are so subtle, within a range of 0.1°C to 2.0°C (0.04°F to 0.08°F), that contemporary hydraulic engineering practice has never felt they were significant. Viktor Schauberger, however, considered the temperature variation absolutely essential for all natural water resources management. He insisted that no artificial constraints on the river could ever be successful unless these variations were taken into account, since whether a river removes, transports or deposits its sediment is dependent upon the water temperature and the temperature gradient predominantly active along its course.

Creating a positive temperature gradient

When water descends a gradient, in the course of flow under natural conditions, it rhythmically first heats up and then cools down. The degree of heating depends on the amount of friction with the riverbed, the external temperature and the extent to which the water is directly exposed to the Sun. Only a minute change in temperature is required for water to pick up, transport or deposit its sediment, but the type of temperature gradient prevailing determines the action. A negative temperature gradient causes the deposition of sediment, and a positive temperature gradient provokes its removal. The temperature gradients alternating too suddenly can, however, cause the scouring or deposition of gravel to become chaotic.

Fig.11.1. Alternate Heating and Cooling (breathing) rhythms in river flow.
Friction with the river bed gradually warms the river (negative temperature gradient) so that it starts to deposit its suspended sediment. When this reaches its maximum, an overfall occurs, producing a horizontal barrel vortex that cools the water (positive temperature gradient), until the river gradually warms up again. Schauberger likened this to the river 'breathing'.

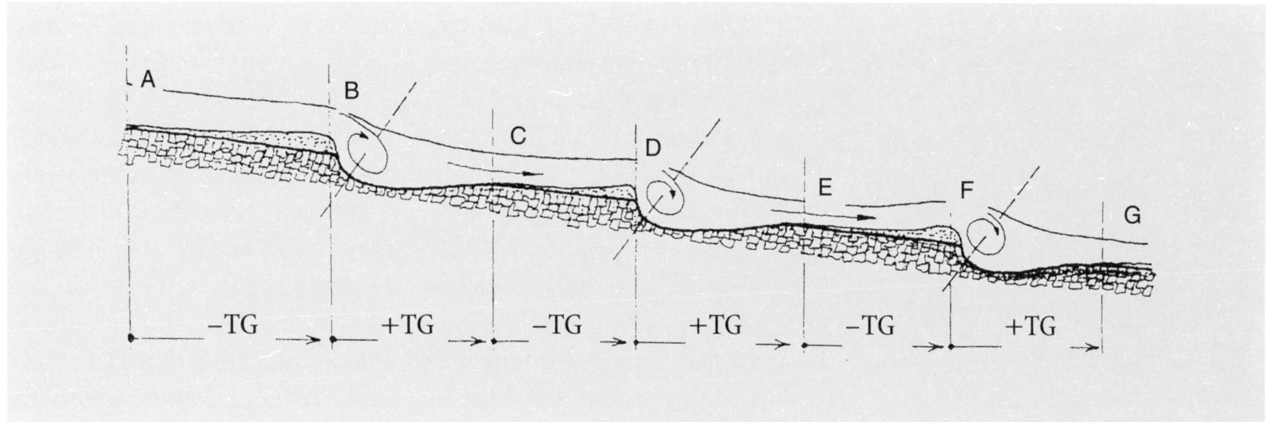

In Fig. 11.1, for example, from A to B the temperature gradient is negative. From A to B the water gradually heats up and in the process is unable to retain the sediment in suspension and drops it progressively as the water becomes warmer. At B, the zone of maximum deposition, the accumulated material results in an overfall that, in turn, creates a horizontal barrel vortex immediately downstream. This vortex, however, cools the water and therefore from B to C the temperature gradient becomes positive. The sediment is once more picked up and transported. Upon reaching C, the effect of the positive temperature gradient gives way to its negative counterpart and the suspended matter is again dropped, reaching a maximum at D.

This pulsation or alternation is like breathing; a positive temperature gradient representing the inbreath, the absorbing, material-collecting movement; the negative temperature gradient representing the outbreath, where the energetically transformed matter is exhaled from the system and deposited. In order to regulate a river naturally and successfully, it is essential to study the alternating sequence of the temperature gradients. A stretch of river with a positive gradient is less likely to flood, since only minor sediment deposition will occur. If the danger of flooding is to be reduced then a positive temperature gradient must be recreated or its duration extended. This can be done in four principal ways:

1. By shading and cooling the river through the replanting of trees, particularly at the bends, where the friction and therefore the warming tendencies are greatest. Tree species with a high evaporation rate should be planted. Through evaporation the sap in the tree is cooled and circulates down to the roots under the river bed, cooling the water as well. This kind of tree therefore acts like a refrigerator.

In order to maintain the health of the river, there should be a belt of trees 500 to 1000 metres wide. Rivers flowing through cleared, barren countryside should be reforested in order to re-establish healthy flow conditions, restore the nutrient supply and recharge the groundwater table in its vicinity (Fig.11.2).

2. By the construction of appropriately designed dams in which the temperature of the discharge can be controlled according to the

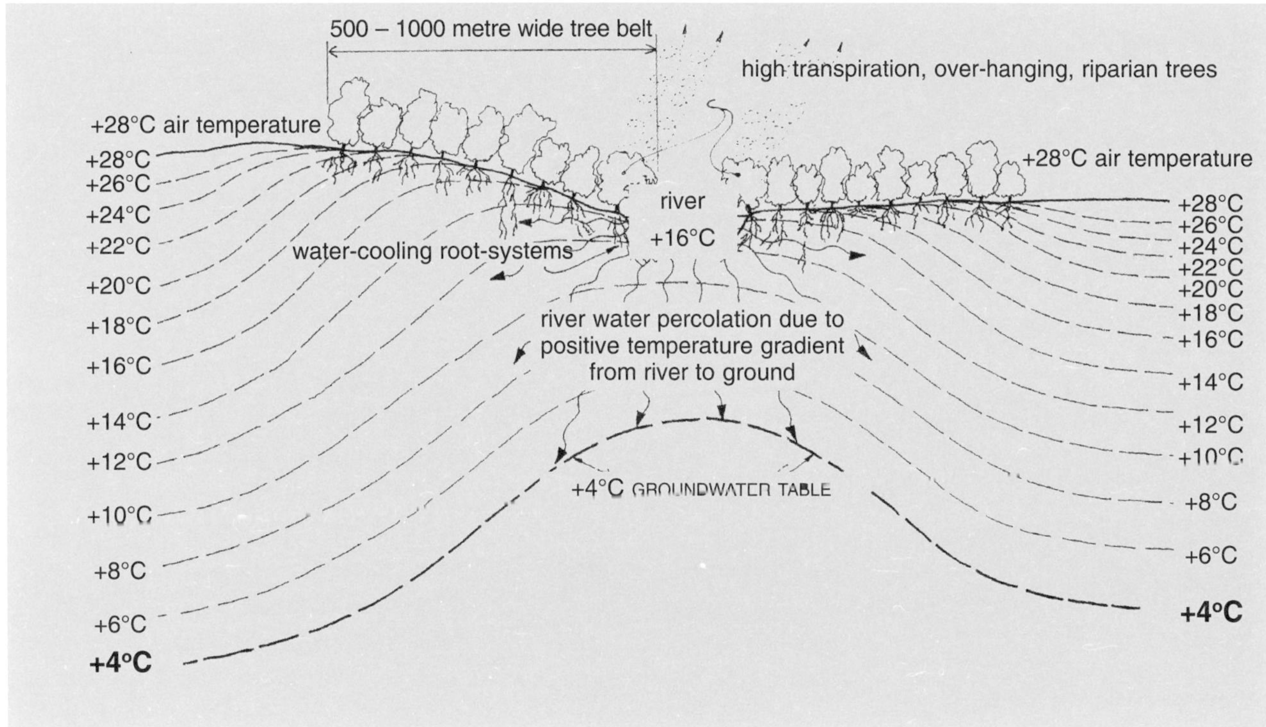

Fig.11.2 Groundwater Recharge through river bank reforestation.
The trees act like a refrigerator, cooling the ground, which allows a positive temperature gradient to draw water from the river to recharge the water table.

prevailing air temperatures and the water temperatures of the flow downstream.

Current practice with most dams and water storage facilities is to release either cold bedwater from the bottom sluices or warm surface water over the top of the dam wall, down the spillway. This can have disastrous consequences unless the temperature of the water released or its possible effect on the downstream flow regime is taken into account. Warm water, for example, discharged into a stretch of river where the temperature gradient is only slightly positive, will effectively cancel the effect of the positive gradient, resulting in the automatic and almost simultaneous deposition of silt and sediment. The result will be flooding.

On the other hand if only the cold bedwater is released, it may overcool the lower reaches, causing excessive scouring and the transport of very heavy sediment loads which the lower flow regime may be unable to handle. This may be because of the slope of the bed-gradient and thereby the speed of flow, the width of the channel — wide, shallow channels dropping sediment more quickly, the temperature gradients operative lower down, etc. Each type of discharge eventually produces the same results — silting up followed by flooding. Such discharges also produce what has recently been termed 'cold pollution,' which can destroy downstream fish life and other aquatic creatures due to the sudden influx of far-below-normal water temperatures.

Viktor Schauberger designed a dam with outlet sluices at different heights on the dam wall to correspond with the temperature layers of the dam water (warmer at the surface, coolest on the bottom). An automatic monitoring of air temperature would determine which outflow would discharge the water from the dam at approximately the same temperature. The aim of this arrangement is to remove large and therefore disruptive temperature differences and to bring the external air temperature and the temperature of the river water into a closer approximation (Fig.11.3.).[2]

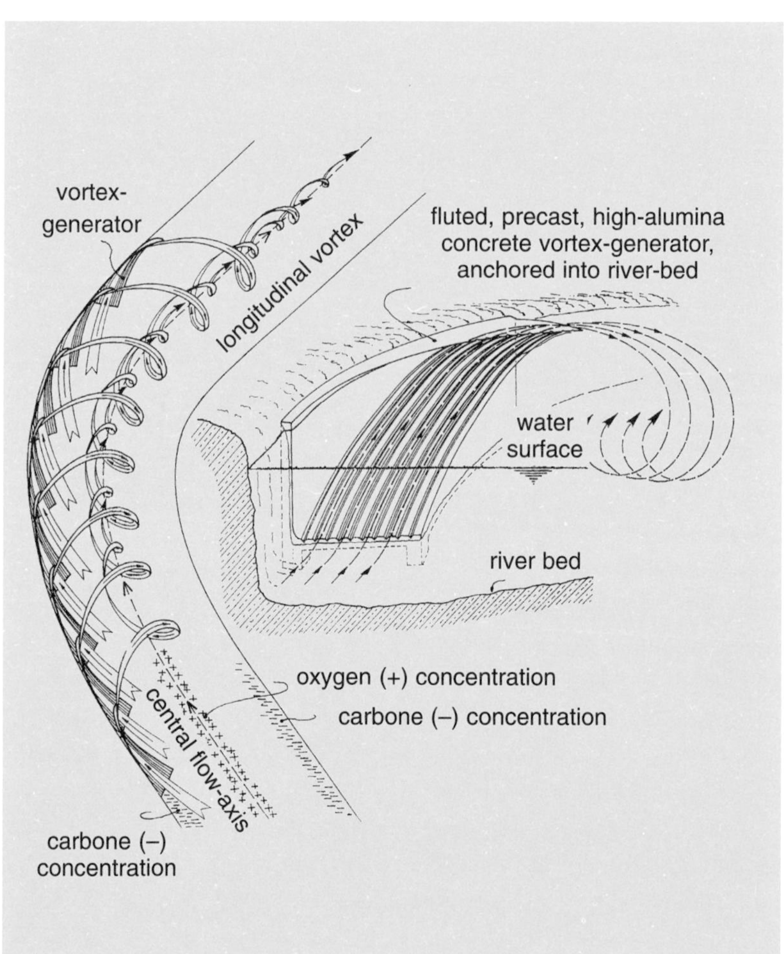

Fig.11.3. An Ingenious (but complex) Method of Freshening and Re-energizing a River.
By installing pre-cast concrete guide vanes that generate a cooling longitudinal vortex on a river bend, which brings the growth-enhancing substances (carbones) on the riverbed and near the banks into contact with the oxygen in the centre-stream; the accumulated energies from this synthesis release nourishing sales into the river banks between the bends.

3. By installing flow-deflecting guides which direct the flow of water at the bends towards the centre of the river and simultaneously cause the creation of cooling longitudinal vortices. Viewed along the direction of flow, these induce anti-clockwise rotating vortices at left hand bends and clockwise vortices at right hand bends.

The *flow-guide* or vortex generator (see Fig. 11.3) is made of pre-cast concrete, its curved surface fluted with grooves running parallel to the direction of flow, to prevent any lateral slip. It is triangular in shape, the apex pointing downstream. The wider, upstream end of the triangle is horizontal and flush with the riverbed, so as to scoop up the onflowing water and curl it over centripetally (inwardly spiralling) into a vortex in the centre of the channel. This movement gathers up the suspended and dissolved growth-enhancing substances (carbones), from near the banks and the riverbed, allowing them to mix with the dissolved oxygen which in all healthy streams collects in the central flow axis.

These (negatively-charged) fructigenic carbones become energized when moved centripetally and are thus able to combine with the fertilizing (positively charged) oxygen. The oxygen is cooled by a positive temperature gradient, resulting in a freshening and reinvigorating of the water. At the shallower parts of the river between the bends, the accumulated energies from this organic synthesis allow the discharge of nourishing salts into the groundwater in the banks.[3]

4. By the implanting of 'energy-bodies' in midstream, anchored to the river bed, which re-energize the water by forming natural longitudinal vortices. These would be used where the flow-guides are inappropriate — in the straighter stretches of a channel for instance — and where the removal of sediment is desirable. Although never described by Viktor Schauberger in detail, these could take the form of egg-shaped longitudinal vortex-generators with neutral buoyancy achieved through small holes allowing penetration of the outer water. Schauberger may have applied this principle from observing the stationary trout.

Vortices may also be introduced by placing large (preferably metalliferous) boulders in the centre of the channel. Schauberger found that the boulders that 'floated' in a very cold stream contained metal oxides and silicates, so these stones would actually increase the

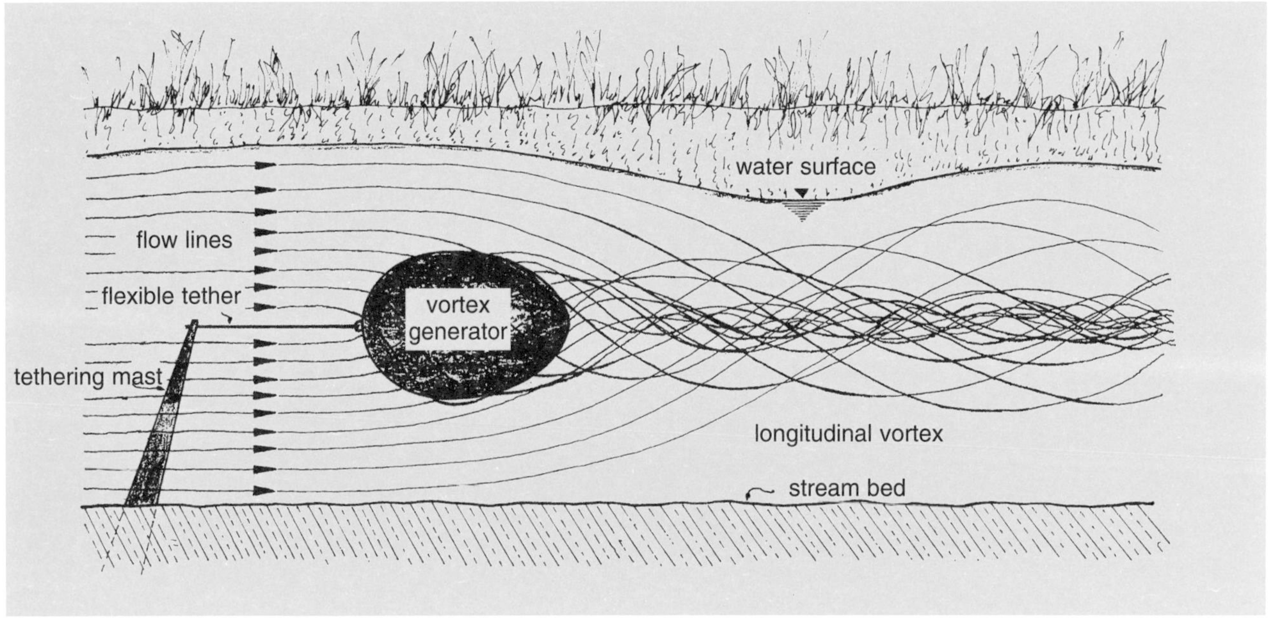

Fig.11.4. An Egg-shaped Body to generate Longitudinal Vortices.
Another way to increase vitality and electrical charge in streams.

energy of the water. Water carries an electric charge. If the water is caused to rotate, a biomagnetic field would be created which would enhance the vitality of the life-enhancing elements (fructigens, dynagens and qualigens) and therefore the general health of the water.

Schauberger once admitted making use of 'energy-bodies,' when he secretly installed them during the night in a sediment-choked stream. By morning the sediment had disappeared, the channel bed deepened considerably and the natural flow of water restored. The engineers in charge of the stream's regulation were amazed.

The formation of vortices and bends

We have seen that energy is always connected with movement. The natural movement of water is sinuous, convoluting and vortical. Without such movement there is no polarity. Vortices, however, cannot form without the existence of polarities. Through the action of vortices come rhythms, the pulsations that act as a gateway — a breathing process that the river performs for the environment.

There are three kinds of vortices that form in a river. The principal one, responsible for the river's health is the longitudinal vortex (see Fig. 8.2) which is naturally generated at river bends. The coldest water filaments are those closest to the centre and they,

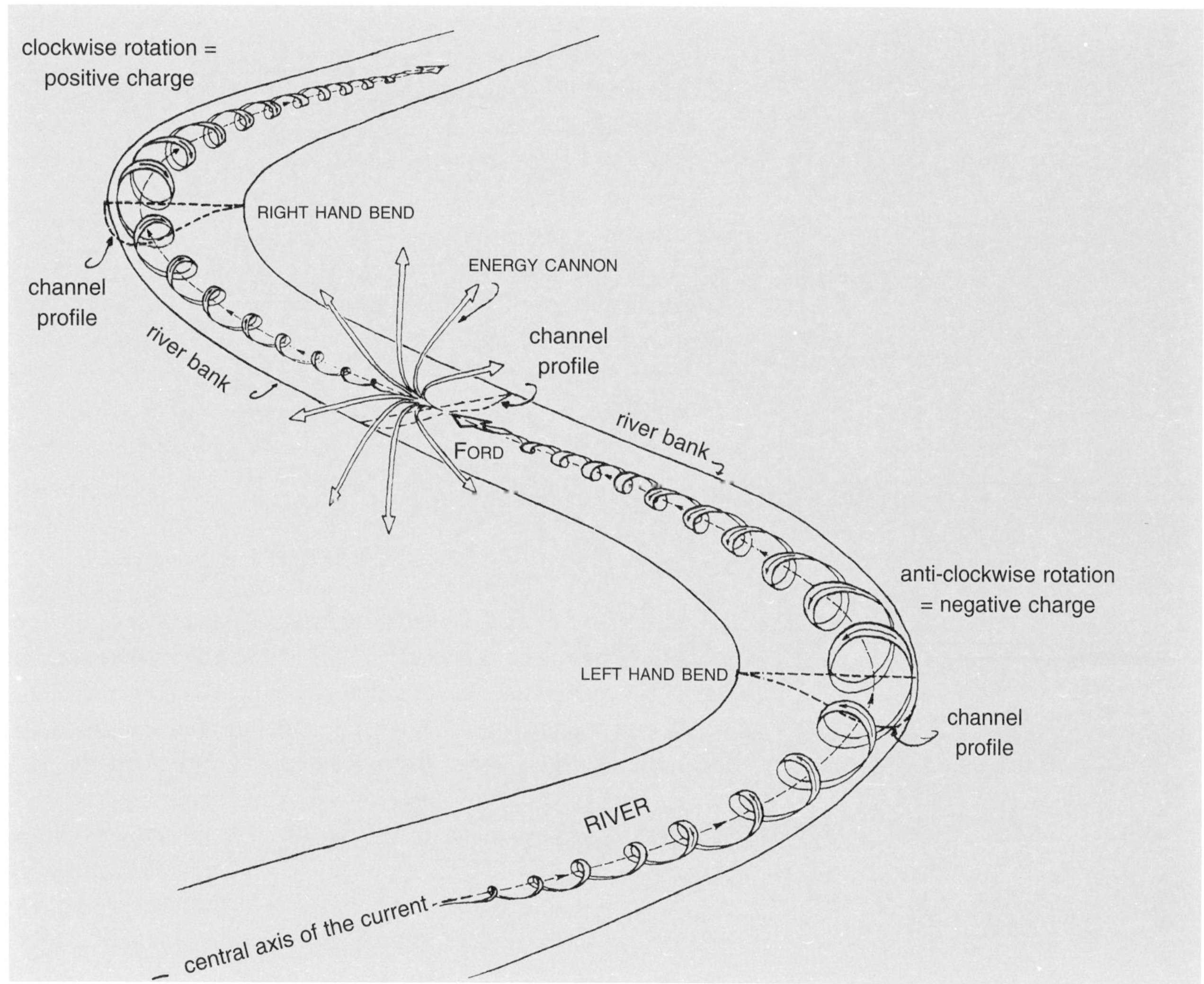

being subject to the least turbulence, move fastest, pulling along the outer water filaments in their wake. The outer water filaments create the turbulence that keeps the riverbed clear of silt, becoming infused with trace elements and nutrients, and building up its internal charge of pure energy that is released as the longitudinal vortex weakens (Schauberger called this release the 'energy cannon').

Then there are the transverse vortices that form at right angles to the bank. These are caused as a lower layer of laminar-structured water slips faster than the layer above it. These mix the water, but at the same time cool it, because the water temperatures within the centre of these vortices are identifiably cooler than those without, the

Fig.11.5. Energy Release in the Environment.
As the longitudinal vortex forms at a bend in the river (see Fig.11.3), the water cools and grinds sediment, releasing nutrients into the river; when the vortex slows down after the bend, the water warms in the now shallower riverbed and begins to deposit its store of nutrients and trace elements; then just before a new vortex starts to form in the reverse direction at the next bend, energy is released into the environment; Viktor Schauberger called this the 'Energy Cannon'. If the river has been badly regulated, this discharge could be of damaging energy.

uppermost vortex train manifesting itself as the familiar backward-breaking ripples seen on rivers at the surface. This type of vortex also distributes the lighter weight sediment and the nutrient material carried by the river from the centre towards the river bank. While they do increase turbulence, their action is more as a brake to slow down the flow of the river which might otherwise be too rapid.[4]

On the other hand, increasing water temperature often weakens the longitudinal vortices, the rising turbulence making the transverse vortices more destructive, and the banks may be breached, causing flooding. The third type of vortex acts vertically towards the river bed. They may gouge out potholes with a boulder as a grinder, but can be destructive by bringing radon-type energies from the ground into the river and projecting them into the immediate environment (Fig.11.5.).

Vortices as the source of creative energy

The longitudinal double-spiral vortex creates a cold dense flow in the middle of the vortex structure. This is called the core-water, or what Viktor termed an 'emulsion' because of its particular qualities. It is the breeding ground for the most vitalizing energies produced by natural river flow. Finely ground minerals, trace elements and

Fig. 11.6. River Bend Formation in plan and section.
If the river is initially shaded on both banks, the profile of the channel at section 1-11 will be symmetrical. The curved line at the top of the diagram reflects the velocity of flow at each vertical, increasing from the banks, reaching a maximum at the centre of the channel.

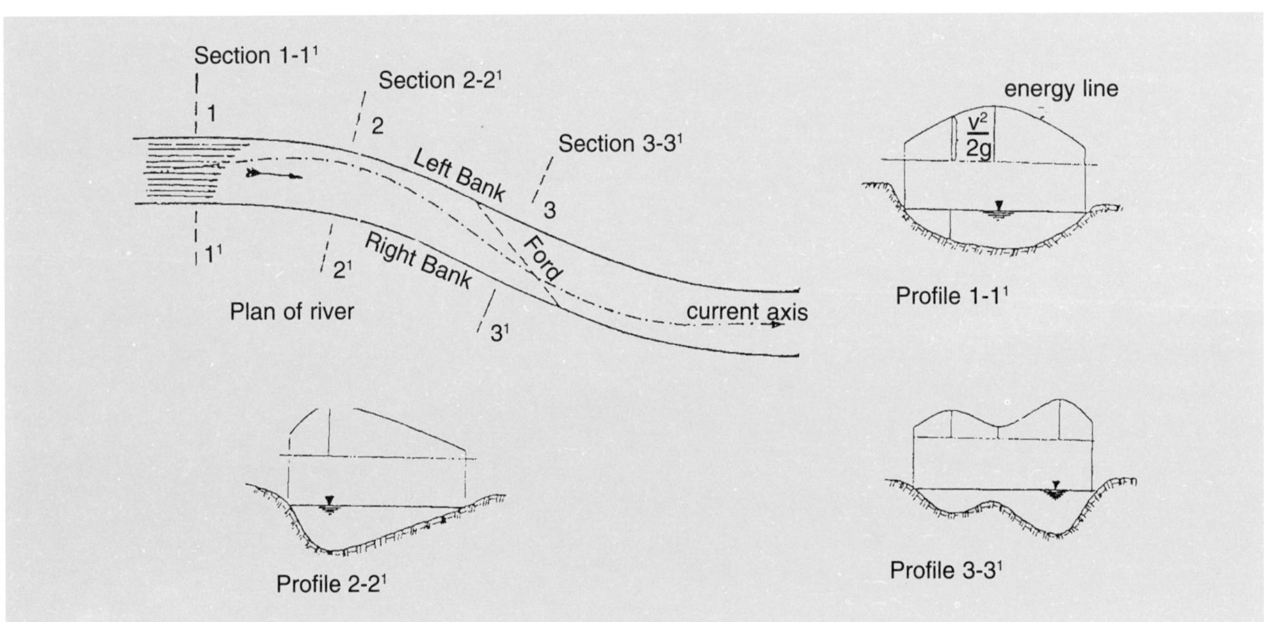

organic substances are spun into this belt of rapidly rotating core water (emulsified) that is composed to a large extent of ionized elements. What this does is to enable new combinations and recombinations of the various elements and suspended substances. This is a process that Viktor called 'cold fermentation,' which is very much associated with longitudinal vortices. These are beneficial because the cooling makes the oxygen and silicates more passive and able to combine with carbones, which then produce a fructigenic or growth-promoting effect.

Overheating of the water creates other types of vortices that are not so beneficial. These might be vortices forming laterally across the river (transverse vortices), or vertical vortices ascending to the surface from the river bed. In these the oxygen is heated, becoming aggressive, and producing low quality, germinating-inhibiting energies or pathogen-producing bacteria. This often happens as a result of poorly conceived river regulation, and can propagate harmful energies to the countryside.

The formation of bends

A river will always follow a sinuous energy-generating path, because this is in its nature, unless mountains or other immovable objects prevent it. Rivers are the mirrors of an unseen flow of energy.

The water on the right bank heats up where it has been exposed to the Sun's heat (see Fig.11.6 section and profile $2{-}2^1$); the water becomes more turbulent and begins to decelerate compared to the main body of water. The water flowing along the left-hand bank which is cooler and faster moving then overtakes the slower moving water and curls towards the right around it, due to the increasing turbulence and deceleration of the warmer water, eventually creating a bend. The faster flow will pull the heavier sediment centrifugally to the left, while sediment on the right is scoured out by the colder water. Meanwhile at this point the cross-sectional profile of the river becomes asymmetrical, due to the varying flows and temperatures, the coldest water flowing in the deeper section of the channel.

The cold water now flows on the other side of the channel; a bend is formed in the opposite direction due to the momentum of the cold water-masses, (see section and profile $3{-}3^1$). This rhythm of the river changing its course from left to right and right to left is an integral part of its pulsating flow. It is our interference of this rhythm that causes the river to become aggressive and flood. The banks will then not receive their recharge from the river, and all life downstream will also suffer. Should any kind of adjustment have to be made to the course of a river, it is essential to know when to encourage a right hand bend, for to put a left hand one there would only disrupt the river's energy flow. Even on a long left or right hand bend, there is still an alternating left-hand right-hand motion, although the motion in the opposite direction to that of the bend may be very slight and of short duration.

This current crossover appears where the river is most shallow and where the slowing down of the flow allows suspended material to settle. So these fordable stretches become the major deposition zones for the river's suspended nutrients and minerals and where the river can transfer these to the river banks. Alternatively the bends are where the rocks and stones are ground down, the trace elements contained in them being taken up by the vortical flow for later nourishment. Viktor Schauberger used to say that this sediment actually helps to sustain the river in it wanderings towards the ocean; he called it "the river's bread". These vital nutrients will be absorbed into the groundwater table.

This fordable stretch is also the place where the energy nutrients created by the river are released into the environment, provided there is a positive temperature gradient in relation to the river bank. As noted above, Schauberger called it the 'energy cannon' (Fig. 11.5). It is the completion of the 'outbreath' part of the cycle. All the energies accumulated in the previous in-winding, longitudinal vortex have to be released before the water rotates in the opposite direction. By this means a river constantly renews its vitality and enriches the land though which it flows.

If the water is sufficiently cold, dense and dynamic, small particles of trace elements and minerals are released from these suspended stones as they grind together, and are partially or wholly dissolved, replacing those previously lost through transfer to the surroundings. In addition pure ionizing energy is released through the generation of the triboluminescence. A golden flash of light is produced when two crystalline stones of similar composition are struck against one another. As it takes place under water it cannot be related to normal combustion, electrical discharges or frictional heat, and must therefore be a process of cold oxidation not associated with the generation of heat.

This is probably the origin of the fabled 'Gold of the Nibelungs,' the 'Rhinegold' that supposedly lay on the bottom of the Rhine in days of yore and which gleamed during the hours of darkness. This legend is also to be ascribed to the phenomenon of triboluminescence. About 200–250 years ago, the water of the Rhine was probably clear enough for people to observe what appeared to be the flashing of gold on the riverbed. The Rhine today, however, is a thick, turbid, grey-green muddy brew, its life force having been extinguished by modern mechanistic methods of river engineering.

Conventional river engineering

Viktor Schauberger's most vigorous campaign was to try to persuade the Bonn government to restore the Rhine and the Danube to their natural courses. He was greatly disturbed by the way in which those mighty rivers' banks had been straightened, so that the water was not able to flow naturally. It was like constraining someone in a straightjacket. This had the effect of overheating the oxygen content, making it aggressive. The water becomes violent, prone to flooding and disease-promoting. Tree felling on the river banks has only exacerbated the problem.

Often the rivers have been regulated through trapezoid-shaped canals in the misplaced belief that the flow would be improved. In fact this almost lifeless body of water was unable to carry its sediment, which settled on the bottom, and the river has to be constantly dredged. Because the flow is uniform, no cooling longitudinal vortices can form and no energizing processes can take place.

The water becomes warmer, sluggish, insipid and murky. With its energies destroyed it becomes a stale and lifeless liquid. Instead of being a carrier, mediator, accumulator and transformer of life-energies, the river has become a corpse (Fig. 11.7).

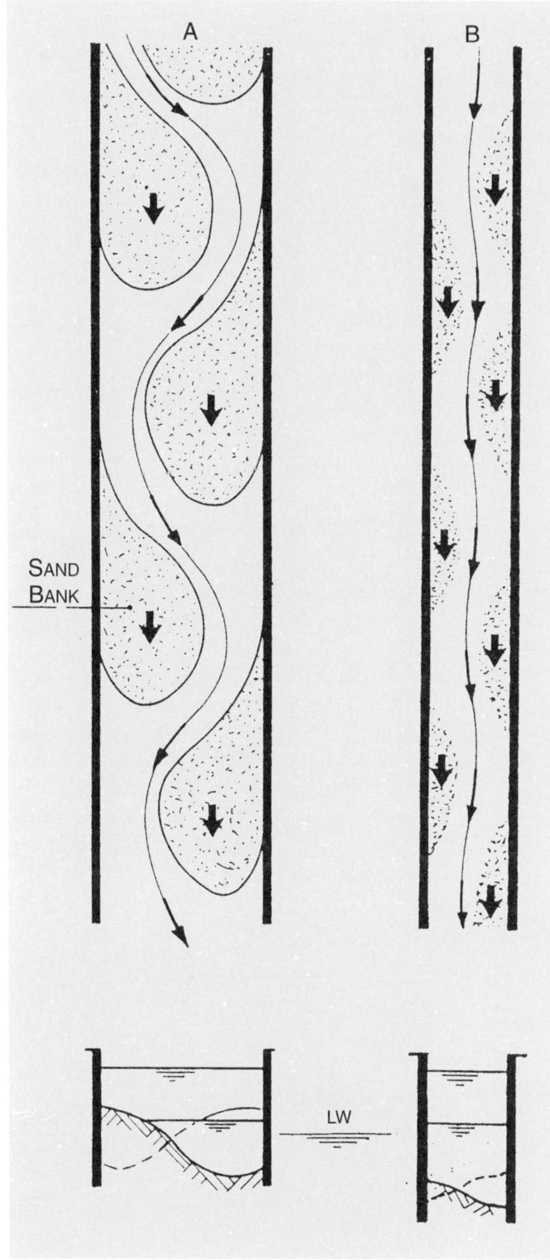

Fig.11.7. Sand banks in Conventional channels.
From a textbook of conventional river engineering. The river still tries to dance and play, but confined to a straightjacket, it silts up and will have to be dredged, to avoid flooding.

Hydroelectric power

Present methods of hydroelectric power generation destroy water in their own way. The present inappropriate design of dams we touched on earlier in this chapter. The water is thrust down cylindrical pipes under enormous pressure. Upon leaving these it is then hurled against steel turbine blades where it is smashed to smithereens. The physical structure of the water is literally demolished and all the dissolved oxygen, and even some of the oxygen in the water molecule itself, is centrifuged out of the water.

Viktor Schauberger had photographs taken through a microscope (Fig.11.8) that show the marked difference in the structure of water that has been subjected to centrifugence on the one hand and centripetence on the other. The fragmented appearance of the centrifugally moved water is unmistakable. The slicing action of the blades causes severe friction and heating which makes the oxygen highly aggressive and it attacks the bare metal, severely pitting the surface, often destroying the blades' efficiency.

This fragmented and largely oxygen-deficient water, a virtual skeleton of healthy water when forcibly expelled into the river, has disastrous consequences for the fish and other aquatic life. Inevitably certain species of fish disappear once these power stations are commissioned, and other forms of life survive with difficulty.

The water is so depleted that it has to build itself up again completely before it can be of any benefit to the environment. So it seeks out new supplies of oxygen and other high quality substances wherever it can find them, including living things. With their particularly intimate contact with this 'ravenous' water, fish are especially prone to attack as it enters their very delicate gill systems and their body's tissues are attacked by oxygen-hungry carbones. The soil bordering on the river is also leached of its

Fig.11.8. Viktor Schauberger's Evidence from the Microscope.

Centrifugally Killed Water (left). The strongly crystalline structure of heavily oxygenated water can be detected wiht a microscope. If warmed it becomes an incubator of dangerous bacteria.

Centrifugally Vitalised Water (right). Magnetically charged water is characterised by an amorphous structure. Its content of oxygen is for themost part bound.

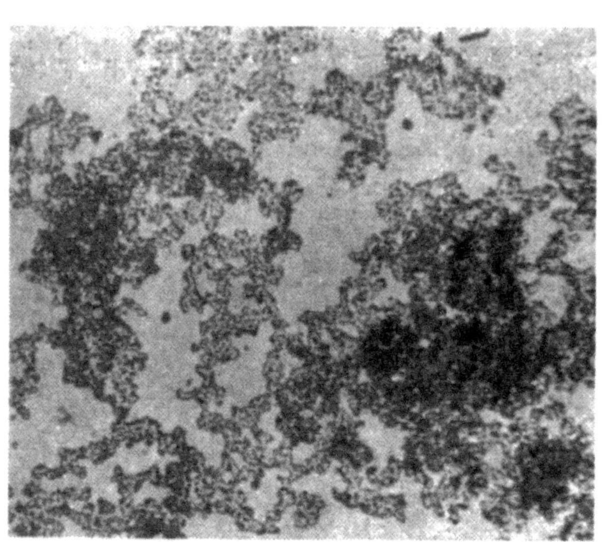

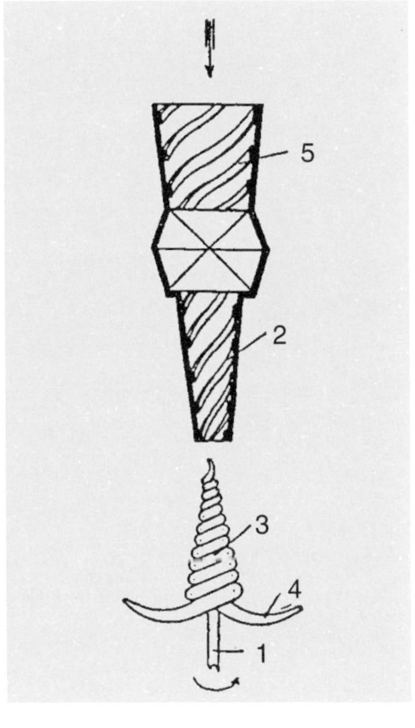

Fig.11.9. An Experimental Egg-shaped vessel for Generating Hydro-electric Power.
The hyperbolic cone device with spiralled nozzles to maximize speed of water flow. This could produce 90% more electricity than a hydro turbine.

nutrients which the water hungrily consumes resulting in a large drop in soil fertility and productivity.

Viktor Schauberger showed how unnecessary is this extraordinarily destructive power-generating process. He devised a novel method in the early 1920s which can produce 90% more electricity from a given flow-volume without harm to the water. Using water from a nearby stream Viktor installed this device to light his forest warden's house, which was too remote to be connected to any other source of supply. The design shown in Fig. 11.9 is very simple, illustrating his belief that what is natural is silent, simple and cheap.

It operates by water being cooled, densified and energized as it passes through a rifled brass nozzle, in a vortical flow, thereby reducing both pressure and friction as the water is centripetally drawn away from the sides. The water is directed against a multiple-spiral, shell-like impeller attached to the shaft of a generator. [5]

12. Supplying Water

Dwindling water supplies

The subject of water is very topical, mainly because usable water is in short supply. Predictions are now common that wars will be fought over access to water. It is easy to see why. Countries that control the headwaters of important rivers can restrict their flow downstream, like Turkey with Iraq, Israel with Jordan, Syria with Israel, Sudan with Egypt, India with Bangladesh. Twenty per cent of the world's population does not have clean drinking water; nearly half the world does not have sanitation. One hundred cities in northern China now ration water, and Beijing's future as China's capital has been under review because its growth has outstripped its water resources. Even those countries which have sufficient water treat it so badly that, when delivering it to homes, kill it with chlorine, fluorides and other chemicals, ostensibly to prevent disease; instead this depresses our immune systems and makes us more open to infection.

How has this come about? Water is in great abundance on this marvellous planet, but less than 0.5% is available as fresh water. The rest is salt water, inaccessible groundwater, or frozen in polar mountain ice. While the world's population is increasing by 85 million a year, cities are expanding at double that rate due to urbanization. Cities and industries consume the most water (industrial water consumption is to double by 2025).[1] Twenty-four countries, mainly in Africa, will not have enough water to meet 2025 projected needs.[2] And, if that is not critical, according to a recent UN report, world population could rise from 6.1 billion in 2000 to at least 8.2 billion by 2050.[3] Today, 1.2 billion people drink unclean water, and 2.5 billion lack proper toilets or sewerage systems.[4] And what will be the situation in ten years' time?

Globally, about 70% of water diverted from rivers or drawn from aquifers is used for irrigation. This is hugely wasteful; leaking pipes and channels, evaporation from reservoirs and from irrigation sprays means that about 60% of the water does not reach the plants' roots. China's greatest river, the Yellow River, has run dry and in several years since 1985 has failed to reach the ocean.[5] The once mighty Nile, Ganges and Colorado Rivers barely reach the sea in dry seasons.[6] The introduction of industrial agriculture into India and Northern China has in those areas led to dangerous lowering of the water table.

The construction of large dams, whether for hydroelectric power or for irrigation does incalculable environmental damage, as well as annihilating viable human communities. Dams destroy ecosystems and sever the balancing of energy from one part of the landscape to another. Since 1970, when Egypt's Aswan High Dam came into operation, the number of commercially harvested fish species in the Nile dropped by two-thirds, and the Mediterranean sardine catch has fallen by 80%.[7]

Water for profit

Traditional societies know how to manage their water, but increasingly the supplies of rural communities are being privatized by companies whose major priority is profit. In April 2000 the protesting citizens of Cochabamba in Bolivia suffered over 180 casualties at the hands of their police before their government revoked the right of International Waters of London to impose a 35% increase in water prices. The Bolivian government has now reconsidered its policy to privatize all public water supplies.

Vast new networks of supply and disposal pipes must be built in the cities if basic water needs are to be met. Governments, unwilling these days to invest in social infrastructure, are privatizing water utilities, and the results seldom benefit the consumer. A shortage in any essential commodity brings out the profiteers and extortionists. Pro-privatization propaganda reached a climax at the Water Forum meetings in The Hague in March 2000, but the abuses and inadequacies of commercial control have become apparent.

One study has shown that Swedish municipal water authorities delivered water at around a third of the cost, had operating costs of about half, and produced nearly three times higher return on capital than English private water companies of similar size.[8] However, since the economic downturn of 2001, several English private water companies have been experiencing financial difficulties. It makes complete nonsense that essential water supplies should be subject to the ups and down of the financial markets.

A great danger to our water comes from the globalization of supply. Multinational companies are unaccountable and self-serving with more interest in profits than in a sustainable environment. A group of water companies tried at the 2001 Water Forum conference to foist a new water order on the world, in effect to encourage water supply to be removed from public control. American companies are negotiating to build dams in India which would displace countless communities and destroy their environments. Three French companies already control more than 70% of the world's private market.[9] Increasing numbers of privatized water schemes are linked to ventures to extract more water through vast dams and reservoirs, with bulk water supply schemes that guarantee profits by requiring consumption regardless of need.

Modern water treatments

Chlorination

Because public water is not treated with the care required to keep water pulsating and alive, it degenerates, attracting pathogenic organisms. As a result, the authorities routinely treat it with chlorine to prevent the threat to the community of waterborne diseases. This powerful disinfectant removes all types of bacteria, beneficial and harmful alike, and in doing so, over a long period of time, destroys or seriously weakens many of the immune-enhancing micro-organisms in the body. It is a major contributor of lowered immune resistance in older people. Medical authorities say that the amount of chlorine is so small that it could not do this, but they fail to take into account that the chlorine accumulates in the fatty tissue of the body, so that the dosage is cumulative, nor that there is a homeopathic action that amplifies the effect on the body.

> Those of us who live in cities and are forced year-in and year-out to drink sterilized water should seriously consider the fate of that 'organism' whose naturally-ordained ability to create life has been forcibly removed by chemical compounds. Sterilized and physically-destroyed water not only brings about physical decay, but also gives rise to mental deterioration and hence to the systematic degeneration of humanity and other life-forms.[10]

Fluoridation

The issue of adding fluorosilicates (fluoride) routinely to drinking water is one of the worst outrages in public health policy. This is not the naturally occurring calcium fluoride that is present in some drinking water, usually at low levels of about 0.1ppm (parts per million). It is a by-product of a number of industrial processes, initially the iron, copper, aluminium and now the phosphate fertilizer industries, and contains also a number of heavy metals; altogether a potent toxic cocktail, the disposal of which would be costly by current environmental standards.[11]

The solution to this problem of industrial waste disposal was to arrange for their addition to public water supplies. In parts of the USA, Canada, Britain, Ireland, Australia, New Zealand, and a few non-English speaking countries, like Chile, this is permitted, usually at levels of about 1ppm (or 1mg fluoride per litre of water), but many other countries decided the risks were too high to implement the policy. The addition of fluoride as a policy is justified by the claim that it reduces dental cavities, especially in children. Independent research actually proves otherwise, and shows that the body accumulates levels of fluoride in the bones and certain organs, and there is evidence of increased risk of cancer, brain function impairment, kidney malfunction and premature ageing.[12] At higher dosages, fluorosilicates are an effective rat poison.

Unfortunately fluoride is also added to many processed foods, fruit juice, milk and, especially toothpaste. Fluoride is released into food cooked in Teflon-coated cookware, so the actual intake may be significant, even if you don't live in a fluoridated area. For reasons that are difficult to comprehend, but which are clearly political in nature, many dental and health authorities seem to support this mass medication of whole populations, and politicians seem happy to go along with it.

Mass fluoridation started in the USA in 1945, backed largely by the Mellon family, owners of ALCOA, the biggest aluminium manufacturer, and one of the biggest fluoride wartime polluters. Starting with Grand Rapids, Michigan it was introduced within two years to a hundred cities. Basically a dirty tricks campaign that labelled opposers as crackpots (and during the McCarthy era as left-wing subversives), it has never completed convincing tests, nor produced adequate evidence of its efficacy or safety. "It was a political, not a scientific health issue" and, like the agenda of the more recent genetically modified foods campaign, became a major US export.[13]

The World Health Organization and the American Medical Association were persuaded to back the policy. The FDA (US Food and

Drug Administration) has backed off slightly from its 100% endorsement of the product, due to public exposure of the scam, but today 130 million Americans in 9,600 communities continue to drink fluoridated water.[14] Like the USA, about 50% of the Canadian population has fluoridated water.

Mass fluoridation came to Britain in the 1950s, and currently 10% of the population is exposed, mostly in the West Midlands and the North-East. The present UK government policy is to require all water companies to adopt fluoridation. In Australia, some of the fluoride laws are so Draconian that people may be prosecuted for speaking out against water fluoridation.[15]

Barry Groves concludes, "Fluoridation is the longest, most expensive and most spectacularly unsuccessful marketing campaign ever to come out of the United States."[16]

Viktor Schauberger was very concerned about industrial pollution of rivers and lakes, but the addition of poisons to our domestic water supply was not an issue of the 1930s. Indeed, he insisted that the way we transport and deliver water destroys the invigorating qualities of healthy water, and he pursued enlightened research on ways of maintaining water's energy. Viktor predicted that one day a bottle of good water would be more expensive than a bottle of wine, and commented on our treatment of public water supplies:

> If we have any common sense remaining, we should refuse to continue to drink water prepared in this way. The alternative would be degeneration into cancer-prone, mentally and physically decrepit, physically and morally inferior individuals.[17]

Transmuting water's memory

Most communities make genuine efforts to remove physical pollutants from public water supplies, but there are so many organic toxins produced by industrial agriculture, that one is wise to consider good filtration to reduce the dangers of these pollutants and of heavy metals that, sadly, are now more common. There are now generally available good and affordable plumbed-in filters that remove most of the physical contaminants.[18] However, what our water treatment policies must urgently take on board is that the physical removal of a pollutant is only part of making water safe.

Typically, in modern cities, public water supplies are recycled as many as twenty times. Even if the physical contaminants have been removed, their vibrational imprint is still carried in the water in its memory bank, no matter how many times it is recycled. Just as water can carry restorative energies, such as in homeopathy, so it can transmit negative or destructive imprints that can cause disharmony or disease in the body.

The purpose of some of the better vortex treatment systems is to recluster the water, in a manner that superimposed natural vibrations will erase the memory of the water's previous abuse. The vortex, being the transmuting instrument or enabling gateway between different qualities or levels of energy, allows the water to absorb the etheric or cosmic level of energy that surrounds us all.[19] Rather as allowing brilliant sunlight and fresh air to fill a musty room will quickly transmute the stale energy, so the more refined energy always prevails over the coarser. We would recommend a combination of an efficient plumbed-in filter with a vortex-type re-energizing system (see Resources, p. 276).

Tubular water movement

We described earlier Viktor Schauberger's almost mystical experience of when he felt his own consciousness enter the stream and how the water consciousness seemed to tell him how it wanted to move. Great pioneers of science have told of similar experiences as a kind of initiation. For Viktor it opened a wider perception about water's behaviour in quite different situations. For example, how water wants to move in a closed system like a pipe is quite different from its movement in a river. His genius allowed him to make the quite remarkable connection between the behaviour of water in a pipe or tube, and the movement of sap in a tree or blood in the human body.

Water main material

Archeological research has shown that in ancient times, from the Babylonians to the Greeks, there was a greater understanding of water and its qualities. In those times, water mains were constructed of high quality wood or of natural stone. In time, these natural materials became more scarce, and the Romans experimented with different metals. Preoccupied with oxidizing corrosion, unfortunately they often used lead which brought its own problems of lead poisoning, particularly in the wine goblets where the vinegar in the wine dissolved the lead.

Before the expansion of cities during the Industrial Revolution, many water mains in Europe, and even in New York, were constructed of wood, which allowed the water to breathe and to interact with its environment. After the water mains in Vienna were extended to new suburbs with steel or iron pipes, internally coated with tar, as opposed to the traditional wooden tubes, Schauberger found that the incidence of cancer more than doubled between 1920 and 1931.[20]

The laminar structure of water quickly disintegrates owing to the chaotic flow through a cylindrical pipe. Friction with the pipe walls heats up the water, decomposing the dissolved trace elements. As the surface of the iron pipes start to rust, oxygen is taken out of the water, and the rust deposits encourage disease-promoting bacteria. The accumulating rust in turn constricts the water flow, so that what is delivered is dead water, disinfected with chlorine.

The wooden water main

Schauberger knew that water can maintain its vitality and energy only if it is allowed to tumble about in a spiralling vortical manner. So in 1930 he set about designing a pipe that would actually encourage this movement. It was constructed of wooden staves, like a barrel, which allowed the moisture to seep through, transferring a cooling effect (as in sweating) to the water in the pipe. The spiralling movement was created by a series of guide vanes, which act like rifling in a gun barrel. These were made of silver plated copper to

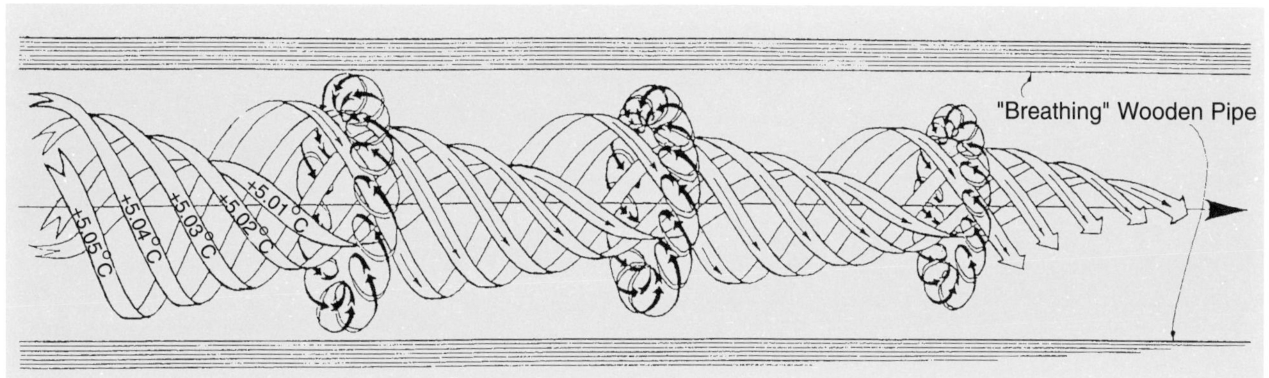

Fig.12.1. The Double-Spiral Longitudinal Vortex.
This is a longitudinal vortex showing the development of toroidal counter-vortices. These occur due to interaction with the porous pipe walls and have an effect similar to ball-bearings, enhancing the forward movement. Their interior rotation follows the direction of rotation and flow of the central vortex. These toroidal vortices transfer oxygen, bacteria and other impurities to the pipe walls, where the concentration of oxygen destroys the inferior, pathogenic bacteria.

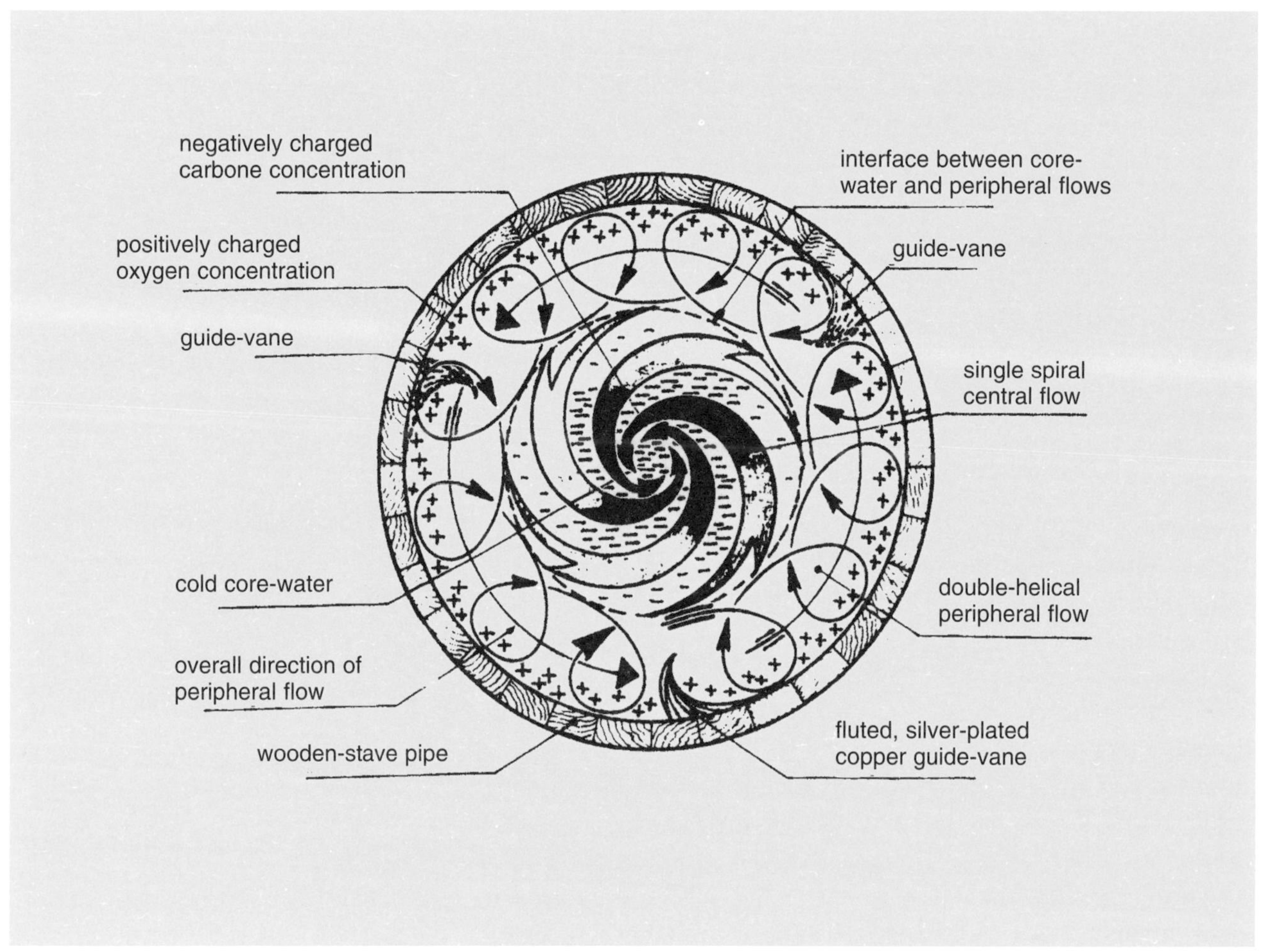

Fig. 12.2. Flow Dynamics of the Double Spiral Pipe (cross section).

enhance the subtle energies[21] and fluted so as to direct movement towards the centre, thus reducing the heating effects of friction.

Figs 12.1 and 12.2 illustrate how this configuration sets up a double-spiral longitudinal vortex, creating a waterflow faster than a conventional cylindrical pipe. The centripetal flow of the main water body helps to cool and accelerate it, this heavier water drawing the specifically lighter outer water along in its wake. The centripetal spiralling of the toroidal 'doughnuts' created by the guide vanes extract oxygen from the main water body, transferring any pathogenic bacteria to the pipe walls where they are eliminated by the aggressive oxygen. The higher quality micro-organisms however, survive, because they require higher levels of oxygen.

It is a brilliant design that imitates the natural pulsating flow of water in a natural vessel and which delivers water that purifies itself and cools through its motion, eliminating the need for any sterilizing or purifying additives. Ideally, these wooden water mains should be embedded in sand, allowed them to breathe, and protected from light and heat. In such conditions they should outlast a steel pipe.

The Stuttgart tests

As the scientific establishment had never taken seriously his ideas on natural water movement, Viktor Schauberger in later life decided to have them subjected to rigorous tests by an independent authority. In 1952 he asked the Stuttgart Technical University to set up the experiments at his own expense. He approached Professor Franz Pöpel, director of the Institute of Hygiene who, knowing Schauberger's infamous reputation, at first refused, saying it would be a waste of his time.

The German Government had been irritated by Viktor's railing about its management of the River Rhine. So, hearing about Schauberger's proposal, it was happy to offer to cover half the costs, thinking that any genuine tests were bound to discredit him. As a result of this, Professor Pöpel changed his mind and agreed to test the various rifled and helical pipes that Viktor supplied.

The object of the tests was to compare how water moves through eight different kinds of pipe, the velocity of the water flow being affected by friction varying according to the form of the pipe. The configurations that produced the most friction were the straight pipes made of glass or of copper. Introducing a sinuosity to the pipe reduced the friction, while Viktor's special 'spiral helicoid' copper pipe directed the water flow in an involuting flow movement away from the walls, giving the greatest reduction in friction, to zero or perhaps even below (negative friction or acceleration) at specific velocities.[22]

Because of expectations of his peers, Pöpel's report played down the significance of the experiment, which in fact in these circumstances disproved the relevance of the Second Law of Thermodynamics, which states that energy in any closed systems must degenerate or run down. The implication of this was that a system can in certain circumstances generate energy spontaneously, that once the initial impetus has been received, no further energy input is required. In other words, energy is not a constant. In this case it was increased through the emergence of fifth or sixth dimensional dynagens (see Chapter 2) created by what Schauberger called 'original' or 'cosmic' movement. Pöpel did, however, admit that in Schauberger's special pipe, friction at two specific velocities appeared to reduce to zero.

The circulation of blood

It is a common experience for those who use the ancient practice of watching the breath when they meditate, of the strange sensation of 'being breathed'; that the process seems to be part of a 'greater breathing.' Viktor Schauberger would often insist in a similar vein, that a bird 'is flown' and a fish 'is swum'. On many occasions he said that the heart is not a pump, that it 'is pumped'. He saw the heart, rather, as a regulator or of blood flow. The spurts of blood that the heart produces during contraction are more like the automatic reaction to having been full, like the outbreath of the lungs.

The Stuttgart experiment had established that when the water flow was in resonance with the configuration of the pipe, there was no friction. Similarly the blood being in resonance with the arteries and capillaries greatly facilitates flow. In addition the blood vessels have a natural pulsating, peristaltic action. About 1927, Professor Kurt Bergel of Berlin University recorded this automatic pulsation a few days after incubation in small warm blood vessels around the egg sac of a bird's egg, although no heart had yet been formed. Professor Bergel also rejected the popular theory of the heart as a pump, insisting that this function was carried out by 'the millions of highly active capillaries permeating the body,' and that 'health and disease are primarily dependent on the faultless or disturbed activity of the capillaries.'[23]

It appears that the pulsation of the capillaries initiate the circulation of the blood, augmented by the configuration of the blood vessels themselves.[24] The specifications for these would have been created with the original energy blueprint for hot-blooded creatures in general, and the human being in particular (see Chapter 2). Included in these specifications was even a provision that the viscosity of the blood would be reduced in the finer blood vessels, so that its ability to flow freely would not be compromised! The same is found with sap at the tree's extremities.

A parallel may also be drawn between the veins and arteries twisting sinuously through the body, bringing nutrients to the tissues and organs and the streams and rivers, pulsating with eddies and spirals, winding their way through the countryside, nourishing the surrounding areas.

Temperature gradients also can influence the efficient circulation of blood. A strong positive gradient (where temperature decreases with movement in a given direction) between the inner core of the body and its outer extremities will stimulate the outward flow. This explains the invigoration of a cold shower. Conversely, a prolonged soak in a hot bath slows down the circulation, producing lethargy. The second is the result of the difference in the physico chemical composition and therefore the energetic characteristics of arterial and venal blood.

Pulsation is assisted by the different electromagnetic charges carried by two principal types of blood. The positively-charged oxygen in the outward flowing arterial blood is gradually absorbed by muscles and skin, creating a partial vacuum. The negatively-charged, carbone-rich venal blood on the other hand returning from the extremities is ready to reabsorb oxygen from the lungs. The contraction of the heart muscle is a balancing response to opposite charges carried by the two types of blood in the relatively large heart chambers. It might also be said that the heart's pulsation is caused by our breathing in positively charged oxygen, (we then expel the negatively charged CO_2 and water), rather than the conventional belief that we breathe because the heart 'pumps.' The heart's real function is to stimulate pulsation in the blood flow.

The situation of the unborn child is different, for there is no temperature difference between the inner core and the outer extremities. It is likely therefore in the case of the foetus that the heart acts like a pump until it is born. After birth the heart would then assume its normal role as pulsator and balancer.

Callum Coats quotes research that calculates the total length of blood vessels in the average human adult to be about 96,500 km (60,000 miles)! On the basis of conventional hydraulic calculation it is inconceivable that the actual power output of the heart, about 1.5 watts, would be sufficient for this huge task.[25] Yet it does so.

Moreover, Walter Schauberger calculated that the annual output of the heart would suffice to raise a weight of about 40 tonnes (44 tons) to a height of 1m (3.28ft).

The Stuttgart experiments showed that a specific configuration is required for frictionless flow to occur. Schauberger maintained that energy creates the vessel most conducive to its desired form of movement in a given situation; and that energy will always try to move frictionlessly in healthy, animate, organic systems. Seen in this light, the pulsating, almost frictionless flow of blood over these enormous distances becomes more comprehensible. It is important that further investigations should be pursued into the lines of research that Viktor Schauberger pioneered.

Water storage

With good water becoming increasingly more scarce, it is important to understand how to preserve its quality. Water's enemy is excess heat and light. Water contains oxygen, a substance that is essential for the processes of growth and decay. Below a temperature of 9°C (48°F), oxygen is used for growth, above that, to promote decomposition. As the temperature rises above 10°C (50°F), the oxygen becomes increasingly more aggressive, promoting pathogenic bacteria which can give us disease when we drink the water containing them.

A tank or cistern that is above ground needs to be well insulated, and painted white to reflect the Sun's heat. If it is mostly below ground, the walls will not require insulation, but the top must be painted white. However, Viktor Schauberger urged us to observe the shapes that Nature uses to propagate and maintain life. Nature abhors squares (cubes), rectangles (water tanks) and circles (cylinders). He said that we should not be surprised that our dependence on these unnatural shapes for storage results in the deterioration of our water. This is probably impractical for larger containers, but we should try a more natural shape for smaller containers.

Because it is a living organism, water needs to be in constant movement to maintain its health. The only container that allows this is the egg-shape. The material of containment is very important, because water needs to keep cool; the best materials are natural stone, wood or terracotta. The ancient Greeks understood this, and kept their water (and wine) in amphorae, egg-shaped vessels that allowed the liquid to breathe. In many amphorae discovered in archaeological digs, grains have been found to be preserved so well after 2000 years that they germinated when planted, proving the effectiveness of the egg-shape for preservation.

PART FOUR

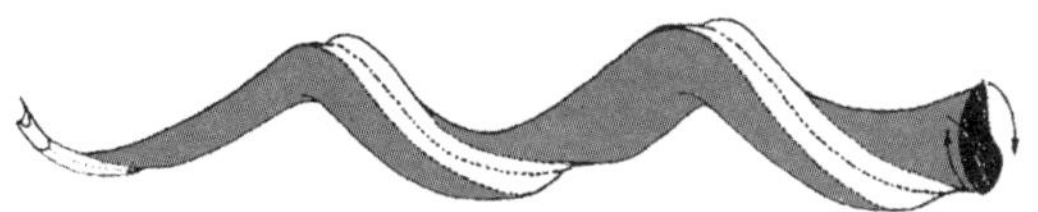

The Life of Trees

13. The Role of the Forest

When someone dies the bell tolls. When the forest dies and with it a whole people, then no-one lifts a finger. Viktor Schauberger[1]

Only people who love it should care for the forest. Those who view the forest merely as an object of speculation do it and all other living creatures great harm, for the forest is the cradle of water. If the forest dies, then the springs will dry up, the meadows will become barren and many countries will inevitably be seized by unrest of such a kind that it will bode ill for every one of us. Viktor Schauberger[2]

Viktor Schauberger, who believed that the highest quality water depends on the forest, predicted that deforestation would bring water shortage and climate change. As equatorial deforestation has greatly accelerated since he died, it might be useful to summarize the effects of this devastation.

Evolution of the forest

Plants have been around for 420 million years, which is only 9% of Earth's history. Without plants there could be no life, for plants are the essential link for converting the Sun's energy into food. Trees are the highest form of the plant, and the most efficient exchangers of energy between the Earth and the Sun. The forests are the main source of oxygen, an essential building block of life; they are the Earth's 'lungs.' There have been three periods when forests have flourished: in the Carboniferous Age 350 million years ago, when land vertebrates became established; in the Eocene, 60 million years ago, when primitive mammals first appeared, and in the last 500,000 years, when the cultures of modern man developed. It seems that in each case a boost in the oxygen content of the atmosphere, which the forests delivered, may have been the trigger for evolutionary explosion of Earth's life forms.

These extensive forests developed in the equatorial regions where the heat was available to prime a remarkable engine for moderating the extremes of temperature and the often chaotic nature of the world's historical climate. In the first case they were evergreen forests, interspersed with enormous swamps. In the Eocene when the modern great mountain ranges were being uplifted, there were large tropical jungles, perhaps not too different from the modern ones which flourished on all the continents until the late nineteenth century, but with less complex fauna.

It is interesting to speculate what caused the forests to establish themselves at these periods. Viktor Schauberger recognized Nature as an intelligent system endowed with meaning and purpose that is concerned with evolving more complex life-forms and a higher level of consciousness. From that perspective it is possible that the establishment of forest might be seen as part of that purpose.

Forest cover varies with climate. Forests have been the natural cover of perhaps three quarters of the Earth's land surface during these periods of evolutionary expansion. This natural forest was an essential prerequisite for the development of the extraordinarily rich variety of fauna and flora (now called 'biodiversity') that makes this planet an important source of life in the Universe.

Destruction of the forests

Either fortuitously or by design, there seems to be a large degree of tolerance in Earth's ecosystems for the amount of forest cover required to support a balanced climate — though what a great reduction of forest does to biodiversity and the quality of life is another question. Over the half a million or so years of humankind's time on Earth, our species has been responsible for reduction of the forest cover to about 25% of its optimum extent. The early agriculturists would burn clearings to grow their crops, and then move on to allow the fertility to be replenished. Early civilizations, some well documented and some which are now folk memories, felled vast tracts of forest.

Many of these lands became desertified, such as the Gobi, Sind, Arabian, Mesopotamian, North African and Kalahari deserts — probably through a combination of deforestation and climate change. Whole nations were uprooted and had to move elsewhere in their search for subsistence. The same is likely to happen today where great swathes of the rich equatorial forests have been cleared. Fortunately in those days there was somewhere else for the displaced to go, because the world's population was still relatively small. Today, however, because of overpopulation and an unsustainable birth rate, any climate changes that produce crop failures can mean only starvation and the loss of life through conflict. In temperate climates, clear felling of forests does not normally lead to desertification, but it affects the biodiversity, the fertility and therefore the long-term health of the environment.

Ten thousand years ago the whole Mediterranean region was covered with forests, mainly of oak. Then about 5,000 years ago the forests of Lebanon provided the timber for the Phoenician empire. We don't know what happened to the forests of North Africa, but two thousand years ago these lands were so fertile that the Romans called them the breadbasket of the Mediterranean. They are now arid desert. A thousand years ago 80% of Europe was forested; today it is about 20%, much of which is monocultured industrial woodland, which lacks the biodiversity and the energy of natural forest. In North America, the forest extended from the Atlantic to beyond the Mississippi, and of course west of the Rockies.

Sometimes the forests were exploited to provide fast economic expansion, regardless of the cost to future generations. In order to provide a navy capable of ruling the seas, in the early sixteenth century Henry VIII ordered the felling of a million mature oak trees, virtually denuding England of its mature oaks. The world's forest cover was reduced from about 75% at its greatest to about 50% in medieval times. By 1900 it had dropped to about 35%. In the frantic rush to get rich quick, regardless of the consequences, the figure has dropped to 25% and every year we are still losing equatorial forest the size of Belgium.

Today, the unstable social conditions worldwide, and irresponsible political leadership favour greedy opportunists anxious to make their fortunes, often illegally, by logging many of the finest stands of prime forests on every continent. This destruction is likely to be seen in the future as dangerous planetary vandalism, because their consequences will bear heavily on the future global environmental balance.

A moral tale

Easter Island, one of the most remote islands in the Pacific Ocean, was occupied by a people about whom we know little, but who had the most remarkable artistic skills (witness the giant statues they left behind), and a sophisticated culture. It had a cover of forest, fertile soil, and at one time supported over 20,000 people. Towards the end of the thousand years of their occupation of the island, their society clearly deteriorated and they had felled all the trees, so that by AD500, there was no way to build a boat and leave the island. The people literally died out.

Of all the violations we have committed against the beautiful and fertile planet we call home, the destruction of the forests is the hardest to comprehend. The effects of such actions are so quickly apparent, in terms of soil depletion, or in extreme cases, of erosion of the living soil layer by rain or wind, and indeed, through climate change. The great floods of the Rhine in recent years, and the devastating floods in Bangladesh and the mud slides in Assam and Honduras have been caused demonstrably by deforestation in the mountains. In spite of this, the tree felling continues. When the European immigrants settled in North America, there was continuous forest from the Atlantic to the Mississippi.

Five thousand years earlier the great Midwestern prairies and the grasslands of Argentina were also forested. The deep soils of the temperate latitudes were created over hundreds of thousands of years by rich natural forest. (Grasslands do not produce deep soils.) And within a hundred years we have ruined these, first by intensive cultivation, and then by chemical poisoning. The American prairies, and the East Anglian wheat fields have lost on average half their soil depth. When in 1999, over 30,000 people died in mudslides in Venezuela, scientists blamed the weather! The obvious lessons are not being learned, which suggests that our 'experts' are completely out of touch with reality, a complaint frequently voiced by Viktor Schauberger!

We are told that the critical point may soon be reached when there will not be enough forest to produce sufficient oxygen to support high quality life. For the forests are the lungs of the Earth, breathing in carbon dioxide (CO_2) and exhaling oxygen (O). When the trees are felled, and again when they are burned, they contribute to the mass of carbon dioxide, the principal global warming gas. Recent analyses of fossilized amber have shown that their air bubbles contained 38% oxygen. Today the average oxygen content of air is 19%, which suggests that the human body was designed to operate at twice today's concentration of oxygen. In some larger cities the oxygen content has deteriorated to as low as 12%.

Crucially, though still little understood, forests create the environment for the propagation of water, the "first-born" of the energies of life, as Schauberger puts it, and they moderate the climate, making it cooler in summer and warmer in winter. They are also responsible for the mineralization and fertilization of the surface soils, essential for the nutrition of higher life forms and, most important of all, the forests create the rich humus and bacterial life, the foundation of a rich biodiversity, which stores and recycles vast amounts of rainfall, preventing floods on lower land.[3]

Tropical rainforests

Everyone who has the opportunity, before it is too late, should visit a tropical rainforest, for they are the priceless jewels of our ecosystem. Important not just for the incredible richness and variety of their fauna and flora, they have had a substantially modifying influence on the world's climate, helping to make most of the Earth pleasantly habitable and very productive. They were on four continents, but are now only about half their extent of 500 years ago: the South American is the most complete, at about 75% of its original size; the South-east Asian, from India, through Indo-China to Indonesia and Australia is about a third of what it was, and the African about 40% of its original size. The Central American has virtually disappeared.

More than twice as much of the Sun's energy reaches the Earth's surface at the tropics as in high latitudes where the Sun's angle above the horizon is very low. The tropical rainforests of the world act as heat pumps, transferring to higher latitudes some of the enormous energy they generate, thus evening out the temperature difference. Without them, the equatorial regions would be much hotter, and the higher latitudes much colder. The larger the mass of a tropical rainforest, the more effective it is as a heat pump.

Now that we know, from a study of the Amazonian rainforest, how the heat pump works, it is possible to conjecture that the African continent would not have been nearly as dry as it is today. In South-East Asia the destruction has reached cataclysmic proportions, with a free-for-all between corrupt local interests and greedy multinational companies who are also extracting minerals at a fast pace, particularly in Borneo, where most of the virgin forests, theoretically protected, are likely to disappear within fifteen years.

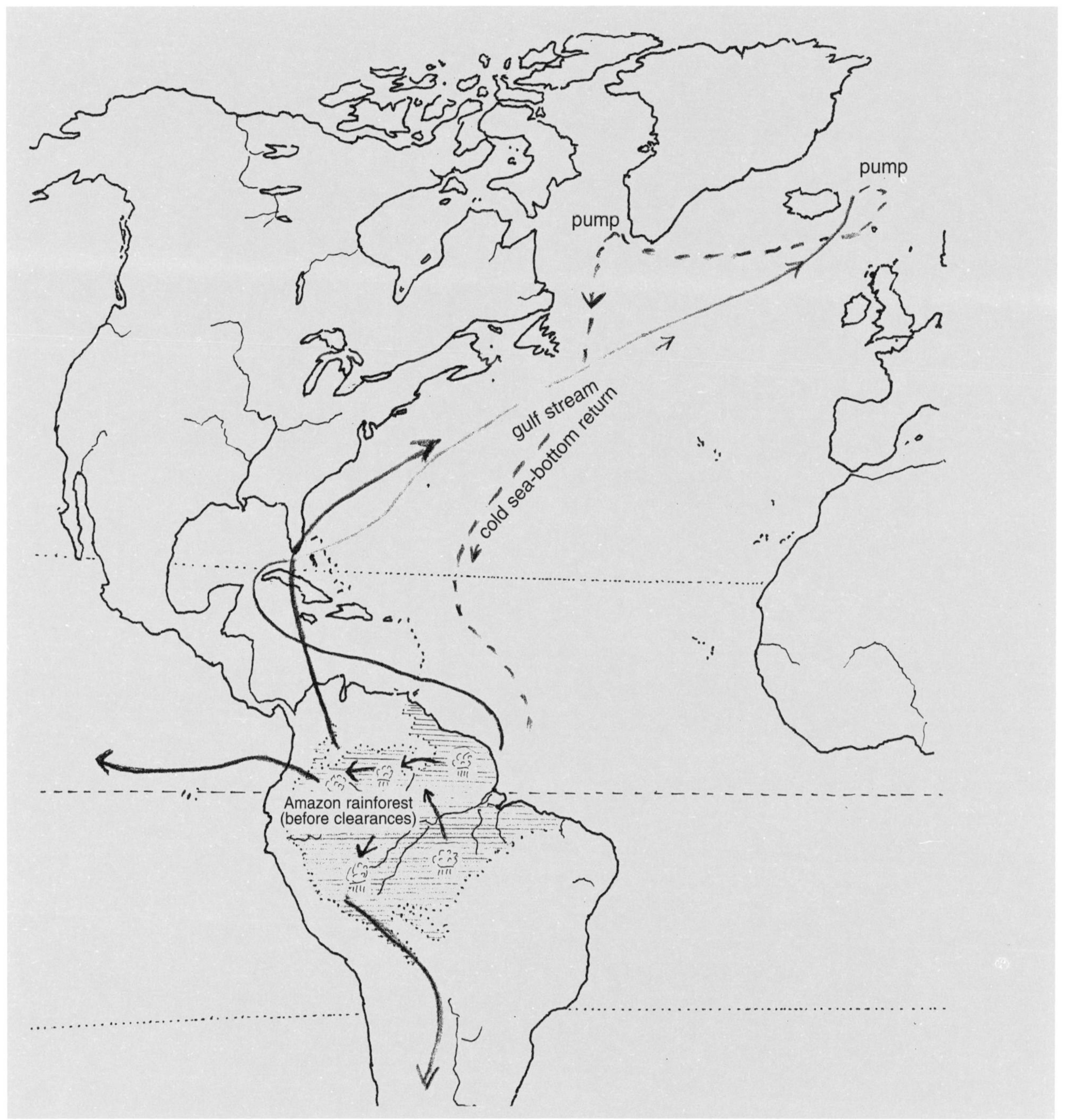

Fig.13.1. The Amazon Heat Engine and the North Atlantic.

The Amazon Basin is the big heat engine that controls the climate of the Northern Hemisphere, but only when the tropical rainforest is largely complete. See Note 13.3 (p. 274) for how the Gulf Stream pump works, and the danger of its failure due to fresh water run-off from the Greenland icecap. Note 13.7 explains how the Amazonian heat engine works.

Within the last decade both droughts and storms have, for example in Australia, become consistently more severe. With the accelerated destruction of the forest, the climatic future of the region looks grim. Amazonia contains two-thirds of the world's surviving tropical rainforest, representing about 30% of all the biological material on the land.[4] You can imagine that when all four tropical rain forests were intact, they must have contained the greater part of the plant and animal life on Earth.

The released energy drives the great air masses across the Amazon basin to the Andes, recycling the rain and evapo-transpiration several times in a leapfrogging process (see Fig 13.1). The airflow then splits into three: the southern part is deflected as far as Patagonia; the central part flows over the Andes into the Pacific, continuing west as the trade winds; the northern airflow crosses the Caribbean, and helps to drive the Gulf Stream north-eastwards to Europe.[6] Rainforests act as thermal engines, rainfall stimulators and as regulators of atmosphere and oceanic systems. They moderate the climate of the whole Earth and help to make it habitable.

The Amazon Basin, which comprises 7 million km^2 of rainforest, is the biggest and most efficient energy transformer on Earth[7]; it is self-maintaining when complete, but 25% has already been lost in the last 35 years. Five million km^2 lie in Brazil which has recently unveiled an accelerated development plan (see below) that would result in the loss of a further 20% by 2020 (a total loss of forest of 45%!). There is a critical size of the Amazonian rainforest below which this complex heat engine and rainfall distributor will fail. Some authorities claim that if it shrinks to much less than the present 75% of its original area, the forest will not be able to perform these critical functions effectively, resulting in more hostile weather patterns and drought across the globe.[8]

Areas that have been clear-felled put at risk the remaining forest for many miles from the edge of the deforested area, rendering the marginal area more susceptible to die-back due to the local increase in temperature. In fact, the Amazonian forest through deforestation is generally losing its ability to withstand the worldwide temperature increase created by global warming. At some point, perhaps in the next twenty years (or sooner under present Brazilian plan), a critical point could be reached, when massive die-back could cause this vital energy transformer to fail.

Preservation of this precious forest is a tough battle. In June 2000, the biggest landowners in Brazil who control 50% of the agricultural land, pushed a draft law through the Brazilian senate committee which would have allowed a 25% increase in annual rates of clearing and burning of the forest. An international email campaign amongst environmentalists, instantly mounted, generated hundreds of thousands of signatures, forcing the Congress to back down. Less than a year later however, the Brazilian government launched the much more ambitious *Avanca Brasil* plan to develop most of Amazonia, with new highways, even railroads; new settlements and extraction of minerals and timber. The whole region will be transformed in the next twenty years, with the remains of the forest chopped into strips and blocks with little chance of survival. This unbelievably irresponsible policy can be stopped only by mass international protest.

Forestry

The death of the forests is only the tip of the iceberg and is a reflection of the deeper deterioration in humankind itself.

Ernst Krebs

If a forest's climate changes over hundreds or thousands of years, the types of trees that grow in it will gradually change, without threatening the survival of the forest. However, if the rate of climate change accelerates, as it is doing today, certain species disappear before new species can take hold. The forest starts to lose its vitality and will gradually deteriorate into an arid wasteland.

The modern science of forestry began in the early nineteenth century. Napoleon in his passage over the Alps removed an unbelievable number of great trees, and the Swiss were determined to restore the damage. Less concerned with mass production than we are today, they insisted that planting must be of appropriate species. Though this sensitivity to landscape and the environment is still practised in Switzerland and Austria, in other countries forestry has deteriorated to the production of timber for cheap furniture, chipboard and firewood, as that is about all the poor quality of timber is good for.

Forestry today is about planting single species' woodland to be harvested within as short a time as possible (while the trees are mere adolescents) in order to maximize the profit. A redwood for example, which has a lifespan of 2000 years, today is harvested after sixty years, before it can be fruitful, at about 3% of its potential. Without mature seed, the genetic base of the remaining seed has deteriorated to the point of infertility. The consequences of this madness are far-reaching, for as the biological diversity is depleted of its highest quality organisms, so too are the energies that support higher forms of life. The destruction of the forest brings with it the destruction of water, with appalling consequences.

Monoculture

If you go into a typical plantation, it is impenetrable, dark, and feels dead — a veritable green desert. No birds sing nor animals scurry, and there is little opportunity for any other plants to grow. Those that do are removed on the theory that they take away nourishment from the trees. In fact their absence increases the competition. The individual trees are all of the same age and species; they vie with each other for space and for nutrients (of which there is a limited amount for each species), for their roots go down to the same level, creating a hard pan of salts which prevents access to the valuable minerals and energized groundwater below. There is only a certain amount of each element and chemical compound available which is suitable for that species and all the trees whose lives are wholly dependent on them must fight to get it.

It is hardly surprising that the wood from such a plantation is of very poor quality. You might compare the composition of a human community to a forest. If all the individual humans were clones of each other, and there were no elder statesmen or wise elders, how creatively barren and spiritually impoverished would be that community! These young trees are clear-felled, leaving a scene of devastation, with the valuable soil vulnerable to erosion. Students of forestry do not yet learn the purpose of a natural forest, nor about biodiversity, which is the keystone of Nature's order.

Without natural forest, higher forms of life on this planet would not have been able to develop. Apart from oxygenating the atmosphere and replenishing the water, both of which sustain life, it contains the vital pyramid of the different levels of life, without which creation would degenerate, as it is doing in our time. By a mysterious process, forests encourage rainfall; appropriate trees planted in an arid or desert environment devoid of rainfall will often cause rain to fall, nourishing the trees, and starting the process of healing that environment.

Biodiversity

A natural, undisturbed forest has a rich diversity in colour and form that brings a sense of inner tranquillity and peace. With our warped sense of order we see the profusion of life as chaotic, whereas in fact it is in the highest state of order. Order in Nature arises from a sensitive state of balance in a highly complex ecosystem. What we often recognize as ordered is usually sterile and uniform.

The natural forest is a community of vast numbers of species of plants, animals and micro-organisms which cannot flourish or even survive without each other. This interdependence is something we still little understand, and the tragedy is that, with the disappearance of the tropical rainforests, we shall lose the vital laboratory that is the most complex ecosystem on Earth. They contain literally millions of species of fauna and flora, most of which we have not yet been able to study. Science does not yet fully understand either the full importance of biodiversity, nor how it is achieved, yet its preservation is essential to our salvation. There is a rapidly decreasing number of places in the world to study it, and they are hastily being converted to monoculture or to arable land, the exterminators of biodiversity.

The rainforest has many layers of trees and shrubs, the high trees, the overstorey, protecting those below that need shade. The trees with deep root systems bring up valuable minerals and nutrients from below, beyond the reach of the more shallow-rooted. The micro-organisms on the forest floor thrive on the rich variety of leaves and provide valuable nourishment for all the plants.

The ground remains cool and moist due to the protection of the trees overhead and the rich spongy humus can retain up to 85% of the rain, which recharges the water table and allows the full circulation of groundwater. This essential element of the natural forest is an early victim to deforestation for, when exposed to the elements, the ground surface quickly deteriorates, its ability to hold water compromised — for warm ground sheds the rain like concrete — which results in floods in the lands below.

The trees that grow the tallest, or on the outer edge of the forest are equipped to withstand the heat and direct sunlight. They in turn protect those that are more delicate and light-sensitive, and the young trees that need the CO_2-rich environment and coolness of the lower layers of the forest.

Those trees and shrubs that are sensitive to light and heat are shielded from degenerative effects by varieties of tree whose structure is designed to resist the heating. By the time the mother tree dies, its young are ready to take over the role of their parents. Because trees are allowed to mature and live out their full cycle, their seeds are of the highest quality, which ensures that the forest stays in good heart. Nature here, with this rich variety, is in a productive state of balance, what Schauberger calls "changeable, unstable equilibrium".

Clearly only Nature, whose very foundation is *interconnectedness,* can truly create biodiversity, albeit slowly. Humanity, now the dominant species, if it is to survive, must replace its present methods of cultivation, for forestry or food, with radically different methods that are sustainable. The most promising experiments to this end have been made by Permaculture, an environmental movement founded by Bill Mollison and David Holmgren in Australia in 1974.[9] They have demonstrated how to create an integrated environment of plants that grow best in association with one another, protecting each other from pests.

In these artificially created natural habitats, horticulture, forestry and animal husbandry are combined into a harmonious and sustainable whole. Shelter belts of trees are planted to protect the cultivated plots. The available water, the microclimate and the soil conditions are taken into account. Each human community is in this way able gradually to become more self-sufficient. Permaculture methods have been introduced, with great success, into countries like India where the levels of poverty often restrict the ability of people to feed themselves. Natural methods of composting and fertilization are used instead of artificial fertilizers.

High quality hardwoods are still coming out of equatorial and temperate forests and used for fine furniture and musical instruments. Soon these resources will be exhausted. Where else are we to find such fine wood? Since mass production has become the norm, understanding has been lost of the natural processes required to produce high-quality timber. Vast areas of land are cleared of trees completely, exposing the soil to the direct heat and light of the Sun. This raises the ground temperatures, the delicate soil-capillaries are destroyed which deliver nutrients and moisture to the soil — and the groundwater table sinks. Hardwoods will not be used in the replanting, as they require too long to mature for commercial exploitation. Reforestation is generally of softwoods such as pine, for contemporary forestry is not interested in quality or in long-term investment.

Energy in the forest

The Sun's energy reaches the Earth' s surface as a full spectrum of light waves. In a natural, mixed forest, this energy is transformed into creative growth, the various plants absorbing different parts of the spectrum. The outcome of this is the production of good water, a humus layer teeming with bacterial life (which is an efficient counter to pollution), and an overall coolness and feeling of harmony. In Nature, a function that maintains any system (e.g. a forest) in a state of stable health and balance is the outer expression of an inner creative force. It is significant that medicinal plants will grow only in a healthy forest where the biodiversity is greatest.

A monocultured woodland, on the other hand, absorbs only a part of the light spectrum, the balance being given off as ambient heat. The Sun's energy is provided to create balanced life forms. If it cannot fulfil its creative functions, it becomes destructive, in this case overheating the monocultured trees. The energies are not balanced, and this discord affects all the creatures. The pulsation and harmonious interaction of the energies are disrupted, encouraging disease and disharmony. Schauberger showed that highly ordered and diverse systems lose their stability when their environment suffers deterioration, indicating that we could expect moral and spiritual deterioration in the human community.

In the human body a blood temperature of 37°C (98.4°F) is regarded as being healthy. Should it rise to 38.5°C (103.1°F), symptoms of distress are felt and we become susceptible to infection by life-forms that are normally dormant in the body, but which become activated between, say 38.2°C (100.6°F) and 38.6°C (101°F). The body will usually respond with a fever, which drives the temperature higher, destroying the bacteria or virus that brought the infection. Schauberger found that it is the same with trees. Their health is stable within a narrow range. When a tree becomes overheated, it becomes susceptible to parasites and fungal attack. It is not the parasites that cause the sickness, but the changes in temperature and energy balance.

14. The Life and Nature of Trees

Trees in the biosphere

Humans have always had a very close interdependence with trees.[1] Hominids came on the scene at one of those rarer times in Earth's history when a forest environment predominated. For the greater part of our short time on the planet, our ancestors grew up among trees. First they would slash and burn small clearings in the forest in order to grow crops. Wood was the greatest single resource to allow population to expand; it was the principal source of fuel and of building materials. These early societies were intimately connected with their environment; their shamans mediated with the life forces and the guardian spirits. The wildwood was treated with reverence.

Part of the forest was earmarked for growing sustainable wood supplies. Mostly this was for coppicing, when the branches are cut just above ground level every five to eight years. This practice produces an abundance of multipurpose straight branches and is eminently sustainable, encouraging re-growth.

The elders and the shamans selected special stands of trees for ritual purposes, for worship and for thanksgiving. These sacred groves were their churches and cathedrals, with altars, nave and cloisters. Later, many groups moved onto the savannahs, but societies like the Druids (*dru* means wood, *wid*, knowledge) in Roman times had complex tree classifications and tree medicines. The wildwood is a magical place, and it is not surprising that there is an immense richness of lore about the healing properties of different types of tree.

There is an area in Gloucestershire, in the heart of England, still known as the Wychwood that was one of the last stands of primitive forest to disappear to the demands of building a wooden navy for English control of the seas. To this day there remains in this area an awareness of the magical qualities of the wildwood, and a memory of the rituals of healing and of working with the nature spirits.

The tree is at the top of the botanical ladder, and is like a gateway between the human and plant kingdoms. The forest is a community with a hierarchy among the trees. Each area has its wise trees or grandfather/grandmother trees. The older parent trees succour and nourish the young saplings.

Water is born from the fusion of molecular hydrogen and oxygen below the surface of the Earth, through the medium of subtle energies. The tree, with its roots deep in the ground, is intimately connected with the evolution of water. As we have seen, water takes the form of blood, lymph, sap and milk, the life-giving and maintaining fluids which are the basis for the growth and development of all life. Every living organism is therefore a column or container of water.

The form of a tree

All trees have a root system that absorbs nutrients from the soil and anchors the trunk; trunk and branches that define the shape of the tree and raise the crown to the sunlight; and leaves that perform the essential functions of photosynthesis, and making chlorophyll and carbohydrates.

The roots are the complement to the branches, securing the tree against wind and absorbing water that contains the energies and the minerals the tree needs to be healthy; they also play a vital part in the role of the tree as a biocondenser of energy. At the ends of the roots are magical organisms called protoplasms that convert the minerals from the inorganic to the organic state that the tree is able to use. There is a complex interaction between the roots and the bacteria, fungi and other micro-organisms in the soil, which is part of the energy exchange between the tree and the earth domain.

The trunk is formed for the most part from dead cells that give it rigidity and stability. The living parts are: the *cambium* that produces new cork or bark to offset what is shed on the outside; the *phloem* with fine capillaries that carry oxygen, nitrogen etc, down to the roots, and the *xylem*, whose coarser channels allow ionized minerals, salts, trace elements, carbonic acid or CO_2 to flow upwards. Phloem and xylem are also found in the structure of leaves, where they perform a similar function.

The crown is the most noticeable part of the tree, comprising branches, twigs, leaves, flowers and fruit or nuts. The leaves receive from the earth minerals and trace elements, CO_2 from the atmosphere and the Sun's energy to drive the process of photosynthesis;

the by-product of which is oxygen, vital for the sustenance of the animal kingdom and for other life-giving processes.

Trees and humans — a symbiotic relationship

The life history of a tree is also the life history of water. Trees are the highest form of plant life, as human beings are of animals. Humans and trees are marvellously interdependent (see Fig. 14.1). Trees, through the process of photosynthesis, exhale the oxygen we need for survival, and in return absorb the carbon dioxide we exhale. Of their total production of oxygen, 60% is released in daylight, the balance being used by the tree or plant itself during the night to produce cool oxidations that help to build the actual structure of the plant. As with so many of Nature's interdependencies, this is a symbiotic exchange, a cooperative transaction. Were there no trees and other vegetation there would be no animal, human or micro-organic life on this planet. Through our mindless deforestation, we have already reduced the amount of oxygen and water available to us.

Fig.14.1. The Symbiotic Relationship of Animal and Vegetable Kingdoms.[2]

An **ANIMAL** is:		A **VEGETABLE** is:
A combustion or oxidation apparatus		An apparatus for reduction or deoxidation
Possesses the faculty of locomotion		Is rooted to one location
Burns	carbon	**Reduces**
	hydrogen	
	ammonium	
Exhales	carbonic acid	**Fixes**
or gives off	water	
	oxide of ammonium	
	nitrogen	
Consumes	oxygen	**Produces**
	Neutralized nitrogenous matter	
	fatty matter	
	starchy matters, gum and sugar	
Produces	heat	**Absorbs**
	electricity	**Abstracts**
Restores its elements to air and earth		Derives its elements from air and earth
Transforms organized into mineral matter		Transforms mineral into organized matter

Trees and colour

Another symbiotic relationship between trees and human beings is found with colour. The graph below (Fig. 14.2) shows the relative intensities of radiation in the electromagnetic spectrum, from the ultraviolet on the left through the visual spectrum to the infrared on the right. The darkest line shows the intensity of solar radiation relative to frequency or to the various shades of colour. In the visible part of the spectrum there is high human sensitivity to the green and low to the red and ultraviolet, whereas with the tree it is the opposite. A tree's sensitivity to light is a mirror to the human's.

The highest intensity of solar radiation is found in the green part of the spectrum. The tree cannot use these frequencies for its growth, for the greens induce dormancy. Whatever colour or frequency is not absorbed, is reflected. A red surface, for example,

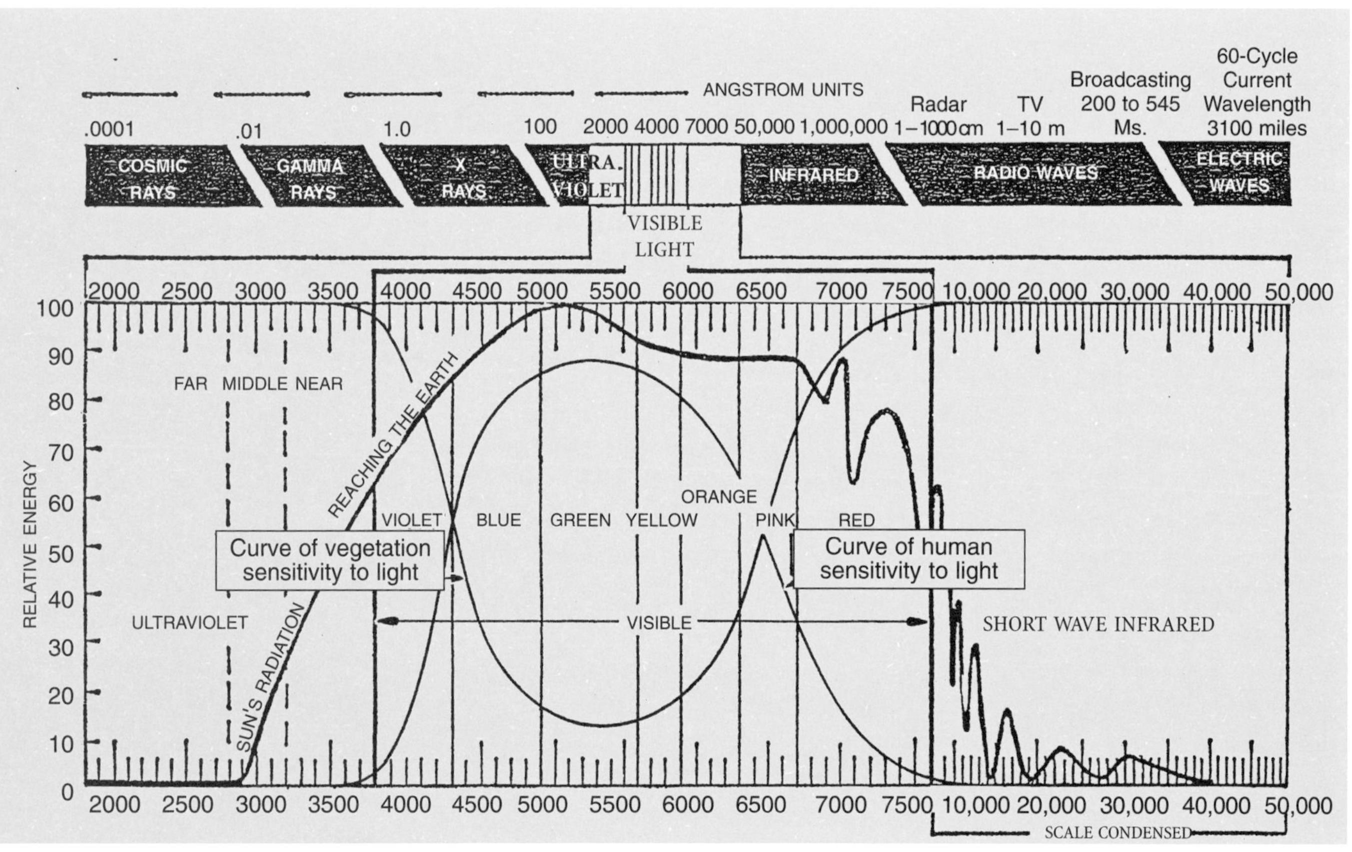

Fig.14.2. The Electromagnetic Spectrum.

absorbs all colours except its particular shade of red. Many metabolic processes are triggered by specific frequencies, and if the required frequency of light is not available in sufficient quantity, then the response is blocked.

A tree will absorb most in the ultraviolet or the red to infrared portion of the spectrum. It is insensitive to green light and, if placed under green light, appears to be in a state of suspended animation. The light sensitivity of the human eye on the other hand is exactly the opposite. It is insensitive to the ultraviolet and infrared frequencies, but very sensitive to the colour green.

Because we cannot observe any green in sunlight itself, without trees and other vegetation, green would be missing in our experience. Green is a very soothing, healing colour for humans, sedating the nervous system and psyche. Its absence in large cities can make us irritable and even violent. Trees and humans have a symbiotic relationship with colour.

The physical nature of trees

The structure of the tree is a record of its various stages of growth, and this is mirrored in the movement of sap over the full span of the tree's existence. As the life energy of the tree recedes with ageing, the sap sinks lower and lower, progressively drawing back from the uppermost branches, which die off. In many cases this is accelerated by human activity and the tree is said to suffer from 'die-back.' Like an elderly human being, the tree's structure stiffens with age, and like an elderly human, its consciousness falls back through all the stages of its previous development, perhaps re-living its earlier experiences.

It is important in times of climate change to realize that the tree is probably the organism least adapted to rapid change. The average lifetime of a tree is the longest after rocks, and therefore many centuries must pass before any real adaptation to changed conditions can occur. Even minor environmental changes, to which other shorter-living things can adapt, can cause trees stress and vulnerability to disease, so that they wither and die.

As long as too much heat does not stress them, trees will moderate heat through their absorption of CO_2 and their evapo-transpiration. When the forest cover is substantial the trees distribute water vapour evenly through the atmosphere, ensuring a balanced distribution of temperature. The evaporating area of a mature beech tree, for example, with some seven million leaves, totals about 1.47 hectares (3.6 acres).

Trees also break the strength of the wind, creating shelter for other life forms and lesser species of vegetation. The planting of shelter-belts (best in spiral form) reduces both the wind speed and the dehydration of the soil, creating microclimates that help the soil against erosion through the provision of additional humus and protection. Indeed shelter belts can influence the evaporation rate over cultivated land by as much as 30 metres upwind and 120 metres downwind, and Canadian research has shown that farms with a third of their land as shelter belts are more productive than farms of equivalent area where there are no trees at all.

These shelter belts also trap carbon dioxide (CO_2), the heaviest naturally occurring atmospheric gas, found mostly in the lowest levels of the atmosphere, and an essential component of photosynthesis. Increased CO_2 under the right conditions will produce stronger photosynthesis. When trees and hedgerows between fields are removed, productivity falls, because this causes a fall in carbon dioxide. Trees should be revered as much as water, for together they are both are the givers of life.

Tree classification

Trees can be classified generally into seven major categories. These can be subdivided according to latitude, altitude, whether they are light-demanding or shade-demanding species (the former having a thick, rough bark and the latter a smooth thin bark), and whether they are hardwood or softwood, broad-leafed, conifer, evergreen and so on.

Before we examine trees and their growth in relation to these categories in more detail, let us look at the specific contribution that trees make to the general environment. We give the example of a 100 year-old tree, whose extraordinary performance was calculated by Walter Schauberger in the 1970s in relation to the average output of European species:

During the course of its life, a hundred-year-old tree:

a) Has processed and fixed the amount of carbon-dioxide contained in 18 million cubic metres of natural air in the form of about 2500 kg of pure carbon (C).
b) Has photo-chemically converted 9,100 kg of CO_2 and 3,700 litres of H_2O.
c) Has stored up circa 23 million kilogram-calories (a calorific value equivalent to 3,500 kg of hard pit coal).
d) Has made available for the respiration of human and beast 6,600 kg of molecular oxygen (O_2).
e) Against the forces of gravity, has drawn from its roots right up to its crown and evaporated into the atmosphere at least 2,500 tonnes of water, every tree is therefore a water-column and if such a column, which continually supplies and recharges the atmosphere with water, is cut down, then this amount of water is lost.
f) Thereby fixing a mechanical equivalent of heat equal to the calorific value of 2,500 kg of coal.
g) Has supplied a member of the consumer society with oxygen sufficient for 20 years, and its nature is such, that the larger it grows, the more oxygen it produces.

In view of such achievements, who in the future could value this tree merely for its timber?
The combustion of 100 litres of petrol consumes about 230 kg of oxygen. That is, after a trip of barely 30,000 km (18,640 miles) (9 6 lit/1000 km), this tree's entire 100 year production of oxygen has been squandered.
Driving an average size car 30,000 km (18,640 miles) = 100 years of oxygen production.

If a person chooses to breathe for three years, to burn 400 lit of petrol or heating oil, or 400 kg of coal, then the production through photosynthesis of 1 tonne of oxygen is required.
1 tonne of O_2 = the O_2 content of 3,620 m^3 of air (+15°C at 1atm)
The photosynthetic production of 1 tonne of oxygen necessitates:
a) The building up of 0.935 tonnes $C_6H_{12}O_6$ (carbohydrate),
b) which process requires 1.37 tonnes CO_2 (carbon-dioxide) and 0.56 tonnes H_2O (water)
c) The transpiration of 230 to 930 tonnes H_2O
d) Light energy equal to 527 x 10^6 quanta ($\nu = 440 \times 10^{12}$) which represents 3.52 million kilocalories.

All this is no small achievement for a single organism!

[Source: Walter Schauberger]

Light- and shade-demanding trees

There are two types of tree with very different requirements of light (see Fig.14.3). The effect of light on tree growth has two principal energy outcomes. Partly it determines the structure of the timber and, secondly, it influences the form and character of the tree itself, depending on whether it is a shade-demanding or a light-demanding species; and these are also related to latitude and altitude.

Trees mirror the quality of light in their natural habitat. If the frequency of green is harmful to them, they will use green leaves as they will screen out or repel that frequency. In general, if the incident light has a greater proportion of high-frequency, high-energy, ultraviolet light, in other words hard light, the wood will be soft. Conversely, where there is a greater preponderance of low-frequency, low-energy, infrared, soft light, the wood will be hard.[4]

Australia's native timbers, notable for their hardness, are a good example of this. Because of Australia's position on the Tropic of Capricorn in the southern hemisphere, the intensity of infrared light is greatest when Australia experiences its high summer, and when the Earth is also at its closest to the Sun at Perihelion in early January. This is increased by the infrared radiation resulting from Australia's semi-desert condition. Along with other countries in the southern hemisphere, Australia is therefore exposed to more intense infrared light than counties in the north which experience more moderate conditions.

The new growth of many species of Australian trees presents a particular mixture of red, violet and blue hues, in order to resist the potentially harmful penetration of those light frequencies. In Europe and the temperate latitudes of North America, on the other hand, with their very different light conditions, most new growth is light green in colour, with some exceptions (like the copper beech).

To summarize: Softwood species, such as pine, are mostly found in zones of high-energy, high-frequency 'hard' radiation, at low altitudes in high latitudes, and at high altitudes in low latitudes. Conversely hardwood trees, with some exceptions, are generally found at low altitudes in low latitudes (tropical rainforests) and at low to middle altitudes at low to middle latitudes — zones of low frequency, 'soft' radiation.

Tree types are determined to a great extent by: **latitude** and **altitude**.

(1) **LIGHT-DEMANDING** timbers — **THICK**, generally rough bark *(e.g. oak, black walnut)*
(2) **SHADE-DEMANDING** timbers — **THIN**, generally smooth bark *(e.g. beech, birch)*
(3) **HARDWOODS** — thick *(e.g. oak, jarrah)* and thin bark *(e.g. walnut, cherry, maple, red alder)*
(4) **SOFTWOODS** — thick *(e.g. redwood, pine, spruce)* and thin bark e.g. *(hemlock, fir, larch)*

GENERAL DISTRIBUTION*

(5) **CONIFEROUS**	(6) **DECIDUOUS**	(7) **RAINFOREST**
(evergreen)	(intermittent)	(evergreen)
(polar latitudes)	(median latitudes)	(equatorial latitudes)
(high altitudes)	(median altitudes)	(low altitudes)

*These boundaries are not necessarily clearly defined.

Fig.14.3. Tree Type Distribution.

High altitude trees such as spruce have a relatively short lifespan. Shortwave ultraviolet light, with its higher energy and intensity, has a faster dynamic motion with a smaller radius and shorter period tend to favour evergreens with soft wood. In contrast, low latitude or low altitude trees like the beech, where long wavelength, low-energy, low-frequency, less intense light predominates, has harder wood and a longer lifespan.

Contemporary forestry practice requires trees to grow rapidly in girth, putting on a profusion of branches. What this produces is a great quantity of poor quality timber, full of knots. The disregard by forestry of the light factor is one of the causes of the deterioration of forests.

The increase of tree diseases in both logged natural forests and in plantations is a direct result of the exposure to direct sunlight and heat of a shade-demanding species. There are two ways to determine whether a tree is a light- or a shade-demander:

Shade-demanding species have thin smooth bark; growing normally in the cooler inner forest, they do not need to insulate themselves from the heating effect of direct sunlight. Light-demanding trees on the other hand have thick, coarse, thermally insulating bark, which is Nature's way of protecting them from heat and direct sunlight.

Shade-demanding trees grow additional branches to protect the trunk when exposed to light and heat, whereas light-demanders do not. The shade-demanding tree is rather like an introvert, reserved and extremely sensitive to external influences. They tend towards introspection, mental activity (predominant development of the tree's crown) and they are inwardly preoccupied and absorbed. They need a certain shielding and protection, peace and quiet to develop to maturity and their full potential.

The light-demanding trees on the other hand are the extroverts that can happily stand on their own, reflecting their need for light and space around them. They tend to be more physically active, with branches radiating outwards. They are independent, outgoing individuals, which are generally more capable of standing on their own feet without support.

Viktor Schauberger showed that the maintenance of an even inner temperature is vital to all trees, as to all organisms. When sunlight penetrates the trunk, the tree's metabolism is disrupted. It becomes overheated, the sap no longer flows as it should and the general structure of the tree becomes very coarse, leading to malformations, cancerous growths in the interior, and so on. All shade-demanding trees, and under certain circumstances light-demanders too, will do everything they can to maintain or reinstate their preferred inner temperature.

This can be seen after a forest fire, when the trees that survive quickly cover themselves with a profusion of small shoots. The fire has blackened their bark so that, instead of reflecting the heat, it absorbs it and other radiation. Without protective cover the interior of the tree would quickly overheat and the flow of sap would reduce, no longer reaching the highest branches.

Every species of tree has its particular pattern of energy frequencies, which determines its shape and supporting metabolism. If you like, Nature has given it a special niche in a particular environment. An increase in temperature changes its microclimate and the plant's naturally established metabolism can no longer operate healthily, and its wave pattern is disturbed. Instead of 'healthy tree,' there is 'sick tree + parasites.' It is important to understand that the parasites do not cause the sickness, but come as a result of it. Viktor Schauberger called them "Nature's health police" because of their role in removing all organisms that are not evolutionarily viable. The tree will rid itself of parasites once its metabolism has returned to healthy balance.

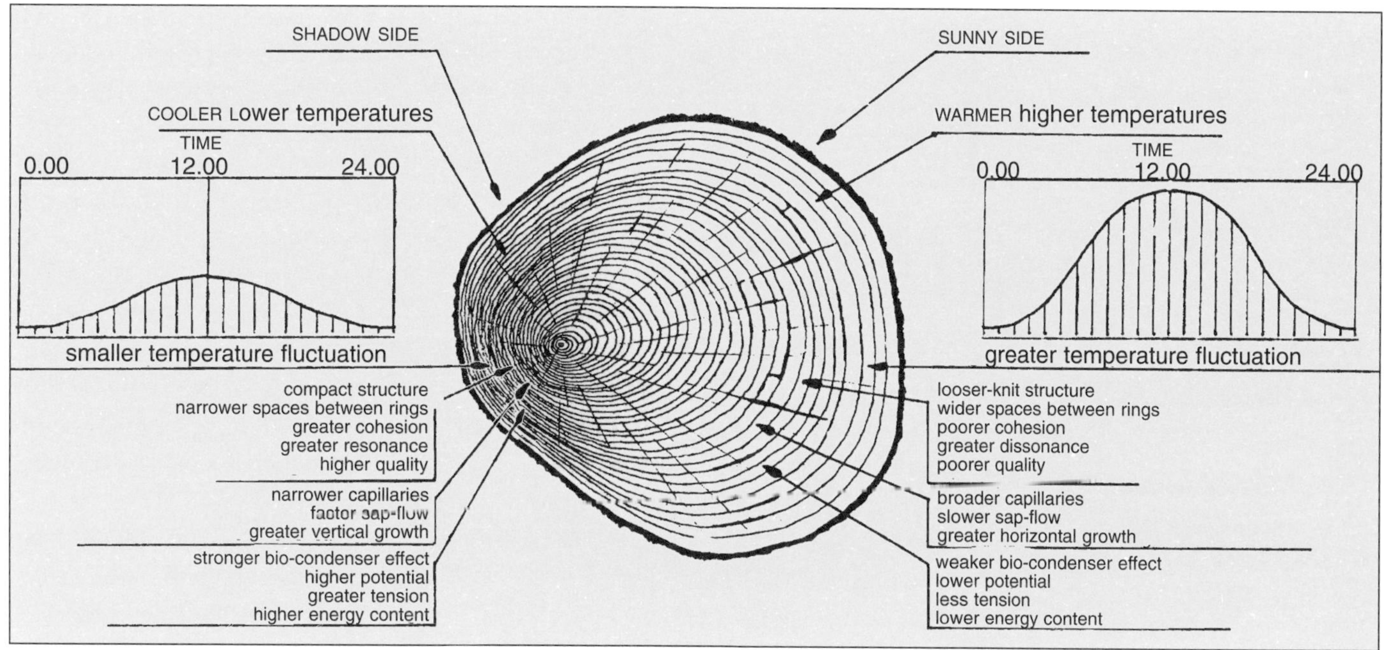

Fig.14.4. Tree Rings showing unbalanced growth.

Light-induced growth

You can tell the age of a tree by counting the growth rings across the cut trunk. These annual rings also tell you something about the conditions under which it grew, and about the climatic variations. Conventionally, a wider space between rings is regarded as a good year for the tree, because it put on more growth; but greater quantity does not mean better quality. What it actually signifies is a tree under heat stress. This is best seen in Fig. 14.4; where the rings are widely spaced on the sunny side of the trunk, the heat caused the wood to expand; on the shaded side the metabolism has not been disturbed and the annual rings are close together.

In a tree that grows in the shade with good soil conditions, the sap-ducts are virtually straight, producing strong vertical growth, and the timber has what might bc termed a 'resonant' quality.[5]

Man-made depredations

Viktor measured the biomagnetic energies in a tree that are responsible not only for its physical upward growth, but also for transferring energies from the Earth to the atmosphere. The tree is in fact a biocondenser, reconciling the Sun's positive, affirming energy with the negative, receptive energy of the Earth. This important role is seen at its most productive in the tropical rainforest, where the enormous fecundity of Nature is best observed.

Biomagnetism, a life enhancing process that puts bioelectricity to work, is present in all living organisms. Man-made electrical systems interfere with Nature's biomagnetism. The shortwave emissions (microwaves) of the world's communication systems have, in many places, seriously interfered with organic life on Earth in the last sixty years. This is seen with the appearance of human cancers near radar establishments or electrical transmission lines, with microwave ovens or portable telephones.[6] It is also damaging trees. Radar seems to be responsible for the destruction of parts of the German forest, and the sub-arctic forest in Canada near the line of Defence Early Warning installations.[7] Viktor observed the early evidence of radar damage to trees; however, most of the destructive effects of microwave pollution have developed since he died.

Microwave transmitters operate with wavelengths between 2cm and 50cm, exposure to which can inflict biological damage. Microwaves have an energetically disruptive effect, triggering deteriorating changes in crystal structure. An example of the amount of free ambient energy being generated can be seen from the use of a neon-filled tube to test the system's working. Held parallel to the direction of transmission from a microwave transmitter, or a high-tension powerline, its spontaneous ignition confirms the ambient energy's strength.[8]

Similar disintegrative effects are found with domestic microwave ovens that operate on a wavelength approximately the same as that of radar. They generate vibrational heat in the molecules of the food.[9] Hydrogen, one of the constituent atoms of the water molecule, has a wavelength of 21cm, well within the bandwidth of current microwave transmissions. It is therefore likely to be damaged by the excessive microwave-induced heating. In the tree this leads to the breakdown of the structure of the sap, which like our blood, is about 80% water. This process also increases the amount of available oxygen within the tree, which results in unnatural metabolic acceleration. The tree, being rooted to the spot, unfortunately cannot escape the radiation emitted by microwave towers and high-tension transmission grids.

Even though we are more mobile, humans too can become

increasingly prone to blood disorders if exposed excessively to such radiation. People living in close proximity to high-tension cables have been shown to have a higher than normal incidence of disease.

According to a study of the Commonwealth Scientific and Industrial Research Organization (CSIRO), an increase in tree ring width of Huon pines in Australia, more rapid in the last forty years than in any other period since AD900, suggests that this internal microwave-induced warming is accelerating. We don't know what happened then; there may have been either a series of gigantic volcanic eruptions or a massive increase in cosmic radiation.

The importance of photosynthesis

Nature works through pulsation, through inhaling and exhaling, like the ocean tides on the shore. The rising Sun draws up the tree's sap charged with trace-elements, gases and minerals, to support the process of photosynthesis and its conversion of CO_2 into oxygen (the inbreath). Photosynthesis, however, is intimately connected with the amount and the quality of the available light. When the level of light falls, then growth, photosynthesis and the creation of chlorophyll diminish and less oxygen is transformed and released into the atmosphere. Then the tide starts to ebb, and the sap ceases to transport the nutrients upwards.

We think of photosynthesis as the process of converting CO_2 to O_2 for us to breathe, but it serves two functions vital for the tree itself: to convert the nutritious sap into carbohydrates (which releases O_2) and to produce evaporation in the form of oxygen and water to cool the tree and release oxygen into the environment. This is not the vaporization associated with sweating, but is the effect of energy concentration or densification. Magnesium is required, in addition to H_2O and CO_2, in order to make chlorophyll, the green protective pigment in the leaves, a third process which releases O_2. These three processes all require light (see Fig. 15.6).

Exactly the same chemical formula that is required to produce chlorophyll, but without light (i.e. underground) also produces hydrogen (and magnesium carbonate). This free hydrogen is an essential ingredient for the production of water, the other being oxygen, which is provided by rainwater percolating into the ground. It is exciting to note that these two identical combinations of Mg, H_2O and CO_2, one with and the other without light, are responsible for the two creators of life, water and photosynthesis (see Fig.15.6).[10]

We have noted a correspondence between times in the past when forests predominated on the Earth, and with major evolutionary surges. It seems that trees have this magical role to fine-tune the proportion of atmospheric gases, particularly oxygen. The 'normal' proportions are O_2 (oxygen) 20.95%, CO_2 (carbon dioxide) 0.3%, N (nitrogen) 78.08% and rare gases 0.93%, though recent years have seen an increase in CO_2 and a decrease in O_2 due to human activities. When we say that life creates the atmosphere (effectively the 'greenhouse'), the symbiotic relationship is exceedingly complex and miraculous.

Fig.14.5. Photosynthesis.

PHOTOSYNTHESIS

Without plants there could be no life. Plants convert sunlight into food by a process known as photosynthesis. They extract carbon dioxide from the atmosphere, water from the soil and exhale oxygen:

1) Carbon dioxide (CO_2) + Water (H_2O) = Photosynthesis + O_2 ⇧
   in this way carbon dioxide and hydrogen combine and molecular oxygen is released (vertical arrow)
2) CO_2 + H_2O + LIGHT ⇨ CH_2O (theoretical carbohydrate) + O_2 ⇧
   ($C_6H_{12}O_6$ = glucose, the simplest form of carbohydrate)
3) Mg + H_2O + CO_2 + **plus** LIGHT ⇨ Chlorophyll + O_2 ⇧
   (green pigment + molecular oxygen)

The same elements in (3) above produce two important further reactions:

(4) Mg + H_2O + CO_2 – **minus** LIGHT ⇨ $MgCO_3$ + H_2 ⇧
   (magnesium carbonate + molecular hydrogen)

or (5) Mg + H_2CO_3 [carbonic acid] – **minus** LIGHT ⇨ $MgCO_3$ + H_2 ⇧
   (magnesium carbonate + molecular hydrogen)

In (4) and (5) the Mg can be replaced with calcium (Ca), which produces calcium carbonate ($CaCO_3$) instead of magnesium carbonate, but with the same release of molecular hydrogen.

These two almost identical, but still different combinations of magnesium, CO_2 and H_2O are the prerequisites for the two principal carriers of life, namely water and photosynthesis (creation of chlorophyll and carbohydrates). One of these takes place in daylight (the visible world) and the other in darkness (the invisible world). In the day zone, O_2 is released and the overall amount of oxygen increased, whereas in the night-zone, hydrogen is released, leading to the rebirth of water through its combination with oxygen.

The creation of water

There is an important relationship between rainwater and trees. Raindrops absorb atmospheric oxygen, nitrogen and other trace-gases in their descent, but their downward spinning movement also generates intense bioelectric and biomagnetic fields. This creates an energy potential which is essentially life-endowing. When the raindrops fall on the leaves of the tree, the oxygen and other gases are absorbed along with the immaterial energies collected, stimulating activity and growth. For this reason plants respond with much greater vitality and activity after a fall of rain than to conventional systems of irrigation where these gases and energies are virtually absent, due to the far shorter fall distance.

It has frequently been observed that the planting of trees in arid or desert conditions causes an increase in rainfall. This is probably because chemicals that are a by-product of photosynthesis are emitted, which helps to generate clouds.[11] This is known to occur in the tropical rainforests, and it is likely to happen in other particularly warm areas. It is one of the most interesting feedback mechanisms that Gaia produces.

When the ground surface is cooler than the air (i.e. it has a positive temperature gradient) rainwater penetrates into the soil. The free oxygen is gradually absorbed by the surrounding soil, activating micro-organisms in the humus upper layers of the soil. As the rainwater sinks deeper into the substrata and continues to release the excess oxygen, it gradually cools towards the +4°C anomaly point. As we have seen, free hydrogen is now available with which the now very passive oxygen is able to combine in the cool conditions, giving birth to new water molecules.

This juvenile immature water, unpolluted by any other substances or ingredients, is born near the temperature when its density is highest, that is, about +4°C (39°F). It begins to rise up through the various energy-horizons (the most finely differentiated temperature strata), acquiring increasing 'information' in the form of subtle energies and resonances.

The water molecules become warmer as they ascend, absorbing salts, minerals and trace-elements on the journey. Becoming ionized in the process they can be taken up by the plants and their micro-organisms. Salt (sodium chloride), for example, is broken up into its two components of chlorine (Cl) and sodium (Na), which develop opposite electrical charges when ionized. It is transformed from an 'inorganic' substance with no electric charge, into two substances which can be combined into organic form ready for combination with its complementary polarity.

The water has now become mature and can contribute life instead of seizing it, creating life-imparting macro water molecules whose nutrients are made more active by the increasingly available oxygen. As these molecules are drawn up through the capillaries of the plants or trees, their size is reduced, as energy and nutrients are passed to structures and chemical processes at different levels, contributing to growth activity. Their potency increases as the molecules become smaller until they are able to pass through the extremely minute foramen and stomata, when their energetic quality reaches a maximum. The greatest growth and maturation occurs at this workface, the furthest extremities of the tree, plant or blade of grass.

The maturation of water

The developmental journey from the deeper strata towards the surface transforms water from a seeking, 'taking' system into a ripe, information-rich 'giving' one, when it is ready to distribute the widest variety of ionized elements in homeopathic doses to the living systems of its environment. It is here that this alive water, rich with minerals and trace-elements, meets the next, young, 'taking,' information-seeking systems — the fine hair-roots of the plant systems and their micro-organisms, or 'microtransmuters.' The water is first taken up by the micro-organisms which transform the raw materials, elements, CO_2, oxygen, nitrogen, etc. into larger molecules and fluid compounds ready for transport as larger molecules by the capillaries of the roots.

The roots eagerly use some of these nutrients for their own development, but the coarse macro-molecules are sucked towards the centre and deposited in order to build up the central structure of the plant or tree. This increasing, but slower flowing quantity of formative material is built into the tree structure up to the level of the ground-surface. Here is the threshold of the visible, energetic world, endowed with a higher dynamic and suffused with radiant, fertilizing energy of the Sun. This is the point where the two aspects of the tree, the two systems of distribution, the seen and the unseen, meet and are united (see Fig.15.6, p. 206).

In the human body, the arteries and veins narrow towards the capillaries and enlarge towards the heart. The blood circulation is managed by subtle differences in temperature and electric charge, by energy density and energetic activity. There are two principal, pulsating circulation systems; one to the lungs to renew oxygen and discharge CO_2 and water; the other from the heart to the rest of the body, delivering nutrients and oxygen to all parts of the body, on its return collecting and transporting CO_2 and waste matter.

The tree, however, has no pulsating heart. The 'pulsators' responsible for the movement of its sap are the Sun and the Moon. As the world rotates, the direction of the Sun's and the Moon's attraction fluctuates from above to below, through which a pulsation arises between inhaling and exhaling. During the day, the sap draws the energies up the tree ('inhaling'), while at night the energy withdraws to the root system (exhaling).

As the sap rises from the ground level, gradually the sap-ducts and capillaries begin to narrow and the coarser elements in the sap, unable to rise further, are built into the tree's structure at the point where their upward movement ceases. As the sap vessels get smaller, the faster the sap streams both upwards and downwards and the greater the homeopathic potential. Ultimately only the most minute particles, which are hardly to be counted as matter, stream up towards the crown or down to the roots with increasing spiral gyration, dynamic and energetic effect.

The growth activity is at a maximum at the extremities of crown and root zones, because all that is active here are the most highly potentiated homeopathic resonances and amounts of barely structured matter. This upward or downward stream of energy also has a nonmaterial, form-controlling aspect. At the outside edge of the growth process, the tree crown, energy radiates into the environment, a process of life giving life, while at the root zone the energetic polarity seems to be that of life seeking life.

A water molecule, when it reaches the crown, carries within it the highly active resonances of the trace elements previously taken up in the root zone. Refined to almost pure water again, with ultra-high potency and trace element overtone resonances, it arrives at the leaves' minute stomata. From these, it ascends into the atmosphere towards its energy and temperature anomaly point at an altitude of 3–4000 metres. Here it is once more in a 'taking' mode, ready to take up the finer and more spiritual energies from the Sun and the cosmos.

This never ending water cycle over time brings a cumulative increase in 'information' which provides a fresh impulse for further processes and development that drive evolution.

15. The Metabolism of the Tree

All the processes that take place in water are reflected once again in the individual forms of vegetation. Viktor Schauberger

Sap movement

Viktor Schauberger has transformed our understanding of the metabolism of the tree. He showed how the movement of the sap under the conditions of both natural growth and of unnatural light-induced growth is determined by the temperature gradient within the tree itself, and by the external light, heat and cold.

The solution, transport and deposition of nutrients, as we saw in Chapter 14, are functions of the temperature gradient. Salts and minerals are precipitated with cooling, when light and air are excluded; however, they are precipitated with heating when exposed to light and air. Under a positive temperature gradient, as the sap cools towards +4°C (39°F) or is maintained at this temperature, the highest quality nutrients are precipitated last. Under a strong negative temperature gradient and with light and heat, the opposite happens; only the lowest quality nutrients are expelled, the highest quality not being transported at all.

We saw that the growth of shade-demanding trees takes place largely in the crown where the air temperature is usually higher than at ground level. The tree's overall shape is cylindrical, with few lower branches, because there is no need to protect the trunk against light. Lacking horizontal lighting, the trunk does not suffer large temperature fluctuations, so it produces closely set annual rings. The temperature in the trunk reduces from the outside inwards, resulting in an even deposition of growth material, which means high quality and dense timber. These shade-demanders have a slender girth because of their strong vertical sap movement, high health and associated levitational energies, that in a mature tree enables it to withstand gales.

When a shade-demander is planted out in the open it has to cope with unnatural levels of light and heat, protecting itself as quickly as possible by sending out branches right down to the ground, at the

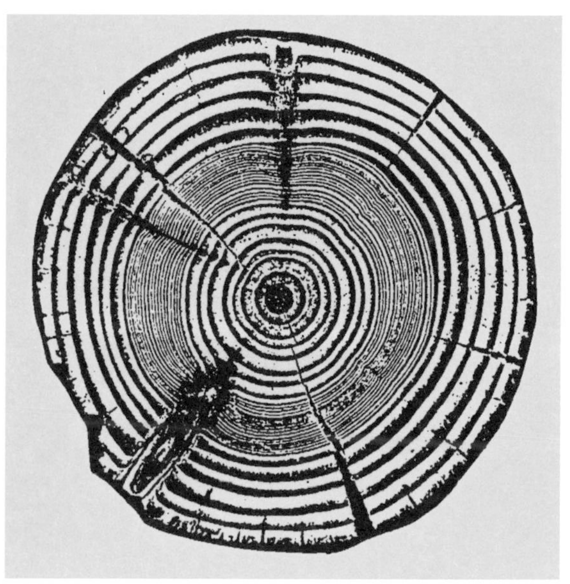

Fig.15.1. Cross Section through Tree Trunk.
The tight inner rings show normal growth of a shade-demanding tree. The outer rings show evidence of too much exposure to sunlight, following its neighbours' removal.

expense of its upward growth. It develops a cone-shaped form, with much growth of branches on the lower part of the trunk. These will tend to grow on the sunny side of the tree, leaving it unbalanced and misshapen.

In its early years, due to high light exposure, a plantation tree exhibits wide annual rings and abnormal lateral branch growth (see Fig. 15.1). Once it receives some protection from its neighbours, the need for lateral branch growth diminishes and it will tend to grow upwards. However, in commercial woodland, the trees are thinned after a prescribed period, those considered suitable for use in construction going to the sawmill and the remainder to the pulp-mill. This thinning out exposes the remaining trees to excess heat and light. All their growth energy is diverted to growing branches on the exposed part of the trunk, mainly on the sunny side, which produces knots and twisted, spongy grain.

The annual tree rings tell the story of a tree's exposure to light. In Fig. 15.1, the rings near the middle show that in its early years, this 33-year old tree was exposed to unnatural levels of light and heat. The healthiest growth was in middle third of the tree's life, revealed by the annual rings at their closest. Its last years show the stress it experienced when its protecting neighbours were removed.

High quality, resonant timber could be cut only from the area of closely spaced rings. A board cut from the full width of the trunk would warp as a result of the unevenness of the grain. For practical purposes the only source of good narrow-ringed timber that is firm and regular in its structure and less likely to warp, is a mature tree from a natural forest. A shade-demander in a natural forest or a plantation that is suddenly exposed to light will show irregular annual rings, an off-centre heart, sometimes heartrot, and radial cracks (called 'shakes') like those shown in Fig. 15.1. Excessive heating, causing sponginess in the wood that often results in heart rot, and encourages bacteria and parasites causes the openness of the grain. This combination of conditions Viktor Schauberger called "tree cancer".

The conventional theory is that the movement of sap is caused by osmosis, or by differences in pressure between air pressure and the pressure in the capillaries. However, the absorbent raising action of osmosis is limited, and cannot account for the rising of sap in the highest trees, which can exceed 91m (300ft). Mechanical suction cannot be responsible either, as the limit for drawing up water is

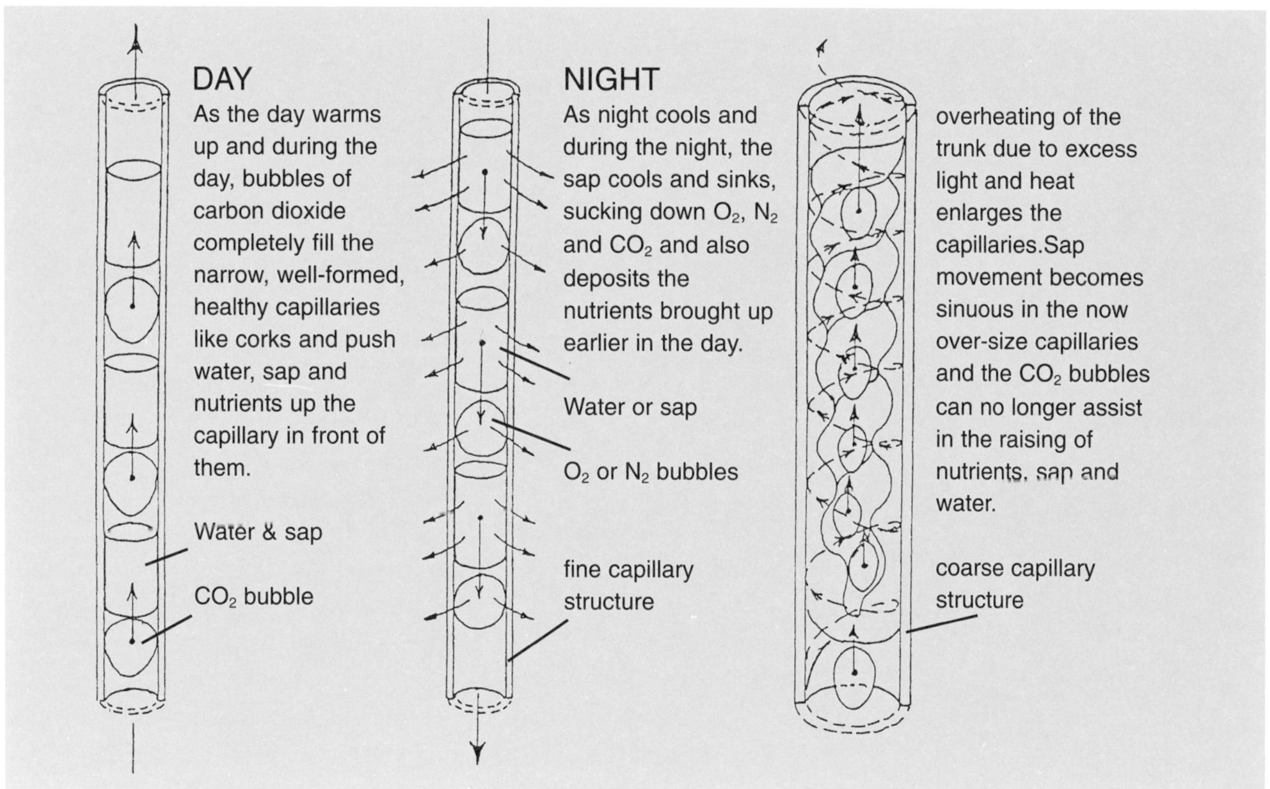

Fig.15.2. Rising Sap.
As the day warms bubbles of CO_2 completely fill the narrow capillaries like corks, pushing water, sap and nutrients in front of them. As night cools, the sap sinks, sucking down the CO_2, the sap and the nutrients.

9.81m (32.18ft). Viktor Schauberger found that it had more to do with a metabolic process:

> On many occasions I have already stated that the rising of sap in trees cannot be explained by the physical factors hitherto put forward alone, such as the effect of the external air pressure, etc., but that its explanation is to be found in the ongoing metabolic processes in constant pulsation in every cell of the tree and is therefore a result of the vital activity of the capillary tree-cell. Professor Kurt Bergel of Berlin came to similar conclusions in relation to the activity of the heart and the blood in animal life.[1]

The healthy movement of sap is stimulated both by the pulsating action and by the extreme fineness of the capillaries to be found in a completely naturally grown tree (Fig.15.2). When the carbonic acid contained in the water and sap is warmed, it is converted into

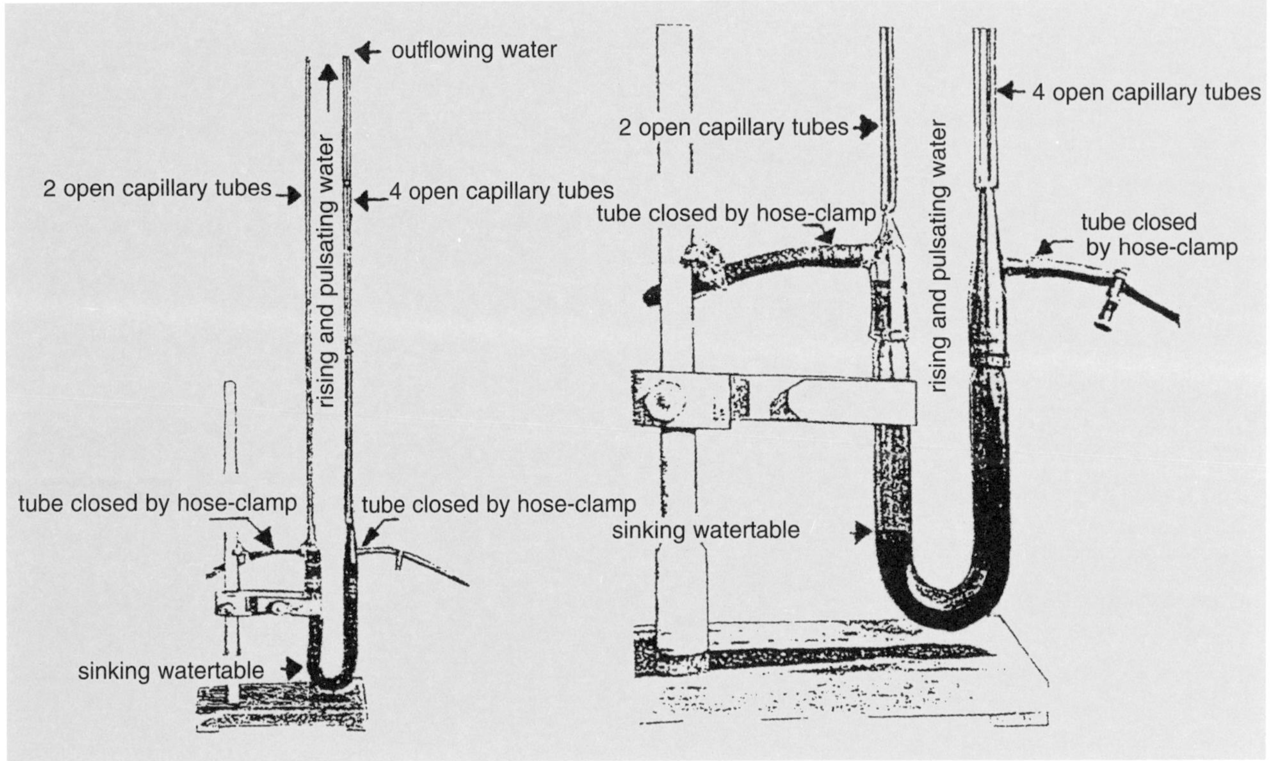

Fig. 15.3. Viktor designed this surprisingly simple but ingenious experiment that anyone can replicate with simple laboratory equipment, which consists of a U-tube, the bend of which is filled with pure quartz sand that is then saturated with salt water. This effectively separates and prevents communication between each side of the U-tube, but the salt water can be displaced laterally when pressure is higher in one arm.

The top of one arm has attached an adaptor to two fine capillary tubes, which allow contact with the air. The other arm has four fine capillaries attached to it. Both arms are now filled with fresh high quality spring water with little oxygen content, which has not been exposed to the Sun, or for long to the air.

The U-tube is then placed in an insulated container, e.g. a bucket, containing ice at the bottom, and then filled with good loam. The ice will create an artificial environment of +4°C (39°F) at the bend of the U-tube, helping to bring about a positive temperature gradient from the top of the loam downwards.

The container is then placed in the heat of the Sun and slowly as the +4°C (39°F) temperature is reached below and the higher water heats up, the water level in the arm with 4 outlets will rise and overflow as there is less resistance on that side, the water on the other side remaining level. The rise in the water level is assisted by the heat of the Sun converting the carbonic acid in the water into carbon dioxide bubbles that push the water bundles ahead of the them and pull the water behind, creating a pulsating effect.

During the night the water on the 4-capillary side subsides, the carbones in the water having absorbed the oxygen and other gases from the atmosphere. This makes it specifically heavier, exerting pressure through the sand barrier on the other side of the U-tube, causing the water level in this tube to rise up its pair of capillaries.

This replicates the natural process of pulsation that happens with all liquids in Nature, a pulsation which is caused by temperature difference, pressure and suction. This experiment sets out to duplicate particularly the conditions under which sap rises in the daytime (the four capillaries representing the xylem tubelets), falling back at night time (the pair of capillaries approximate the delivery of the phloem tubelets).

To demonstrate the action of a natural spring, the adaptor with four capillaries is removed, leaving the shorter side open, so that the water rises and overflows on that side when the temperature difference is greatest between the +4°C (39°F) environment at the bottom of the bucket, and that at the surface of the loam. At night the water drops on the open side, rising on the side with the two capillaries.

carbon dioxide, which forms bubbles. These bubbles act like little plugs and, as they rise, push the intervening packets of water, sap, etc, ahead of them, pumping the water with the nutrients and the sap right up to the furthest extremities of the crown.

The sap rises during the day when the tree exhales oxygen through photosynthesis. When the Sun sets and the temperature drops, this process is reversed as it breathes in oxygen to help build up the root system and the trunk of the tree. Nightfall initiates the retreat of the sap, which becomes denser through cooling and is drawn towards the root-zone. The capillaries in the crown of the tree are evacuated, creating a partial biological vacuum as the CO_2 gas-bubbles condense and begin to sink (see Fig.15.6).

The CO_2, nitrogen, oxygen, starches, sugars, and trace gases formed during daytime photosynthesis are drawn down through the minute stomata and pores in the leaves, down the trunk, some of them reaching the hair-roots. Their purpose here is to nourish the life-functions of the tree during the night and provide the material for building the structure of the inner fabric of the tree as a whole. As the crown and the trunk cool down, the root-zone warms up and the opposite happens to what took place during the day. This keeps the soil warm during the night and in winter, and cooler during the day and in summer. The ground temperature in this way is prevented from overcooling or overheating, greatly benefiting the micro-organisms in the humus.

Light-demanding trees are able to work in the same way because they have thick bark or, in some cases, a light-coloured bark with a high reflective factor to protect them from the greater heat and light which would interfere with this delicately balance metabolic process.

The cambium layer (see Fig.15.4 on p. 204) is the active zone where the growth of the tree takes place through the interaction of two electrically charged fluids. The negatively charged phloem containing oxygen, carbon dioxide, nitrogen, etc, flows down the inner side of the dielectric, while the positively charged xylem, containing ionized minerals, salts, trace-elements, carbonic acid or CO_2, flows up the outside. Between these two streams and through their interaction, the proto-annual ring is transformed into a proper annual ring. The life history of the tree is imprinted on these annual rings.

Fig.15.3. (opposite) Rising Sap Experiment. *The constant pulsation in the capillary tube mimics the principle of rising sap in the tree, just like the pulsation that causes blood circulation in the body (a propos of which Schauberger also said "There is no condition of equilibrium in Nature")*

Fig.15.4. Horizontal Section through Trunk.
This shows how the growth rings act as charge separators or dielectric layers.

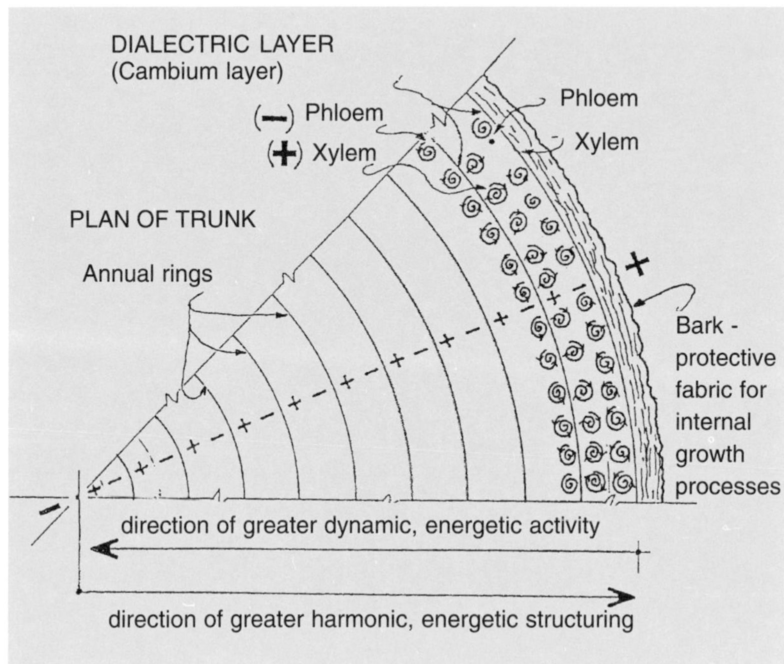

Temperature gradients in the tree

Temperature gradients are important in tree metabolism. The areas of active growth in the outer trunk and in the branches need heat energy to sustain the formative elements in a productive, ionized and fluid state for the processes of combination and re-combination to take place.

During the daytime, a positive temperature gradient is active from the outside inwards, the cooler, more internal sap rising faster, transporting the finest nutrients up to the top of the tree. They are taken to the foliage, for the small green shoots, flowers and reproductive elements required for the highest quality growth. Viktor Schauberger's measurements showed that this upward flow could be as fast as 3m (10ft) per hour, or 50mm (2ins.) per minute. The lower quality, coarser nutrients present in the outermost layers of the cambium ring (just inside the bark), needed for building the structure of the tree, are raised only as far as their fineness permits, the coarser being deposited in the trunk, the finer later in the branches. The effectiveness of this process depends on a negative temperature gradient being active from the outside inwards (cooler outside > warmer inside) during the hours of darkness, in its function as depositor or precipitator.

With rising air temperatures, the point where the positive and negative temperature gradients meet within the tree shifts to deeper levels. The flow of the sap becomes more sluggish and the positively charged nutritive elements are held in near stationary suspension at various heights to await the arrival of the negatively charged elements from above. This may be the reason why the Amazonian rainforest stops producing oxygen towards midday. The positive nutrient-transporting temperature gradient soon changes to a negative one as the temperatures rise rapidly during the morning. This arrests the supply of nutrients; photosynthesis ceases and with it, the expiration of oxygen is interrupted.

With nightfall and the cooling air, the temperature gradient reverses to positive from the inside outwards, so that the outer layers of the tree become cooler than the inner. The crown cools faster, causing the sap to sink quickly. The higher temperatures of the Amazon rainforest cause fast evaporation, to bring accelerated cooling of the

Fig.15.5. Vertical Trunk Section.
This shows ring temperature decreasing inwards, and the flow of nutrients in the xylem, upwards in daytime, descending at night.

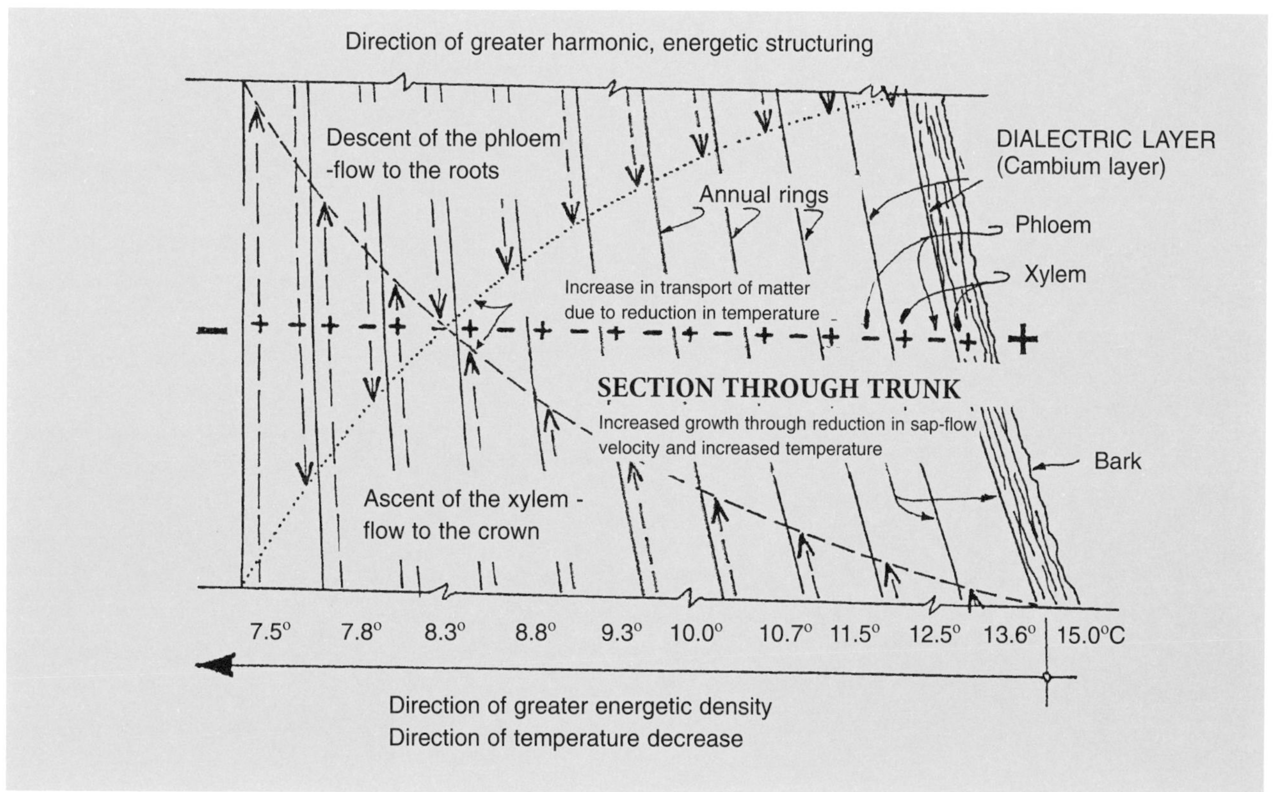

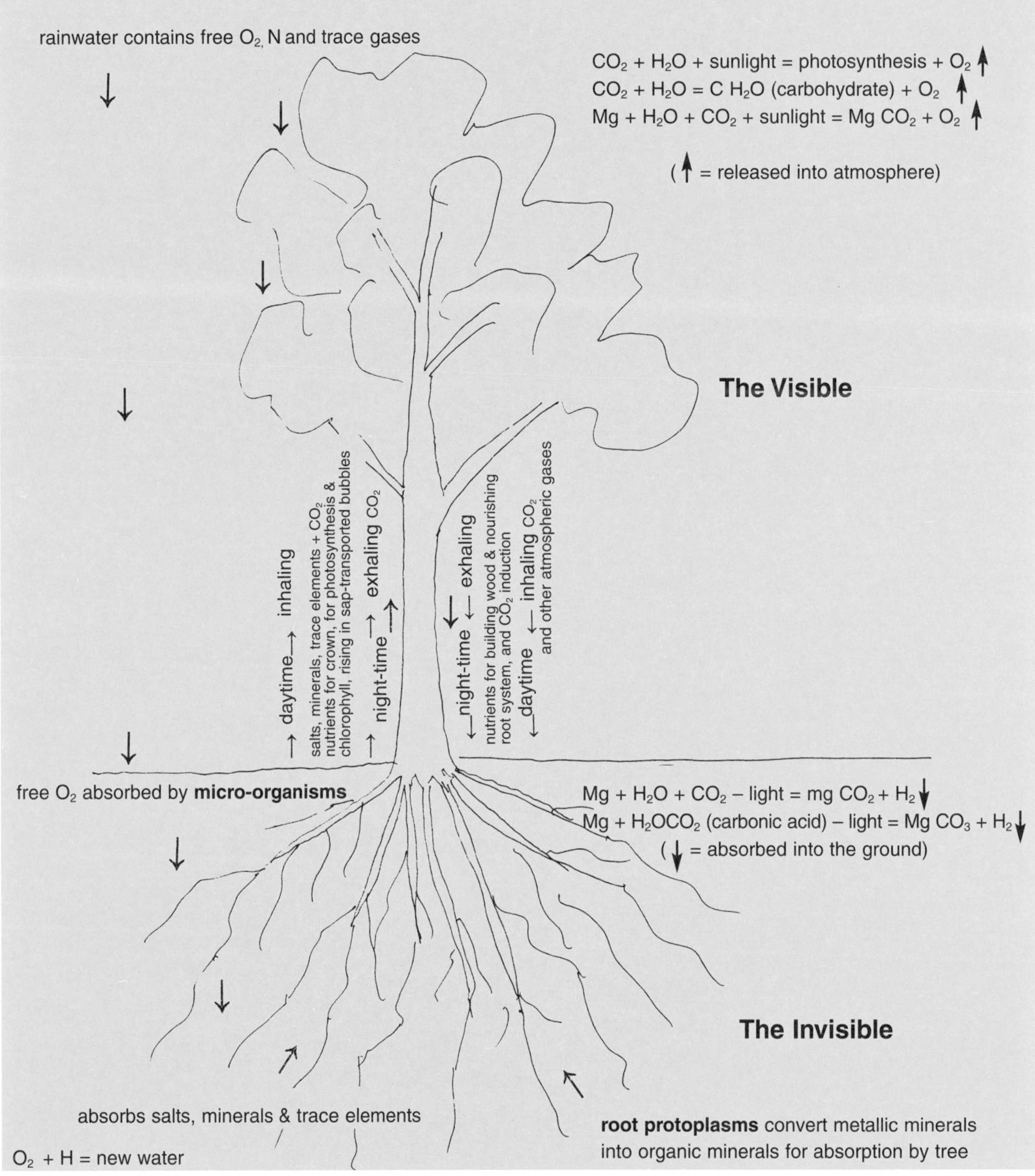

Fig.15.6. The Metabolism of the Tree.
The vital exchange between the yang solar and the yin earth energies for the production of photosynthesis, chlorophyll and carbohydrates and its role in the production of water.

sap which, sinking after midday, does not reverse direction until the following day. The oxygen and other gases contained in the negatively-charged phloem are drawn down towards the root-zone. By this means, oxygen is made available to assist decay in the upper reaches of the soil, and to stimulate growth around the root tips (Fig.15.6).

During the night the descending phloem plays another important role. It interacts with suspended positively-charged xylem and because of the prevailing positive temperature gradient (Figs. 15.4 and 15.5) is drawn towards the exterior of the trunk. This produces new wood growth that is made denser and harder with winter cold, forming an annual ring.

In a commercial plantation a shade-demanding tree grows more branches in order to protect itself. The sap is therefore diverted from its normal progress up the trunk to nourish the spurious branches, twisting around the extra knots in the trunk. The excess heat also makes the sap ducts larger in diameter so that the carbon-dioxide bubbles are not able raise the fluids required for healthy growth. Insufficient nutrients are able to reach the crown of the tree, which is likely to suffer die-back; high quality timber is no longer produced, and the tree will have a limited lifespan. Sprouting foliage shows the height to which the sap is able to rise.

Because of unnatural high internal temperatures there is premature deposition of nutrients, a condition akin to arterio-sclerosis in the blood vessels of humans. The higher temperature also limits the rise of these coarse materials, which are deposited near the base of the trunk, causing a cone-shaped trunk. With its levitational energies thus weakened, such a tree more easily falls victim to storms.

The tree as a biocondenser

We discussed earlier how the formative energies (which belong to the fourth and fifth dimensions) carry the blueprint for the evolution and physical manifestation of all organisms. This life-force carries with it an electrical charge. The process of growth and development of any organism requires that this life-force is enhanced or potentiated by a process known as biocondensing.

As part of its important role in Nature associated with the two creators of life, water and photosynthesis, the tree acts as a biocon-

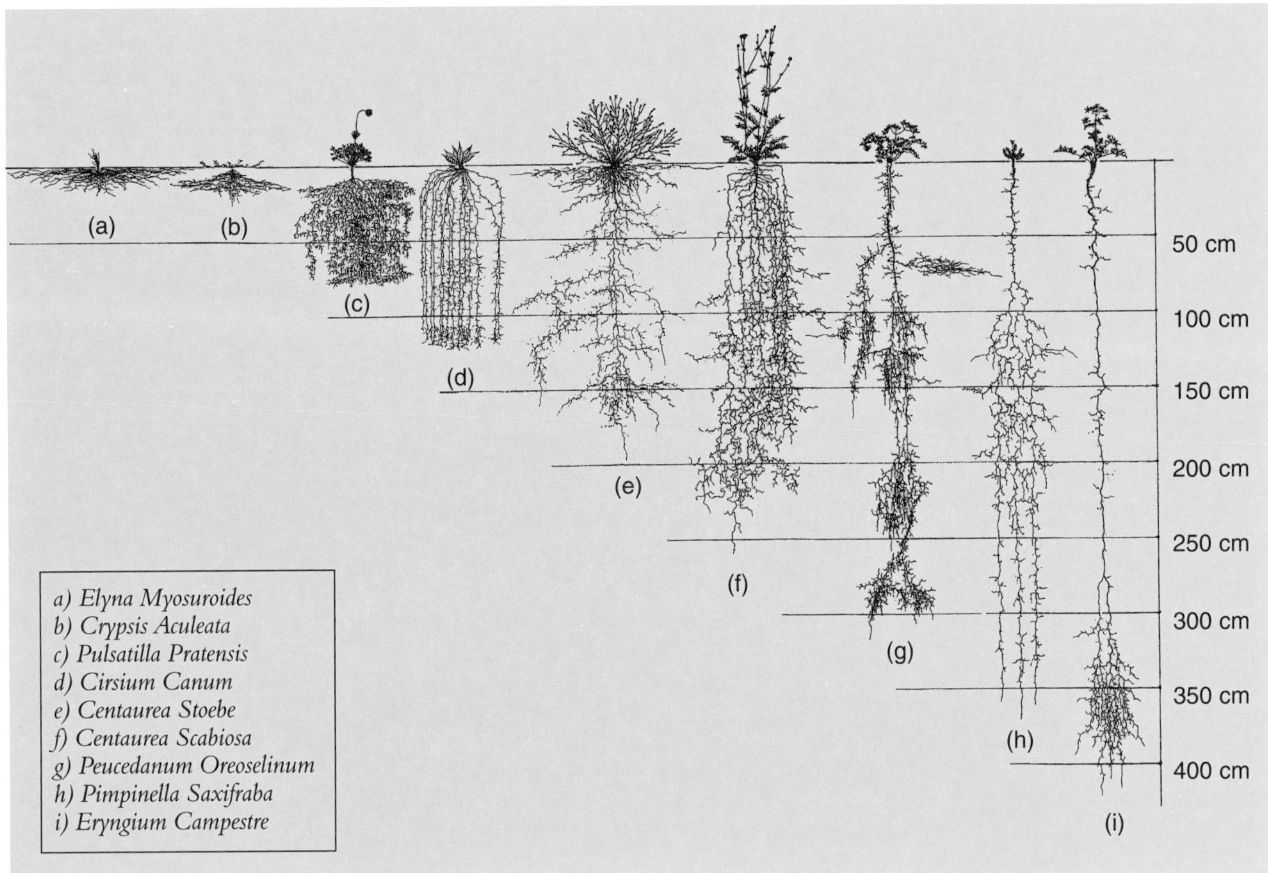

Fig.15.7. Various Root Systems.
In the evolution of plants, first primitive ones (a & b) take root, making use of the low-grade nutrients at the warm surface. They allow a little soil and moisture to accumulate. As the soil cools off, the water table slowly rises, bringing up deeper minerals and nutrients. This allows higher plant forms to develop (c to i), which hold the soil together and encourage humus to form, which attracts micro-organisms that break down the soil, increasing the fertility and richness, causing the pioneer plants to die off.

denser, whose purpose is to increase the potency of the life force towards the tips of both branches and roots.

In Chapter 7, we saw how the Earth may become charged with life energy through its terrestrial biocondenser. Trees work in a similar manner, the annual rings forming the dielectric separators between the electrically charged areas. When these are closer together, the potential (the dynamic energy) is increased, which occurs higher up the trunk. In the central part of the trunk some growth takes place, but the most energetic growth happens at the ends of the new shoots.

The diameter of the trunk reduces as the tree grows taller, which makes the annuals rings grow closer together, increasing the bioelectric potential. At the very top of the tree the potential is very high. Finally in the leaves themselves the energy potential is at its maximum. This is necessary for the critical process of evapo-transpiration to take place. The sap capillaries are extremely small, so that the substances having only the finest materials with the highest of nutritive qualities remain, the coarser having been left behind to build up the structure of the lower part of the tree.

In addition, this refinement of the energy at the leaves gives it a kind of increased homeopathic potency; so that when they receive the highly energized drops of falling rainwater there is an immediate transfer of pure energy or life force. It is therefore hardly surprising that this is where the most intense growth takes place.

These areas of dense growth where the biocondensers are located are finely structured and susceptible to damage, either by being pierced, or disturbed by excessive warming. If this happens, the biocondenser fails, disease sets in and the tree dies.

By inserting copper probes, Walter Schauberger was able to record significantly high electrical charges between the cambium layer and the heart of the trunk, sufficient to light a small flashlight bulb. The healthier and more naturally had the tree grown, the brighter the light observed.

Root systems

The root system, being the invisible part of the tree, has an aura of mystery. A germinating seed puts down a root into the darkness before it sends a shoot into the light. The root system is the complement to the canopy, and its energy exchange system is just as complex.

It is important to see the whole tree as an energy pathway that brings about a marriage of the negatively charged energies of the Earth (a receptive, female system) with the positively charged energies of the atmosphere and the Sun (a radiating, male system). Out of this union comes the primary manifestation of the organism, 'tree' — with its secondary life-enhancing processes of chlorophyll production and photosynthesis.

We are taught wrongly that there is a one-way transport of nutrients from the roots to the leaves. The very fine root tips, with their tiny capillaries, correspond to the new, growing leaves in the tree canopy, and at night the descending energies and nutritive elements contribute to the important processes that these root tips perform.

At the ends of the root tips are tiny protoplasms, little chemical factories that perform the important task of converting minerals from their natural metallic to the organic form that the tree is able to absorb. They are also responsible for transferring yang energy and nutritive elements derived from the tree crown, to increase the vitality of the soil, without which the micro-organisms would be unable to flourish. In addition, they release hydrogen, which combines with free oxygen in the soil to give birth to new water. So it is clear that these protoplasms perform invaluable functions.

Even a gardener probably has only the vaguest idea of how a root system develops. To hold up the plant stem is one purely physical function. There is, in fact, the widest possible variety of root forms and systems, the diversity of which is essential to healthy micro-environment, because each species' roots go down to a different level in the soil, bringing up different nutrients and energies.

Trees are described as being flat-rooted, heart-rooted, tap-rooted and deep-rooted, the last evaporating more water than heart-rooted trees, and flat-rooted trees evaporating least of all. Each plant species, therefore, has its own particular root structure, which penetrates to a different soil horizon to withdraw the elements it needs. But other plants will share some of these nutrients also. Fig. 15.7 illustrates the wide variety of root systems.

When plants first appeared, about 420 million years ago, climatic conditions were inhospitable, with severe storms and heavy rain. Only the most primitive plants could gain a hold, feeding on the salts and metallic minerals. Although they had very little root growth, the stems above ground were able to trap some nutritive wind-borne dust to form very primitive soil, their shadows having a slight cooling effect on the ground, allowing some moisture to collect.

Soil and nutrition

Cooling was the key to the appearance of water, and as the ground cover spread, the lowering temperature affected the deeper ground, allowing the water table to rise, bringing with it minerals, trace elements and nutritional substances nearer to the surface. This created the conditions for higher quality plants to evolve. Requiring better quality nutrition, these higher plants had deeper root systems that brought up minerals from a different horizon, but were no competition for the pioneer plants.

The more evolved plants held the soil together, trapping more moisture that helped to attract micro-bacterial activity to break down the mineral particles into finer dust, the first step towards the humus that is necessary for even higher plant forms. The root systems become more complex, interweaving at different levels, so that they cannot easily be separated. Greater fertility brings a richer soil that is of too high a quality for the pioneer plants, which will now disappear. A more favorable microclimate in the higher soil increases the diversity of the bacteria, encouraging more complex root systems.

There is a magical and symbiotic relationship between the various root systems that we cannot easily observe below ground, more complex than the interrelationships of the plants above ground. With greater complexity, and the evolution of trees, the soil takes on the full yin energy potential of Mother Earth, and with it the creation of virgin water, an essential requirement for higher life forms.

This process of soil formation took several million years before larger plants, such as small bushes and trees, were able to gain a hold; and they had to go through thousands of years of evolution before a forest was possible. The forest is the most productive environment for the building up of soil and fertile humus. It is self-fertilizing and self-sustaining. The great forests were able, over a period of thousands of years, to build up twenty feet or more of soil depth. With our heedless disrespect for Nature's bounty, in one century we have allowed these great soil banks to be eroded and destroyed, first through deforestation, and then by careless tilling of the unprotected soil surface.

The web of life that evolves in a natural forest is so complex and sensitive that the removal of key species can cause a depletion of the energy that can lead to a progressive decline of the system, as more species fail for want of the sustenance that was provided by the missing species. A hole is created in the complex root network that is the interconnecting link between the deeper ground and the surface. The root system raises the water table. A missing species also means a hole is created in the water system that supplies the nutrients. Over time, a shortage of nutrients puts more plants under stress, leading to more species disappearing.

Something like this happens with our monoculture systems, for the nutrients are not able to rise through the crusty layer formed at the level to which all the same species' roots descend. This leads to depletion of fertility and all the energies associated with it; uniformity means sterility, something that Nature abhors.

PART FIVE

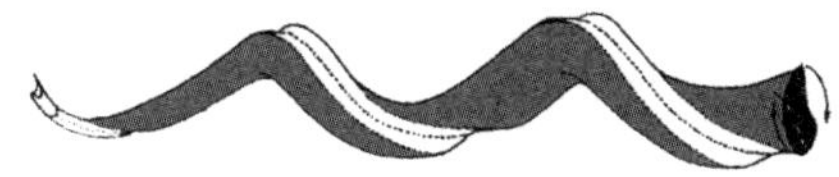

Working with Nature

16. Soil Fertility and Cultivation

Our primeval Mother Earth is an organism that no science in the world can rationalize. Everything on her that crawls and flies is dependent upon her and all must hopelessly perish if that Earth dies that feeds us. Viktor Schauberger[1]

The crisis in intensive farming

When there was great enthusiasm in the 1930s for the much publicized glamour of industrialized agriculture, Viktor Schauberger was very aware of its pitfalls, developing a number of field tests which demonstrated the fallacy of the new technologies. Though he did not live to see the dramatic agricultural catastrophes of the 1990s, to a large extent he predicted them.

Intensive farming developed first in the Americas, where the limitless vast open plains could be cultivated or grazed in only very large units. At first in North America, and then on the South American plains, this meant enormous herds of cattle or highly mechanized crop cultivation. Because of the inevitable depletion of minerals and, as a consequence of monoculture, intensive farming of this kind soon leads to the widespread use of chemical drugs or artificial fertilization with animals, and herbicides with cultivation. By its very nature intensive agriculture is unsustainable, but it is a big and profitable international industry and, as we all know, we are living at a time where big profits count for more than human or ecological values.

There is a growing interest in sustainable cultivation, and there are many books on the topic. It is impossible to grow crops without a loss of fertility in the soil. We shall be examining different methods of fertilization from the inorganic to increasingly higher organic and energetic processes. Viktor Schauberger's whole research was deeply committed to improving food quality and soil fertility. He had original ideas about fertilization, but his most intriguing ideas were concerned with amplifying the subtle energies of the planet to bring about higher quality in the plants themselves.

Ploughing methods

Viktor Schauberger's interest in soils was initiated during a visit to Bulgaria in the 1930s where he had been commissioned to build a log-flume. King Boris asked him to look into the decline in soil productivity and the shrinkage of the water table in the northern parts of the country since the introduction of modern mechanized farming methods. The southern part, on the other hand, was still fertile, with abundant moisture.

Viktor found that in the poorer southern part of the country, populated largely by people of Turkish origin, the fields were tilled with traditional wooden ploughs pulled usually by teams of women. These fields remained very fertile and productive, with high crop quality. In the north, however, the fields were ploughed with tractor-drawn steel ploughs. As he was aware of the destructive effect that steel and iron have on water in the soil, Schauberger attributed the disappearance of the water and the poorer yields to the use of the steel ploughs and the faster ploughing in the north. This knowledge led him to invent a new kind of plough and to do a number of experiments on improving soil fertility. Before going into this, however, we need to understand more about electromagnetism.

Two kinds of electromagnetism

Viktor already recognized that in Nature there are two types of electromagnetism, just as there are two kinds of temperature change. The one that encourages growth and stimulates energies in all organisms he called biomagnetism or bioelectricity; the elements connected with this form of electromagnetism (diamagnetism) are copper, bismuth and gold.

The other, ferromagnetism, usually just called magnetism, when combined with an electric current, is the form that is commonly used in electric motors and dynamos for the generation of electricity. In Nature this form of energy is used to break down substances. In water's case it disintegrates the water particles into its constituent atoms. The elements of ferromagnetism are iron, nickel and cobalt.

The golden plough

Wherever we look, the dreadful disintegration of the bridges of life, the capillaries and the bodies they have created, is evident, which has been caused by the mechanical and mindless work of Man, who has torn away the soul from the Earth's blood — water.

Viktor Schauberger[2]

Viktor observed how steel ploughs damage the soil. Drawn rapidly through the ground, the hard steel ploughshares generate minute ferro-electric and ferro-magnetic currents that decompose the nutrient-laden water molecules in the soil, in a manner similar to electrolysis, resulting in water loss. The surface tension of the water molecule is reduced, the soil loses its energy potential and its nutritive subtle energies are dissipated. This not only destroys the soil's subtler energies, but also converts the nutritive elements or removes them from the mature water molecule. The residual water becomes pure juvenile water that has no nutritive value.

Abrasion with the soil removes tiny particles of steel from the cutting surface of the plough, which break down to rust, an ideal breeding ground for harmful pathogenic bacteria. An increase in the iron content of soil inhibits its water retention. On the other hand, soils high in copper have the capacity to retain greater quantities of water.

The delicate soil capillaries that deliver nutrients and water to the surface, and some of the micro-organisms that process them are destroyed by the heat–producing friction and the compacting pressure of the steel plough. As the normal supply of nutrients from below is cut off and the water table falls, the soil fertility suffers.

Schauberger started to experiment with copper, initially as a plating of thick copper over a conventional steel plough. The destructive ferro-electromagnetic effects of the steel plough were thus replaced by beneficial bioelectromagnetic ionization, enhancing growth and soil fertility. Because of the remarkable results it achieved, this came to be known as the 'Golden Plough.'

Field trials were conducted near Salzburg in 1948 and 1949 to compare the results of the new plough with the conventional steel plough. Fields strips were ploughed, alternately using steel and

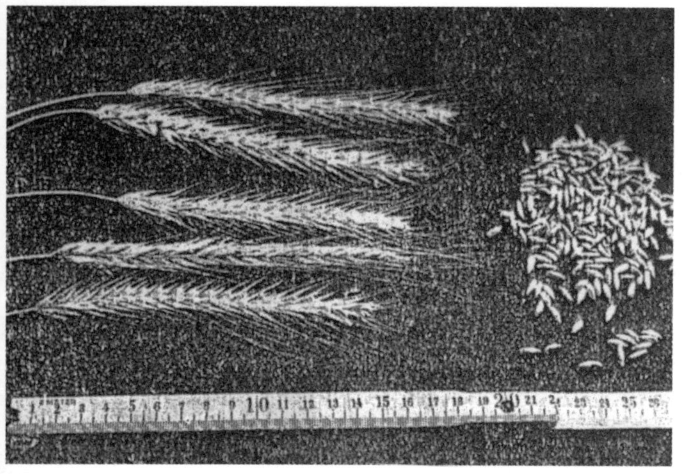

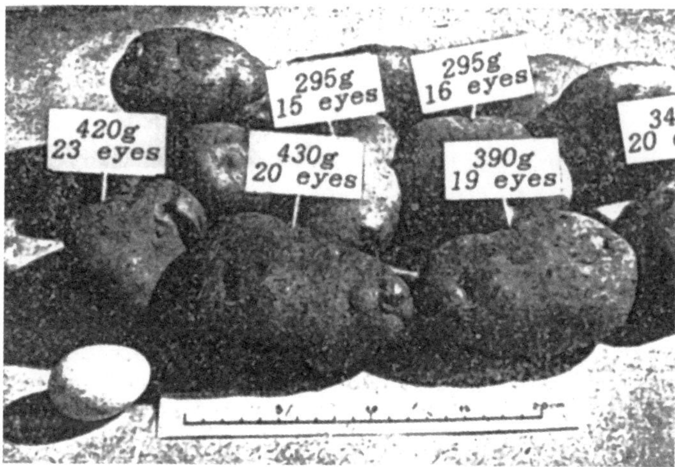

Fig.16.1. 15 cm long ears of rye with up to 104 grains/ear.

Fig.16.2. Potatoes grown on alpine farm at Kitzbühel, Tyrol.

copper-plated ploughs. When the grain came up the differences between the alternate strips was quite apparent. Where the copper-plated plough had been used the water content and the nutrient energies of the soil had been increased, and the corn stood about 6–8 inches higher with a much fuller head. Some yields in the strips ploughed with copper-plated implements increased by up to 40% compared to the control strips where conventional steel ploughs were used. As all other factors of soil chemistry, orientation, furrow width, etc., were identical, the difference in yield was clearly due to the use of the copper plated plough.

With two crops there were spectacular results. 15cm long ears of rye produced an average of 104 grains each (Fig. 16.1). In another experiment in Tyrolean Kitzbühel potatoes weighing nearly half a kilo, containing over twenty 'eyes' (the source of next year's crop), were produced (Fig. 16.2).

The Bio-plough

The conventional ploughshare forms a pressure wave and makes a crushing cut that destroys the soil capillaries. Schauberger in 1948 encouraged a Hamburg engineer Jürgen Sauck to develop a sharp curved blade to create a long slicing cut before the soil is centripetally involuted in a figure of eight motion through the curving wings of the phosphor-bronze ploughshare, copying the burrowing

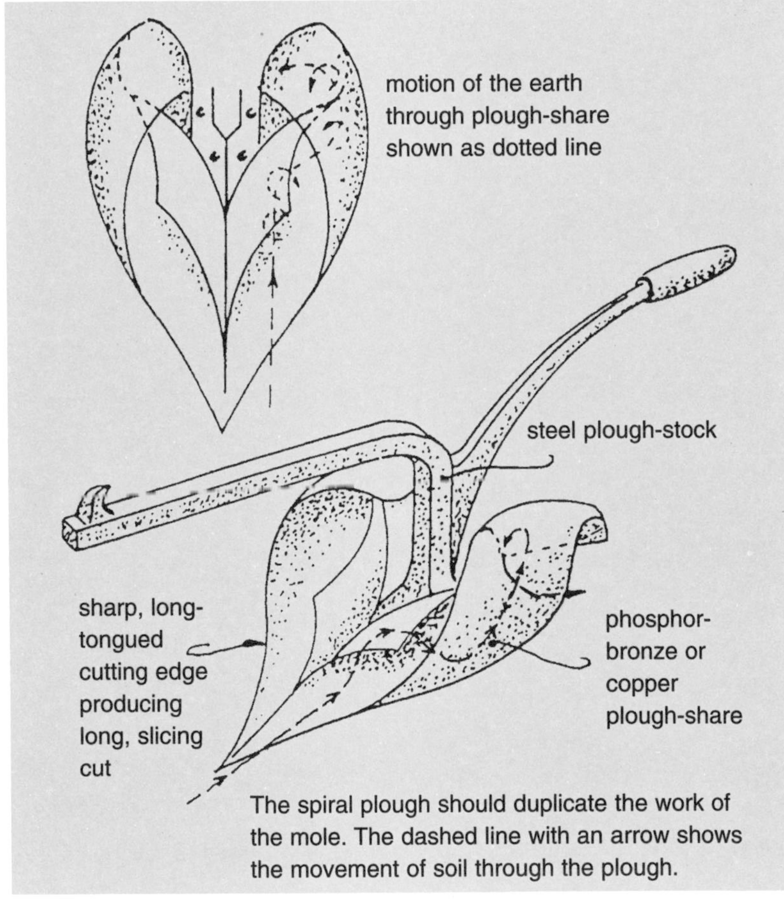

Fig.16.3. The Bio-Plough, 1948.

action of the mole. This was called the bio-plough (Fig. 16.3) because it enhanced the energy in the soil. Its action was to rotate the soil through 360°, so that what was originally on the surface was returned to the surface. This minimized water loss and the sub-surface micro-organisms were never exposed to direct sunlight (heat) and could continue their work undisturbed.

These experiments clearly proved the great advantage of the copper-based ploughs. The great increase in productivity with their use would quickly recover the cost of replacing iron or steel ploughs. The trials had created a lot of interest, but Viktor came up against bureaucratic corruption that defeated his plans. Copper being in short supply just after the war, he had to go to the Ministry of Agriculture to obtain what he needed. It is alleged that the Minister was being seduced with large bribes by the chemical companies to introduce chemical fertilizers, and indicated that he expected Viktor to do the same. Of course Viktor would not, so the copper ploughs never went into production. Because Viktor's research is not publicized in other countries, the copper ploughs were forgotten about, though the Schauberger research institute, the PKS, has encouraged the development of copper gardening tools that are now being marketed in many countries (see Resources).

Alignment of furrows

In his study of crop yields in Bulgaria, Viktor Schauberger realized that there were factors other than the use of steel versus wooden ploughs to explain the differences in productivity between the north and south. The fields in the north were also harrowed, which broke the soil into much smaller particles and made it more vulnerable to drying out in the hot sun to several inches of depth.

In the Turkish south of the country, the farmers could not afford to harrow, and their ploughing was much more rough and ready. The furrows they made were irregular and rough, producing large clods that fell in different directions. The unevenness of the furrows meant that there were no large flat surfaces to absorb the heat of the Sun. This messy looking surface also had the advantage of holding the moisture in the top layers of the soil.

The lesson to be learned from these examples was to cut sinuous furrows so as to vary exposure to the Sun's rays, but in addition to give them a north–south alignment, so that the inclined surfaces of the furrows would be shaded for part of the day and exposed to the Sun only when it was low in the sky. This meant that the young growing sprouts had the maximum amount of moisture when most needed.

Grazing and grass cutting

Conventional mechanical grass mowers have an effect on the grass similar to that of the standard iron plough on the soil. The inclined blade uses a crushing action that damages the capillaries of the grass stalks, and shreds the top of the stalks for several millimetres, allowing the grass to bleed and bacteria to enter. Instead of applying its energies to new growth, the grass stems have to heal the wounds, which can take a week.

Viktor Schauberger's observation of animals was profound. He would watch the cows on the fertile high alpine pastures. The grazing animal gathers the grass stems together in a spiralling movement with its tongue, cutting them with a jerk of its head so as not to damage the stalks. It then seals the ends of the stalks with its moist nose to prevent the loss of moisture and energy.

The alpine farmers needing as much winter fodder as they could get, would crop the grass sometimes three times in the summer. Their implement is the much-cherished scythe that delivers a long, slicing cut, thereby keeping the wound area to a minimum. But more than that, their method of sharpening the blade imparts to it an ionizing energy that draws together the damaged fibres and rapidly seals the wound.

Those who have lived close to the land for many generations use Nature as their teacher. These farmers knew that sharpening a scythe with a stone robs it of its charge of energy. Instead they would hammer the blade on a block of hardwood which enhanced the electrical charge. Mounted on a wooden handle, wrapped in cloth and stored in darkness ensured that it would keep its charge.

Schauberger understood that the Sun's light and heat would discharge a newly sharpened scythe and, for that reason, these farmers would do their blade hammering early or late, and their scything in the early morning or evening. The accumulated energies could be seen as minute glowing sparks on the blade, leaping from one serration to another in the growing darkness of a summer evening.

We have lost this knowledge, and today soil fertility and productivity are in dangerous decline, ironically, because of the heavy use of artificial fertilizers as well as misguided techniques.

Artificial fertilizers

Contemporary agriculture treats Mother-Earth like a whore and rapes her. All year round it scrapes away her skin and poisons it with artificial fertilizer, for which we have to thank a science that has lost all connection with Nature. Viktor Schauberger[3]

The pioneer of modern artificial fertilizers was Justus von Liebig (1803–1873), a German chemist. His research into the elements and chemicals required by plants for growth found that four principal minerals were often deficient in agricultural soils. To increase fertility he advocated the supplementation of calcium (Ca) in the form of lime, nitrogen (N), phosphorus (P) and potassium (K), the last three often referred to as NPK.

These products are soluble and mostly they are by-products of what Viktor Schauberger called "fire-spitting technology". They are produced by heat, which is structure-disintegrating and energy-depleting and applied by either spraying or by powder diffusion.

Chemical companies were quick to manufacture these new products as a way of turning waste material to profit. Liebig later realized that the ingredients necessary for healthy plant growth were far more complex than simple NPK. Indeed he warned that dependence on these basic chemicals could irreparably damage the soil, but nobody was listening. The rapid spread in the use of artificial fertilizers led to a systematic depletion of soil fertility as it lost its organic base. A highly mechanized system of cultivation, using steel ploughs and artificial fertilizers reduced large tracts of mid-western America to dustbowls, forcing the ruined farmers to leave their land. The same is now happening in many third world countries, like India, where multinational chemical companies are demanding the replacement of traditional methods in favour of chemically dependent agriculture.

When the dependence on chemicals was first exported, it was called 'the green revolution,' because their use was linked to increased yields. However, this was quantity at the cost of continually decreasing quality, profit at the expense of life (see Chapter 5). Artificial fertilizers are stimulants to growth and act like narcotics on which the soil becomes reliant. The soil, now dependent on the chemicals — rather like drug addicts who as their physical condition worsens, require more and more shots to extend their lives a little further — is also dying.

In their finely powdered form, artificial fertilizers are moisture demanding, robbing the lower ground strata and the young plants of moisture. With insufficient moisture, transpiration is reduced and the plants' internal temperatures rise, making them more susceptible to disease. These fine powders block the vital capillaries, which supply naturally derived nutrients, mature water, and conduct rising immaterial energies. This makes it more difficult for the plants to absorb rain, resulting in rapid runoff and faster re-evaporation. Irrigation, with virtually worthless water, now becomes a necessity. It is not surprising that the crops grown in such conditions are neither particularly tasty nor nourishing.

Excess nitrogen can also introduce another problem — which makes ionized substances less available for root development, leading to further water shortage for the plants. Nitrates have negatively charged ions (anions $^-$) that capture the positively charged ions (cations $^+$) of elements such as magnesium and calcium, removing them from the root zone. Magnesium is essential for chlorophyll production.

Nature's remedy is to bring in parasites (the 'Health Police') to remove the diseased organisms, requiring the application of pesticides and fungicides. After passing on a pesticide-treated crop to the consumer, the ground is fumigated with poisonous gases injected through plastic sheets, to eradicate these supposedly pernicious pests. Everything dies — earthworms, micro-organisms and beneficial bacteria alike. A diverse biosystem gives way to a lifeless desert. The green revolution was justified as a way of feeding the world, just as is biotechnology today. The holistic biologist Mae-Wan Ho gives many examples of how sustainable organic agriculture can be more productive than chemical farming, which is both unsustainable and destructive of life.[4]

17. Organic Cultivation

Biological agriculture

The health of the topsoil is the most important factor in sustainable agriculture. Topsoil is created by decayed vegetable matter, and can vary in depth from a few centimetres to several metres. Forests created the deep soils of the world over millennia, and many of these have shrunk by as much as 80% in the last two hundred years through our disastrous agricultural practices.

Under natural conditions the friable soil is populated with an abundance of earthworms and other creatures and is usually capped with a layer of humus, formed of decomposing leaves and other vegetable matter, and colonized by a profusion of microbial and creepy-crawly life. This rich mixture of life forms makes up a processing factory essential to soil health and fertility, and everything should be done to help it flourish.

Soil remineralization

In 1894 an agricultural chemist and contemporary of Justus von Liebig, Julius Hensel, published *Bread from Stone,* a valuable book describing the beneficial effects of fertilizing with rock dust, a by-product of road metal quarries. His book, posing a significant threat to this new chemical fertilizer industry, quickly disappeared, bought up and killed off by those who felt challenged by it.

Ideally ground in a cold process that retains its inherent energies, this rock dust in composed of finely ground, mainly igneous rocks (such as granite, basalt, etc.) with a broad mineral spectrum. Because of its great range of minerals, trace elements and salts, when spread on the ground, it encourages a wealth of different micro-organisms.

There has been limited use of rock dust in Switzerland for 150 years. However, its reintroduction has been encouraged by John Hamaker and Don Weaver who in 1975 brought out *The Survival of Civilization.*[1] They describe how important are mineral and trace elements to plant growth and quality, but also that trace elements are a vital moderator of climatic extremes. They also tell how John Hamaker was able to increase the depth of the topsoil at his Michigan home, from about 10cm (4in) to about 1.2m (4ft) over a period of 10 years.

More recently in Western Australia, an experiment by Barry Oldfield for the 'Men of the Trees' showed a remarkable increase in the growth and health of seedlings planted with rock dust compared with those without. Rock dust is easily available as a by-product of road metal quarries.

An initial application of very fine rock dust will quickly attract micro-organisms, but a mixture of small and large grains will allow a slow release over a longer period. Rock dust has been shown to be a buffer against nitrate, sulphur dioxide and nitroxide, and it absorbs and fixes the negative ions while saving the positive ions for the plants' use. Normally rock dust is applied about every five years, the quantity depending on soil deficiency, although it is always beneficial.[2]

It is thought that the remarkable longevity (up to 140 years) and health of the Hunza people of Northern Pakistan is as much due to the mineral-rich glacial water, as to the clean mountain air. Callum Coats tells of his neighbours in Queensland who fertilized their fruit trees from a bucket of rock dust. Their dogs, who would eagerly drink rainwater from this bucket, while leaving their usual water bowls full, clearly knew what was best for them.

Organic farming

Organic farming normally uses manure (generally cow's), farmyard slurry and composted vegetable matter to increase the soil's fertility. The introduction of chemical fertilizers in the nineteenth century was popular and soon supplanted the traditional organic method, because it was much less labour intensive, and appeared to give higher crop yields. A few farmers retained the traditional methods and, as the evidence has built up of the pollution of the water table and rivers by these chemicals, there has been a renaissance of organic farming in the last fifty years.

The sustainability of organic farming derives from the recycling of organic material to maintain its fertility, just as in a natural forest. Modern organic composting tends to use green vegetable matter rather than dried, interleaved with layers of earth. Significant

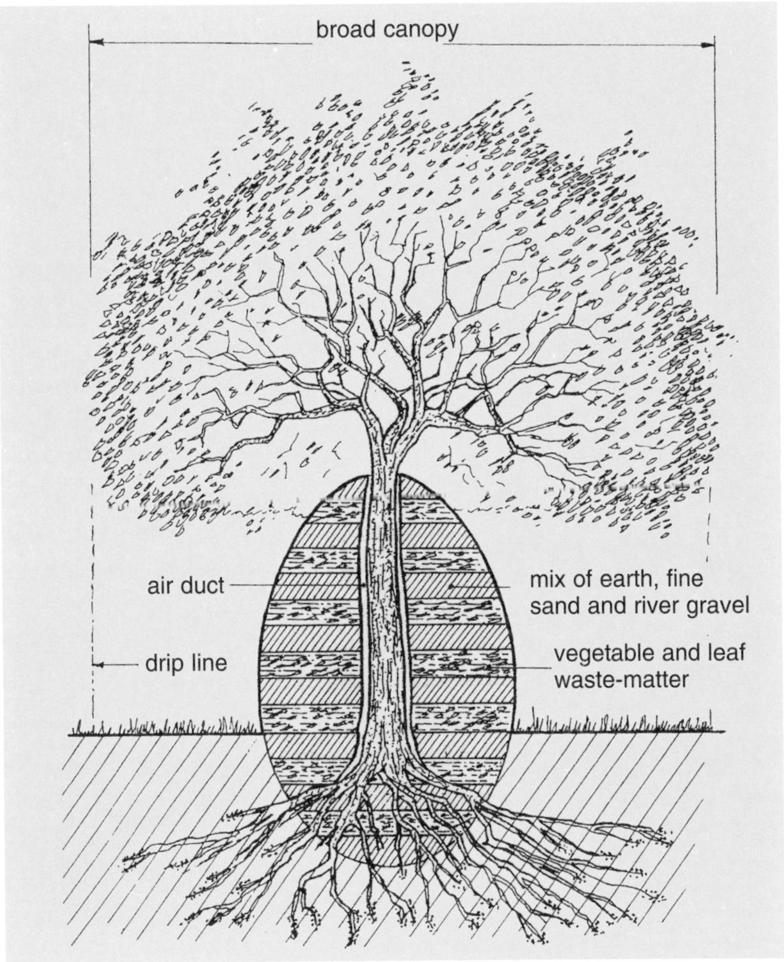

Fig.17.1. The Egg-shaped Compost Heap.

heat is generated in the pile in this way. Though the compost may seem to be of good quality, Viktor Schauberger believed that as the heat discourages earthworms, it will not be of the best quality. His preference is a cold process that produces a higher content of protein and other immaterial, fructigenic energies. He also believed it important to protect the compost from element-hungry juvenile rainwater that will tend to leach out some of the nutrients.

Although shown here on a small scale, the same principle can be applied to larger compost heaps. Schauberger preferred an egg-shaped compost heap built up under a large fruit-tree with a broad canopy as shown in Fig. 17.1.

A hollow is dug out of the ground round the base of the tree whose trunk is then wrapped loosely with several layers of newspaper, which not only protect the tree but, once decomposed, provide an air duct for ventilation. Into the hollow is placed a 20cm thick layer of Sun-dried leafmould and vegetable matter. This is covered with an equally thick mixture of earth, river gravel and fine sand. This is similar to remineralization, just described. A small amount of copper and zinc filings is added to this mixture (see p. 232).

To stop the compost heap getting wet, it is then temporarily covered with clay or some other waterproof material. Insects, earthworms, and micro-organisms are quickly attracted into the heap because it is a cool process. Helped by the diffused oxygen, nitrogen and other trace gases penetrating the newspaper round the trunk and the layer of earth and sand, they begin to break down the refuse.

The heap is built up into the stable shape of the egg shown in Fig. 17.1, as more vegetable refuse becomes available. To protect the cold decomposition from being spoiled by rain, the finished heap is then coated with a layer of clay. Any rain will run down the near vertical surfaces.

The earthworms and microbes will now have multiplied in their thousands through the whole pile and aerated it. As they will begin to die off, their bodies add nutritive value to the compost heap, having by now infiltrated the whole of the compost heap. As the autumn Sun loses its strength, the ground starts to cool and a significant positive temperature gradient is established between the ground and the air. The compost heap is now ready; it is taken down to ground level, and what remains in the cavity is left to nourish the tree.

The material is spread evenly over adjacent fields towards evening, for under the positive temperature gradient — most powerful at this time — rain or dew will carry the nutrients into the ground. This method produces a far richer and higher-quality natural fertilizer, which not only maintains, but actually increases fertility. The host tree also benefits and will produce a copious crop of healthy, tasty and blight-free fruit. Such compost heaps may be built under different trees each year, eventually fertilizing all the fruit trees. If there are no suitable trees, similarly constructed heaps can be built as dome-like humps or barrel-shaped clumps, protected from rainwater and insulated from the heating effect of the Sun.

Biodynamic farming

Dr Rudolf Steiner (1861–1925), a teacher and philosopher born in Austria, and founder of the Anthroposophical Movement, devised biodynamic farming. According to anthroposophy the human being is the highest expression on Earth of the Divine, incarnating all creative power and patterns of physical manifestation. The world is studied through the inner and outer natures of humanity. Its approach to farming is very similar to Schauberger's, the assumption that energy is the primary cause, and growth the secondary effect. While it has been mooted that Rudolf Steiner and Viktor Schauberger did have fairly lengthy discussions, if such was the case, it is not clear how much either might have influenced the other.

Biodynamic farming recognizes the very ancient practice of burying cow's horns filled with cow dung deep underground in the autumn. At this time the active Earth's energies are drawn into the horn because of its vortex shape, transforming its contents into powerful fructigenic energies by the cold process of fermentation encouraged by the low temperatures. The cow horns are disinterred in early spring, their contents having been converted into a sweet smelling, highly active substance.

This empowered material is the basis of the natural fertilizer known as '500 mix.' Since 1947, it has been increasing widely used, and over a 1¼ million acres are fertilized in Australia using this system. The land where it has been spread, when seen from the air, stands out clearly from neighbouring farms, due to the much greener pasture. Some cows from farms bordering Alex Podolinsky's did not eat for two or three days after they had broken into the biodynamic farm, so high was the quality of the grass they had consumed.[3]

The '500' mix fertilizer is produced according to an ancient Alpine tradition which Schauberger himself once observed being practised by an old mountain farmer who achieved amazing results from his fertilizer. The principle is like that of homeopathy. When a homeopathic medicine is made, the original remedy is stirred and shaken between the dilutions, which increase its potency. With the fertilizer a small quantity of the converted cow dung is added to water and stirred first in one direction and then in the other, so as to create vortices rotating about the vertical axis

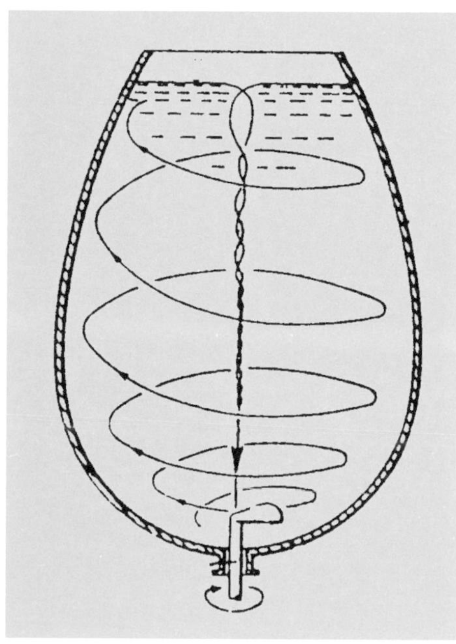

Fig.17.2. Motor-driven Mixing Device with golf club-shaped impeller.

of the mixing vessel. A left-hand vortex builds up the positive energy and the right hand vortex creates a negative energy that draws in the inseminating O_2. The alternating energy charge builds up the inherent energies of the 500 mix. This recalls the alternating left and right hand bends in a river building up its energy in a longitudinal vortex (see p.143).

This method of progressively raising energy is analogous to the Japanese art of sword making. The base material is heated in the furnace, and then beaten out or 'structured' with a hammer as it cools. It is then further heated to incandescence, folded over on itself, fused together and beaten out again. Each time the heating partially breaks down the structuring created by the beating. But with repetition, the structure is cumulatively enhanced and the level of chaos is diminished, ultimately producing a razor-sharp blade whose structure is both laminar and flexible. In a similar way, as the vortices are alternately formed and destroyed in making the fertilizer, the level of energy rises and the degree of chaos decreases until, after about an hour, the product is ready for use. This is sprayed on the fields towards evening within two to three hours of preparation and before the accumulated energies have dispersed.

In order to produce larger quantities of the 500 mix, motor driven paddles are used in cylindrical vessels. Viktor's son, Walter, found that the energies build up more strongly in an egg-shaped vessel, and he devised one (Fig. 17.2) using a simple blade like a gold golf club head as an impeller to infuse carbon-dioxide permanently into water under a partial vacuum.[4]

The farmer that Viktor watched also sang into the brew, rising tones as he stirred to the left and falling tones as he stirred to the right, adding crumbling pieces of aluminium-bearing clay into the water. The chanting builds up creative energy in the water's memory (see p.108, *homeopathy*). After about an hour the mixture was ready to be spread over the fields. The following morning he did this by dipping a branch with small leaves into the barrel and then flicking the energized clay-water emulsion over the ground, rather like holy water is sprinkled with palm fronds on Palm Sunday.

Viktor Schauberger's methods of producing natural fertilizer were similar to Rudolf Steiner's biodynamics, but they did not depend on the thousands of cow horns used by Podolinsky, which are available now only because of the high demand for beef. Ultimately such a supply is non-sustainable, when you consider that in

Costa Rica, a recent study showed that for every beef carcass exported, 2½ tonnes of top soil were irretrievably lost through erosion. For a year's food, a meat eater requires the produce from about 1.6 acres, a vegetarian only 0.66 acres. (These are good arguments for switching to vegetarianism).

The role of subtle energies in nature

As you may remember from our discussion of energies in Chapter 2, though our physical existence and ordinary level of consciousness are based in a material third dimensional world, our psyche and our spiritual nature can be influenced by energies from the fourth to the sixth dimensions. Some people more than others are attuned to these immaterial energies. Viktor Schauberger undoubtedly was, as were other visionaries, such as Goethe and Rudolf Steiner.

Although Earth is called a third dimensional environment, all life and creativity is fundamentally dependent on fourth and fifth dimensional energies. Viktor Schauberger identified these aspects of the Sun's fertilizing role (the spiritual driving force of life), according to their different purposes in Nature (as described in Chapter 2). Dynagens generate higher intrinsic energy; fructigens are those subtle energies that produce greater fertility; qualigens create greater quality. Schauberger believed that there was no more powerful way to stimulate high quality growth than by seeding these dynamic energies directly on the soil. As in any area of creativity, the balance of the positive and negative, the male and female energies are all-important.

The Tibetans, who had a practice to bury so-called 'treasure vases,' knew long ago about the seeding of the soil with immaterial energies in certain propitious places. Filled with precious stones and metals, these containers were believed to discharge beneficial energies that enhanced and protected the environment. The Tibetans believed that gold and other precious metals were best left undisturbed in the ground as they help to balance the earth energy, just as the Hopis and the Australian aborigines regard places with uranium as sacred.

Schauberger's vision was to create a greater abundance of creative animating energy, of fertility and rising quality. To do this involved a process that sounds more alchemical than scientific. It

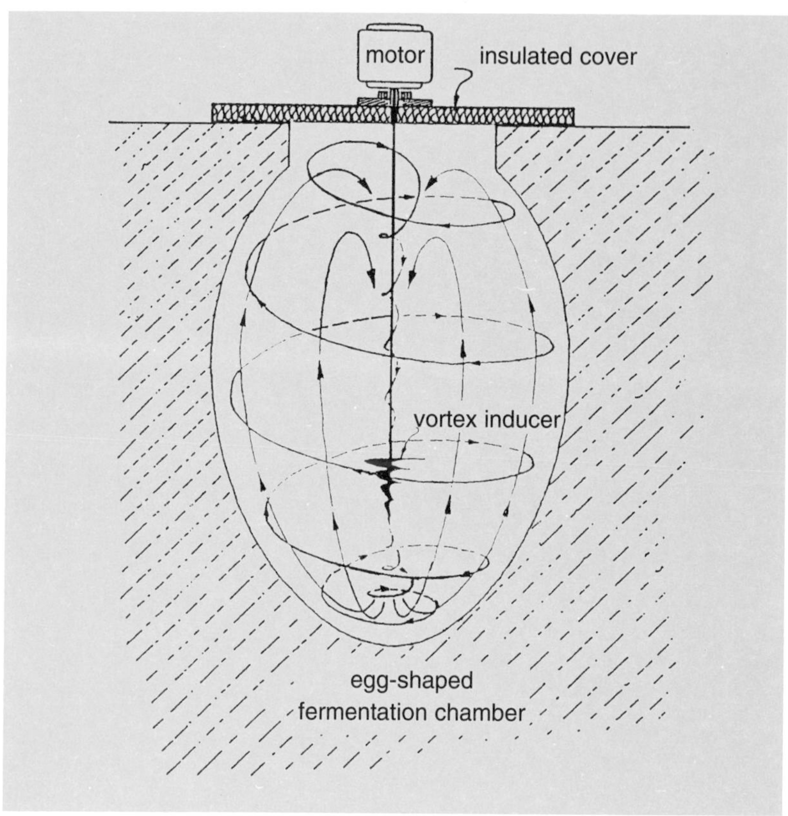

Fig.17.3. Egg-shaped Fermentation Chamber.

required the mixture of small amounts of the male elements of silver, zinc and silicon, with the female gold, copper and limestone, brought together in a special container. For the more precious elements, gold and silver, only a few particles will easily raise the quality of the resulting fermentation. The copper and zinc are in the form of filings or powder.

As a container he used an egg-shaped fermentation chamber scooped out of the ground about 2m (6½ft) deep, and lined with aluminium-bearing clay (Fig. 17.3). A wide range of organic material, kitchen refuse, animal and human waste, as fresh as possible, is now added, up to one third of the volume. The remaining space is then filled with well-oxygenated, juvenile rainwater or surface water, well exposed to the Sun. The top opening is now sealed, so that energies emanating from the interaction of cosmic and geospheric forces will not be dissipated. A bronze rod with a biometal (silver plated copper) vortex-inducer driven by a small motor is inserted through a hole in the cover.

The liquid is stirred in a clockwise (what Schauberger called 'planetary') motion:

> 'Planetary motion' produces an inward spiralling of the liquid, reducing the outward pressure on the peripheral wall-surfaces, while cooling and densifying. This planetary motion, or vortex, involves the natural, animating, centripetalizing acceleration of mass, which initiates higher-grade fermentation processes of an invigorating nature in the bipolar mixture of basic elements. The end-product is biomagnetism, a reproductive, regenerative and upwardly evolving form of energy.[5]

As well as the biomagnetism there is produced a cooling towards the pivotal +4°C (39°F) anomaly point due to the vortical movement in the liquid. The egg-shape ensures that the particles are thoroughly mixed and reduced to the smallest possible particles, homeopathic in their effect, which Viktor notes:

> In terms of homeopathic principles and attempts to produce super-dilutions in order to still the 'specific' hunger of the plants, the more dilute the fertilizing agent, the more it approximates the character of the above ethericities, thus facilitating further interactions that in turn result in increased growth.[6]

There is a mystical dimension to this process, which is like mixing elements of Earth and Heaven. This produces a highly active negative or fructigenic potency, which combines with the water, making it crystal clear. It is also free of unattractive odours and indeed is sweet-smelling, like Podolinsky's '500 mix.' Viktor Schauberger claimed the fertilizer is so powerful, that two such fermentation chambers would be sufficient to permeate the soil over several square kilometres with fertile substances that will encourage germination.[7]

Viktor compares this process to winemaking, where sweet and turbid grape-juice matures into clear, relatively dry wine in a cool cellar. The maturation of good wine, however, may take a year or more, whereas this extraordinarily procreative liquid takes only two to three nights to prepare, weather conditions permitting. When broadcast over the fields in the evening, it absorbs the predominantly positive atmospheric energies ready for fertilization by the Sun's energies the following day. As Schauberger observes: 'Thus, apart from a purely sexual process of procreation, a process of higher genesis here confronts us with the ability to endow quantity with quality.'[8]

Cold fire

Viktor Schauberger has described an eerie experience he had with dynagen ethericities, which in this case produced what is known as 'cold fire,' a strange bioelectric phenomenon:

> Over thirty years ago, walking in a virgin, alpine forest, I came upon a flattish mound covered with vivid green grass and a profusion of bright flowers that did not seem to belong in those surroundings. It was close to a gamecock's courtship display ground, so I decided to spend the night in this remote spot, in order to witness these fine birds display at daybreak. Towards midnight, I was roused by a bluish-white flame curling up from the mound and jumped up to extinguish this incipient forest fire.
>
> In the meantime the flame had grown a metre high and took on an egg-shaped form, similar to those that now and again issue from rock fissures and, like shining dewdrops, stand on the point of a rock. Many years ago a chief forester from Vienna, Walter Hackel, photographed just such a strange light over a metre in height. A copy of the photograph was unfortunately lost at the end of the war, or rather was stolen by looters of my apartment.
>
> However, at that time I knew nothing of these things and so I backed away in horror, as I stood in this pitch-black darkness before an ever more powerfully flaring and heatless flame, which threw a pale glimmer into the surroundings. At first, like a man possessed, with my heavy mountain staff, I hit at the place from where tongue after tongue of this mysterious egg-light sprang up. When I noticed that this shaft of light sprang from the rock at only one point, I ceased to flail away at the supposed forest fire and loosened the surrounding soil. This, however, had no effect.
>
> Then I held my hand in this egg-light and instead of feeling the anticipated heat, experienced an icy coldness and

saw the bones standing out on my hand. An icy chill ran down my back. I returned to the tree where my gun lay, released the safety catch and sat down in my former bivouac, waiting to see what else would happen. After about two hours the sky at last began to grey. A few hundred metres away the gamecock began his courtship, the actual reason for my early visit. I didn't move from my position, watching how this uncanny glow slowly extinguished, and suddenly the whole specter was over.

When at last daylight came, I returned again to the source of the flame and on every tip of the lush green leaves I saw oversize dewdrops, again in egg-shaped form, standing motionless like glittering candle flames. As the first rays of the Sun pierced the tangle of leaves, the grass-tips bent under the weight of the *ur*-water, which visibly grew as the Sun's heat increased.[9] One by one, the now finished dewdrops fell down.

Now I began to dig into the hillock with the tip of my mountain staff and underneath a peculiarly smelling layer of humus, I felt a resistance, which after further digging, turned out to be the almost undecomposed corpse of a chamois buck, which had a clearly distinguishable bullet entry hole above the left foreleg. There was, however, no exit hole. According to the time of year, it could have been shot only by poachers, since the hunting season was long past. It was only later that it became clear to me that the buck must already have lain underneath this mound for a longish period, because it was covered by a thick layer of humus upon which vegetation had apparently sprouted. On even closer inspection, I found a sort of mass grave before me.

The old hunters used to insist that chamois (as also happens with elephants) seek out special places to die where slow decomposition rather than putrefaction takes place. Sick wild animals are attracted to such places which remain equally warm or cold in winter and in summer, seeking either a cure or a painless death. Expressed scientifically, constant anomaly states prevail, which permit decay-free decomposition. This is why, as a particularly sly old forester explained, the high clergymen had themselves buried in a constantly cool church crypt, or why the more common

> priests at least had a little roof built over their graves along the cemetery wall at the eastern side in order to protect them from rainwater. I realized later that, because of its free oxygen content, which activates decomposive forces, rainwater actually promotes decay or rusting.[10]

Fertilizing energies

Schauberger's buried fermentation chamber is sited so as to be a meeting place for the male seminal energies of the Sun (acting perpendicularly to the Earth) and the female fertilizing energies of the Earth (acting horizontally at or near the Earth surface). The residues or fallout of their combination result in physical growth. As Schauberger describes:

> Having been created out of the most thoroughly rotted elements of former life, these emanations are the most natural fertilizers, which have metamorphosed their erstwhile spatiality (spatial volume) to such a degree, that they can only manifest themselves as highly dosed (concentrated) energetic matter.[11]

This is what sustainability is all about. Matter being the energetic waste products of higher (fourth or fifth dimensional) energies created through heat and light, their reconversion into energies make them the best possible natural fertilizers. There is virtually no limit to the charge that can be built up with these energies, as they are nonspatial.

The fertilizing energies (which may be a combination of dynagens, fructigens and qualigens) enter the plant itself through the root protoplasms, the little sacs or vesicles of proto-water or amniotic fluid attached to the root-tip. Like dew, another form of proto-water formed on the tips of blades of grass during the night and early morning, these vesicles, too, collapse if exposed to light and heat. This is why the greatest care must be taken when replanting small seedlings or saplings, which should be done only at night in order to keep injury to a minimum.

Absolutely essential to the plant, these delicate root protoplasms convert the nutritive energies and the minerals into a form that it can absorb. Viktor Schauberger's sketch (Fig.17.4) illustrates the process, which he describes:

No plant is actually nourished by dissolved matter, but rather by the nutritive entities of geospheric origin, 'ascended' in a fourth dimensional state. These diffuse ethericities can enter the sap-stream only through the root protoplasms, where they are fertilized by diffuse oxygenic ethericities. The higher outbirth of this emulsion (*ur*-procreation) is an ethericity that belongs to fifth dimension. These concentrations of matter-energy emit negative, hyper-charged emanations in all directions and bind the positively-charged ethericities entering through the skin or the bark. Some of this emulsion solidifies and whatever is subsequently manifested, is what we call 'growth.'[12]

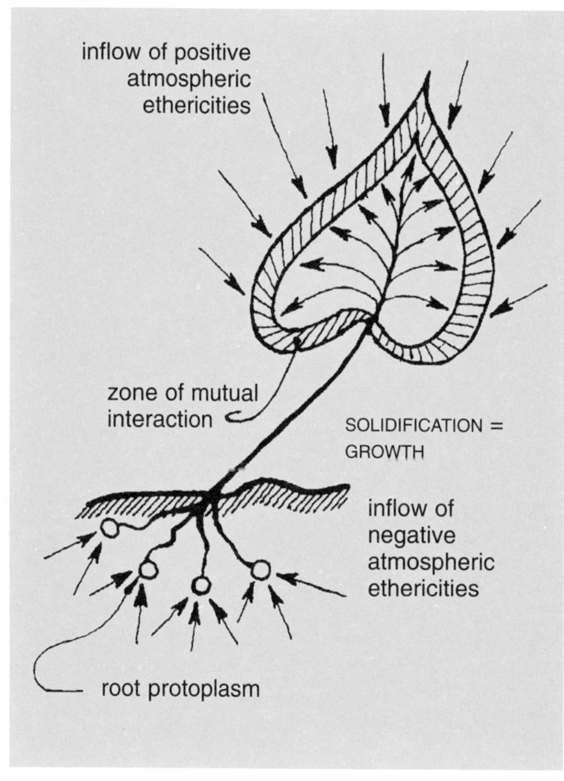

Fig.17.4. Viktor's Energy Exchange Diagram.

With these natural methods of fertilization there is therefore much that we can do to promote healthy and sustainable growth in agriculture. With this technology we have the ability to restore the soil, our only source of wholesome food, to its former state of high productivity and fertility, and even to increase it. These means are not only far cheaper than the use of harmful artificial fertilizers and noxious pesticides, but they increase both the quantity and quality of food. Schauberger held that conversion of agricultural practice to sustainable organic fertility, forestry to biodiversity and water resources management to take into account Nature's more subtle processes, would halt the present deterioration both of the environment and of the human condition.

First we have to understand how Nature works, and accept her laws. Schauberger's life was devoted to this challenge. Let us hope that his work will empower people to seek this goal, and to encourage the changes needed to change our materialistically oriented society. In Schauberger's own words:

A free people can grow only from a free Earth. Any people that violate Mother-Earth have no right to a homeland, because high-quality races cannot survive in soils destroyed by speculation, i.e. because they are divorced of all connection with the Earth. Human societies without roots perish. They have to experience the path of decay until, like unsuitable fertilizers, they give up their stubborn wills and only then will they be allowed to start again and re-enter the mighty course of evolution.[13]

PART SIX

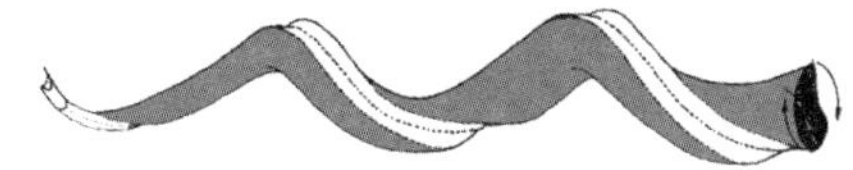

The Energy Revolution

18. Harnessing Implosion Power

'In the whole machine there is no straight line and no circle.'
(Viktor Schauberger's comment to a visitor to his workshop in 1936.)

Arthur C. Clarke, the futurologist, recently commented that we were on the verge of a breakthrough in how we access energy. This was before the giant aerospace company Boeing of Seattle announced new research with a practical anti-gravity device developed by the Russian scientist Evgeny Podkletnov.

The obvious area that would be affected is transport; space travel would suddenly become easy. Aircraft could carry us swiftly and silently without polluting the atmosphere. Surface transport could become swift and cheap. Building methods could be transformed; it could even help with advances in medicine.

But the principal gain would be virtually free, unpolluting energy, which could be produced even in our own homes. Gone would be the necessity to be dependent on an expensive national grid. These changes might not happen smoothly, because political and economic power revolves around the carbon industry, principally oil, and the utilities. Are these power brokers going to give up their control without a fight? Additionally our present, morally bankrupt societies seem always to give the military industries first choice of employing new technologies.

Because Podkletnov's invention was inspired by Viktor Schauberger's research, it might be interesting to follow how his discovery of anti-gravity came from devices he had developed through observing Nature.

The beginnings of implosion research

During the 1920s, Viktor Schauberger had made a bit of money (as well as a reputation) by building his revolutionary log flumes. This enabled him to design a prototype power plant to extract energy directly from air and water, based on the powerful energies he had identified in Nature. The first experiments he undertook with a Viennese engineer, Dr Winter, in 1931–32 were inconclusive, and made him realize he had to undertake much more precise observations of how the trout actually transmutes the energies of the stream into such powerful forward motion.

The principle of the trout turbine was that air and water should be directed through spiral shaped pipes with a specially shaped cross section that moved the substance in such a way as to transform it into a 'living' state. After a certain number of revolutions the air or water would be induced through a specific corkscrew motion into a highly energized state, from which the energy could be released. What Schauberger was producing was a reaction at the atomic level. However, instead of violently compressing atoms in hydrogen gas to create helium and an energy release, he was able to twist all the elements together in the quiet, but powerful, way that happens in Nature; this was more comparable to atomic 'fusion.'

As we have seen, one of Viktor's brilliant insights into Nature's methods was the concept of reciprocity. Many of Nature's processes depend on the alternating of complementary, but opposite, forms of energy, e.g heat and cold, gravity and levitation, electricity and magnetism, centrifugence and centripetence, both aspects of which combine to create a wholeness through their synthesizing, reciprocal action. Thus he found that alternating pressure and suction could be employed in this way on the axis of the machine to produce a powerful propulsive effect.

This 'biotechnical' fusion created what Schauberger called 'diamagnetic' or higher quality substances which had levitational tendencies that were the principal feature of the machines he designed at the beginning of the war. The first, built by a Berlin company in 1940, disappointed him because of the poor workmanship. So he moved assembly closer to home, to a Viennese plant where, in an unscheduled test, his first flying saucer-shaped prototype broke away from its anchoring bolts and smashed a hole in the factory's ceiling. The infuriated owner never forgave Schauberger and was uncooperative about testing a second model.

The German culture has a reputation for being open to new ideas. Indeed, a German industrialist who had heard about Schauberger's strange inventions recommended him to Hitler in 1934. Viktor made a strong impression on the Führer who, after the interview, requested all assistance be given to his research in fuelless energy production. The scientific establishment resented this upstart; indeed, the father of quantum physics, Max Planck, who had been present at the interview, when asked his opinion of Schauberger's theories, retorted: 'Science has nothing to do with Nature.'

Professor Ernst Heinkel, who developed the innovative aircraft that bore his name, also heard about Schauberger's revolutionary power source, and stealing his confidential patent application, attempted in 1938 to incorporate it into his new jet aircraft, the under-performing HE 280. Heinkel persuaded the patents office to restrict Schauberger's technology to water purification projects, so that he would be free to develop Schauberger's innovations in his aircraft research. However, it dawned on him that the conventional aircraft frame was totally inappropriate for Schauberger's suction engine. The development in 1940 of Schreiver's 'Flying Top' in Heinkel's Rostock factory suggests that he had more success when the power generator was transferred to the new model of prototype flying saucer.

In 1943, the Schreiver saucer and its subsequent developments were moved to a secret location in Czechoslovakia to which Schauberger was from time to time seconded. Word of this new 'aircraft' reached Himmler's ears; he was drawn more to unconventional science as a source of new weapons development. Viktor's activities were at that time highly secret, moving from one project to another, but he was apparently not at that time given responsibility for research and development. However, in 1943 Himmler entrusted to the SS the role for developing German secret weapons.

The SS established production facilities for these new secret weapons in giant cave complexes in Poland and Czechoslovakia, safe from Allied bombs, using prisoners of war as labour. Had these underground facilities been set up earlier in the war, its outcome might have been different. The level of secrecy was extremely high; so much, indeed, that at one crucial location at the end of the war, the SS lined up 62 of the scientists and laboratory technicians, and shot them, to save the secrets of that complex 'free energy' atomic installation falling into the hands of the approaching Soviet troops.[1]

The SS decided in 1944 that Schauberger's machines were ready for production. They drafted him and ordered him, under pain of death, to employ prisoner engineers from the Mauthausen concentration camp near Linz to develop five projects. In addition to the high priority flying saucer programme, there was a water purifier, a high voltage generator, an air conditioner and a machine to biosynthesise hydrogen from water. However, because of the success of the Allies' bombing, Schauberger moved his operations to Leonstein in Upper Austria, and the improved Repulsine was finally ready for testing the day the Americans arrived; the SS guards had disappeared the day before.

A British engineer, John Frost, who emigrated to Canada shortly after the war, developed a flying saucer project called the Avrocar at a Canadian aerospace plant, funded largely by US capital. It was to take off and land vertically, and to fly at high altitudes at 1,500 mph. They were having trouble with its stability and, realizing that the power plant was inadequate, approached Viktor Schauberger with a generous offer to buy his propulsion system. Viktor declined, because they refused to promise that his invention would be used only for the good of humanity. Schauberger reported that he had a second offer of $3.5 million from an American company, which he refused for the same reason. This was not long before the Gerchsheimer consortium contacted him.

The American consortium

Karl Gerchsheimer, initiator of the American consortium that tried (see p. 13) to extract Schauberger's secrets in 1958, as head of all civilian administration and logistics had been the most powerful non-military presence in the U.S. zone of Germany from 1945 to 1950. He was a Bavarian who thought he understood where Schauberger was coming from — he had read some of Viktor's papers, and felt he shared the same love of the mountains and their pure water.

Gerchsheimer formulated a plan with industrialist and financier Robert Donner to bring Viktor and his son to the U.S. to help develop radical power technology, although by that time Schauberger was in very poor health. In May 1958 the group assembled in a secret hideaway in the Texas desert. There were many delays and serious communication problems. Gerchsheimer and Donner had a disagreement with Donner's financial adviser, Norman Dodd, their production director, whom they fired in contentious circumstances. Viktor eventually became convinced, probably mistakenly, that the consortium was part of a U.S. government plan to make a very powerful atomic bomb by developing his research trail, and refused to cooperate.

Basically, they had different agendas; the Schaubergers, Gerchsheimer and Dodd all gave varying accounts of what actually happened. Gerchsheimer complained that Viktor's explanations of his theories were unintelligible and suspected that they were flawed. He gradually came to the conclusion that Viktor would not be able to deliver what they wanted. Viktor, for his part, rebelled when it was finally made clear that he must stay for eight years, whereupon he effectively refused to engage in any further communication.

Only after he and his son had agreed to sign a new contract (which was not translated into German for them), effectively consigning to the consortium all rights to his documents, designs and models and to any future ideas and inventions, was Viktor allowed to return to his beloved Austria, a broken man.

A new kind of aircraft?

The Wright Brothers' plane a century ago had wings, a tail fin and rudders. All our commercial jet aircraft today are built on the same principles, but are far less fuel efficient, requiring hundreds of times the energy to push through the atmosphere. More and more power is expended to counter both the air resistance and the pull of gravity, at quite astronomical costs in terms of materials and development. It was to reduce the force of gravity that some of the large aerospace companies in the U.S.A. were undertaking research in the early 1950s. One researcher, Townsend T. Brown had designed a saucer-shaped craft whose weight was significantly reduced by energizing the skins with massive amounts of electricity and which happened also to make the craft invisible to radar.

Conventional scientific theory states that certain laws are inviolable, like the Second Law of Thermodynamics, Einstein's Theory of Relativity or the Law of Gravity. We learn this at school, and anyone who claims otherwise is treated with suspicion or derision. Researchers now working at the frontiers of science, such as in quantum physics, are discovering that these laws apply only under conventional physical conditions, though this is not yet widely accepted.

The discovery that the force of gravity can be reduced or even cancelled has profound implications for humanity. It is as though we can add another dimension to our world, one that had always been present, though not in our awareness. For many people (especially conventional scientists who like events to be predictable) this may be a scary and unwelcome development.

The appeal of anti-gravity is powerful. Passengers travelling in a plane that was able to cancel out gravity would not experience any discomfort, no matter how fast it accelerated or changed course. It would revolutionize space exploration. Put to work in other fields, the absence of gravity would solve the problems of power transmission from engine to wheels, would facilitate fuel-less heating for homes and industry, and have many other uses, even in medicine. Predictions were being made in 1956 that a new kind of aircraft using anti-gravity would be developed within five years. All that was required to usher in an era of efficient, economical, clean and quiet, fuel-less propulsion, of free energy technology for industry and the home — was investment and a little encouragement from the U.S. government.

It never happened; or did it? All discussion about anti-gravity ceased in the U.S. in 1957. But that was the time when the research and development arm of the military-industrial complex went underground, or 'black' as the popular idiom has it, becoming completely unaccountable to government, with astronomical procurement budgets carefully hidden from the scrutiny of the legislative branch. This was justified for reasons of national security during the Cold War, and so it has remained ever since. In fact, America was following the example of Nazi Germany, where the initiative for developing new weapons was taken from the armaments industry in 1943 and entrusted to a very secret (mostly literally underground) programme run by the SS.

There have been various reports of secret aircraft being developed by the black side of the U.S. aeronautical industry. The most noteworthy was the triangular-shaped Northrop B-2 Stealth Bomber which has an electrogravic drive system; it had followed the Lockheed Stealth Fighter (the term 'stealth' signifying their invisibility to radar). Some believe that the B-2 has a system to reduce gravity; what is more accepted is that it envelops itself in a shield of static electricity which both acts like a cloaking device and reduces its air resistance. Since the B-2 went operational in 1993, twenty have been built at a cost of $20 billion each.[2]

It has been suggested that test flights of experimental flying saucer aircraft may account for UFO sightings. While this is certainly possible, evidence is still lacking of the significant development of a successful U.S. saucer programme. The evidence, however, for visitations by craft from extraterrestrial sources, and for the US government's undercover research with recovered alien craft is rather more tangible, despite continuing and complex official denials and disinformation campaigns.[3]

Nick Cook, in his book *The Hunt for Zero Point,* comes to the conclusion that the giant aerospace industry is essentially conservative. They could not take on the kind of anti-gravity research pioneered by T.T. Brown in the late 1940s because they would have lost their credibility within the science of aeronautics, and the industry would have suffered.

> What I have learned is that there are two kinds of science. The stuff they teach you in college, and all the weird things they don't. This knowledge is dangerous. It's change with a capital C and it's not easy to get your head around. The aerospace and defense industry says it likes people who think out of the box, because they're the guys who give us the breakthroughs … radar, the bomb, stealth and all that; but think this far out and they look at you like you're crazy. They might even put you away.[4]

The other, often overlooked, reason for conservatism in technology is the extent to which political and economic power is centred partly in transportation, but especially in the carbon fuel industry. As long as there is plenty of oil to be pumped, why risk destabilization of this power by investigating virtually free energy sources that would inevitably bring with it much more freedom for countless millions of people who are currently dependent on the expensive central distribution of oil products and electricity?

Schauberger's search for free energy

However, in July 2002 *Jane's Defence Weekly* announced that they had seen secret research papers from Boeing, the aerospace giants, confirming positive development of a Russian device — which comprises rapidly spinning superconducting ceramic discs suspended in the magnetic field of three electric coils enclosed in a low temperature vessel.

The man behind this research is Dr Evgeny Podkletnov, a Russian scientist then working in Finland. When he first published details of his anti-gravity device in 1996, he was ostracized by his colleagues and then fired by his university, for the Law of Gravity is inviolable! He subsequently admitted that his father, a leading authority in hydro-engineering, had acquired original Schauberger papers at the end of the war.

The most creative pioneers of new scientific vision are essentially practical people who have an urgent need to see their ideas put into practice. Viktor Schauberger was no exception. Realizing that the machines our technology has developed are not only very inefficient, but that they are also largely responsible for the destruction of our environment, he set about designing appliances which used Nature's creative methods, but which were capable also of producing vastly more power at little cost.

Schauberger abandoned the Euclidean model of straight line and circle. All the functional surfaces of his machines employ the spirals, sinuosity and curves of the open forms of non-Euclidean geometry that are found in Nature. The egg-shapes and spirals that he employed produced life-affirming energies that stabilize, enhance and rehabilitate natural processes.

When Schauberger designed his prototype machines it was extremely difficult to perfect complex curvilinear surfaces. Now, with computer programmes, it is possible with ease to replicate Nature's eggs, spirals and vortices. A design breakthrough to designing benevolent systems would be theoretically simple; what is lacking is the insight and the imagination.

During the 1930s and 1940s, he developed a number of prototypes: of a machine which produced high quality spring water, a domestic air conditioning appliance, and various machines which produced prodigious amounts of motive power. All these machines worked on much the same principles, and had in common a virtually silent and inexpensive operation. All the important elements of Nature's repertoire come into their own, such as male and female ethericities, creative vortical movement, temperature gradients, bioelectricism and biomagnetism. As Schauberger commented: 'At the intersection of two temperature gradients atomic energy is released. Whether it is a formative or destructive energy is determined in each case by the type of movement and the composition of the alloys used to build the motion-producing machine.'[5]

The biological vacuum

I can generate suctional forces which act indirectly and are entirely undetectable. No current of air can be noticed; only an almost imperceptible cooling, as occurs when air is sucked in strongly with the back of the hand held in front of the mouth. It is therefore incorrect to say that I have copied the cyclones and typhoons of the tropics.[6]

The mechanical principle of all of Schauberger's machines is that of suction, the simplest form of which we experience when we place our hand over the plug hole in a bath of deep water; taking it away and replacing it illustrates the enormous power of suction. Professor Felix Ehrenhaft, who helped Viktor with his calculations, worked out that the power of suction, or implosion as it is called in energy terms, is 127 times more powerful than explosion.

Bathtub suction is powered by gravity, which is related to centrifugence, the complement to centripetence. In a similar way that the aircraft jet engine uses the interaction of suction and pressure on a common axis, Schauberger used the balance between centrifugence and centripetence on a common axis to produce a biological vacuum.

This is created by spinning the gas or liquid at high speed in a vortical manner so that it becomes dense and cool. If water were used, every 1°C of cooling would reduce the volume of the gases contained in the water by 1/273. However, if air containing an average amount of water vapour is used, the amount of compaction of air to water is in the ratio of 816 to 1. One litre of water at +4°C (39°F) weighs 1kg, compared to one litre of normal air which weighs 0.001226kg. This is the basis of implosion energy.

In 1939 the American airship the Akron was destroyed when its helium mysteriously reverted to water, reducing in volume 1800-fold in a massive implosion. This immense reduction in volume creates a biological vacuum that can be an ideal and environmentally harmless source of motive power. Gases are converted into water and those contained in the water are further transformed into energy in the process of continuous cooling which occurs in the formation of a biological vacuum.

Viktor's machines, besides spatially reducing physical matter, also converted it into immaterial energies, in reality a translation from the third to the fourth or fifth dimensions. Callum Coats writes:

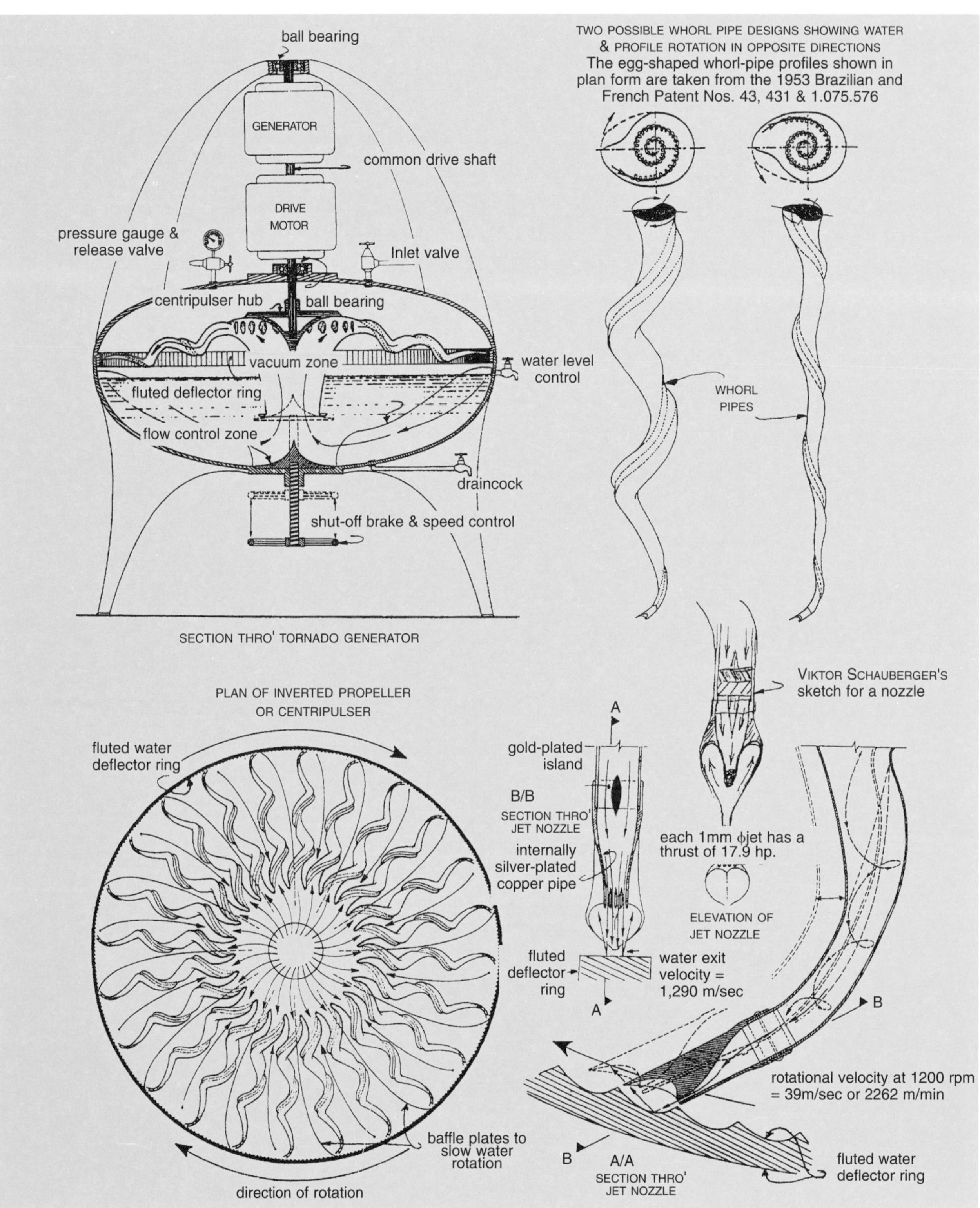

Fig.18.1. Tornado Home Power Generator. *Schematic design based on patent applications and other data.*

This higher realm of being is what Theosophical teaching refers to as the 'laya point,' the point of extreme potency, the eye of the needle as it were, through which and from which all manifesting energies are propagated. Viktor called this process a 'higher inward fall,' noting in his diary of August 14, 1936:

I stand face to face with the apparent 'void,' the compression of dematerialization that we are wont to call a 'vacuum.' I can now see that we are able to create anything we wish for ourselves out of this 'nothing.' The agent is water, the blood of the Earth and the most universal organism.[7]

Viktor Schauberger demonstrated how to remove matter from the physical dimension, and to pack the resulting nonspatial other-worldly vacuum with almost unlimited amounts of pure, formative energy, the counterpart to the physical substance that had been transformed. Simply the appropriate trigger, usually light or heat, could unleash this huge potential and source of power.[8] He described his aim as follows:

I must furnish those who would protect or save life with an energy source which produces energy so cheaply that nuclear fission will not only be economical, but ridiculous. This is the task I have set myself in what little time I have left.[9]

Nuclear fusion

The dichotomy between centrifugal and centripetal technologies is never clearer than with nuclear energy. Viktor frequently inveighed against the dangers of nuclear fission (explosive), and he came near to the unveiling the secrets of nuclear fusion (implosive), the Shangri-la of our technical age. The key to it was the extreme biological vacuum, achieved most nearly in his 'flying saucer,' described later. The process can be described as 'cold fusion.'

Walter Schauberger, with his physics and mathematical background was able to describe the process of conversion of matter into 'virtual' states in a way that other scientists could understand; in this way the approaches of father and son complemented each other. Richard St Barbe Baker, the prominent environmentalist and founder of 'The Men of the Trees' movement, impressed with the potential of the Schauberger physics tried, sadly without success, to interest Clement Atlee's UK government in supporting Walter and Viktor's implosion research.

Instead, Baker brought Walter to England in 1950 to lecture to and dialogue with top scientists. First, at Oxford, there was a gathering of physicists, chemists and forestry researchers, who affected polite interest, but refrained from comment. However, at Cambridge Sir James Chadwick, who with Rutherford had first split the atom, was most impressed with Walter, introducing him to other atomic physicists.

A group of top atomic physicists at Birmingham showed lively interest in this new physics, and admitted to being inspired. A few weeks later Baker was again in Birmingham, and asked the scientists if they had held a postmortem on Schauberger's presentation. "Yes, indeed," they admitted; they had decided that it was "unchallengeable." "Then what are you going to do about it?" asked Baker. "Nothing," was their retort. "Why not?" "Because it would mean rewriting all the textbooks in the world."[10]

The repulsator

Viktor started work on this machine (Fig. 18.2) early in the 1930s. It was designed to convert degenerated or distilled water into invigorating fresh water with the qualities of a mountain spring. A 10-litre egg-shaped vessel made of copper, with some active surfaces silver-plated, was used, insulated to retain the biomagnetic and bioelectrical energies. A powered impeller near the pointed base created alternating right and left handed vortices in the water body, duplicating the negatively and positively charged longitudinal vortices at the bends of naturally flowing rivers. It was inevitable that for his energy-generating machines Viktor Schauberger would choose the egg as it is the only closed shape that will naturally generate vortical movement.

The in-rolling and out-rolling movement allows the water to absorb carbon dioxide and various trace elements that are added in a specific order to approximate the chemical composition of mountain spring water. Some four litres of water are drained off while carbon dioxide is introduced. Once the motor has been started, the carbon dioxide is absorbed into the water. Through the vortical action and resultant cooling, it is changed into carbonic acid, which creates a vacuum. When the water has cooled down to 4°C (39°F), cold oxidation takes place, allowing the assimilation of the trace elements and minerals.

The process takes three-quarters of an hour, and the water is then left to stand in a cold temperature for 24 hours. The water, when sipped slowly straight from the egg at a temperature of not more than 8°C (46°F) will neutralize any over-acidity in the body, allowing the cells, by taking up oxygen (which is passive at this temperature), to return to health.

The implosion motor

This ambitious machine was designed as an electric power generator, though it did also produce high quality water. It worked on the same principle as the Repulsator, being first filled to exclude air and then drained sufficiently to allow the simultaneous introduction of carbon dioxide.

It was difficult to build, being dependent on a series of identical whorl pipe water jets conceived to replicate the shape of a Kudu antelope horn. This intriguingly shaped tube, which has an egg-shaped cross section, allows an almost perfect hyperbolic double spiral flow to manifest. The shape of the pipe and reducing diameter follow the proportions of the Golden section (see p. 69).

This configuration operates in the same way as Viktor's pipe in the Stuttgart experiment, where the shape of the pipe directed the water in an involuting flow away from the pipe walls, significantly reducing the friction. In the two forms of whorl-pipe shown in the diagram (see Fig.18.1), the water rotates either in the same direction as the spiral twist of the pipe, or in the opposite direction, depending on which whorl-pipe is selected, the hydraulic efficiency of either being determined by experiment. In practice only one or other of the whorl-pipe configurations would be attached to the central hub.

This centrifugal/centripetal effect creates a double spiral motion to the water, cooling and condensing it; it also allows the energies to change polarities, eg from magnetic to bioelectric or from electric to biomagnetic. This change of polarities would convert resistance-producing energies into motion-enhancing ones, such as levitational and diamagnetic dynagens.

When the centripulser is rotated by the motor at 1200 revolutions

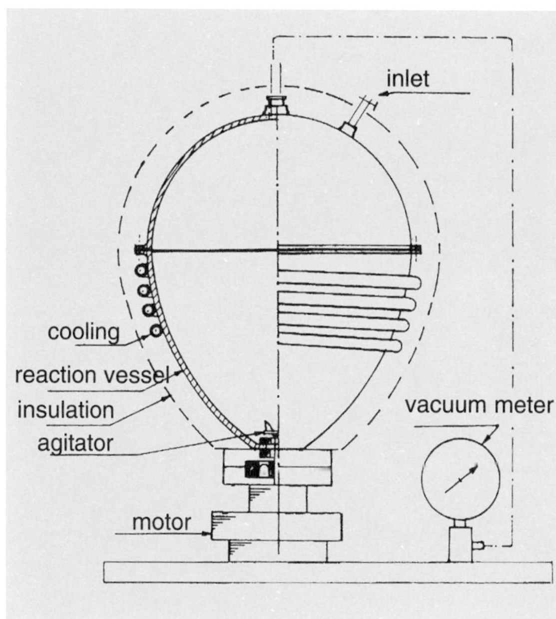

Fig.18.2. The Repulsator. *For the biological synthesis of spring water:*
(a) Alexandersson's (above)
(b) Schauberger's (below)

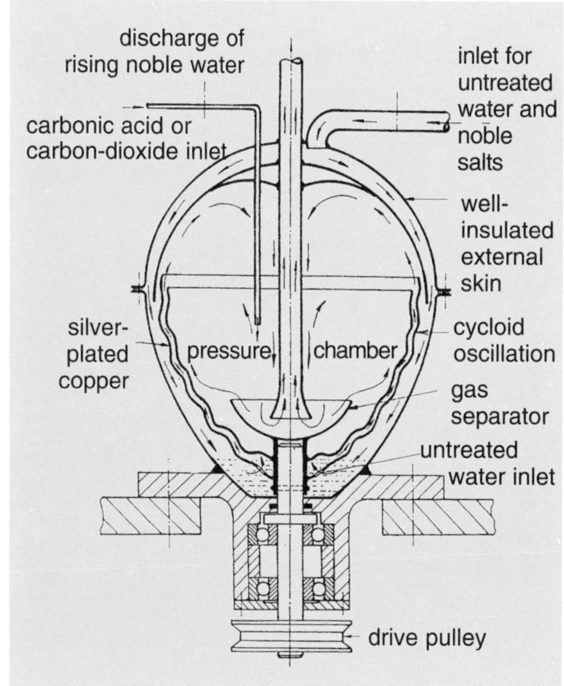

per minute, the water is centrifuged down the whorl pipes while undergoing a double spiral centripetal contraction. It leaves the 1mm diameter nozzle (there are 4 per pipe) with tremendous force because of its density and high velocity. The exit velocity of the water is about 1,290m/sec, (four times the speed of sound), which makes it as solid and hard as steel wire.

The following is the eye-witness report of Gretl Schneider, who accompanied Arnold Hohl, one of Viktor's observers:

> Mr Viktor Schauberger has demonstrated the machine to me. The previous huge construction is no more. It has been reduced to half its former size and in operation develops enormous power. I poured a pot of water into the bottom of it. The machine produced an almost inaudible sound and then a 'pfft' in the same instant and the water pierced right through a 4cm thick concrete slab and a 4mm thick super-hardened steel plate with such force that the water-particles, invisible to the eye due to their high velocity, penetrated right through all clothing and were experienced as lightning needle-pricks on the skin. Water glass was also passed through and solidified in 5cm long hairs on the outside of the casing, like bristles.[11]

Some of Viktor's machines did not need a starting motor, and would get going on their own with a few cranks of a manual starting handle. The heavy centripulser perhaps required one, but after gaining sufficient speed would produce sufficient energy to self-rotate. If the machine works as Viktor claimed, the generator should produce ten times more power than the motor needs, or a ninefold surplus of electric current. One of the problems with Viktor's machines was more how to stop them than getting them started. Another was keeping the machine anchored to the floor to stop the strong levitational energies that were generated from lifting it into the air.

The repulsine and the flying saucer

As we described in Chapter 1, there were several models of this machine developed, the first in 1940 to investigate free energy production, later to validate Viktor's theories about levitational flight, but in the mid-1940s as prototypes of a new secret weapon of the Third Reich:

There are many rumours about what Schauberger was actually doing during this period, most of which suggest that he was in charge of developing 'flying discs' under contract to the army. It later become known that 'the 'flying disc' launched in Prague on the 19th of February 1945, which rose to an altitude of 15,000 metres in three minutes and attained a forward speed of 2,200 kph, was a development of the prototype he built at Mauthausen concentration camp. Schauberger wrote, 'I first heard of this event only after the war through one of the technicians who had worked with me.' In a letter to a friend, dated the 2nd August 1956, Schauberger commented, 'The machine was said to have been destroyed just before the end of the war on [Field Marshal] Keitel's orders.'[12]

This was a much larger version of a 20cm diameter one that Viktor built at the Schloss Schönbrunn which was called the Repulsine. It contained a small high speed electric motor capable of producing up to 20,000rpm at which point the auto-rotation of the centripulser was initiated. 'This machine generated such a powerful levitational force, that when it was started (in Viktor's absence), it sheared the six quarter-inch diameter high-tensile steel anchor bolts and shot upwards to smash against the roof of the hangar.'[13]

There were in fact two different types of the Repulsine. One was secured to the ground and designed to produce power by means of a horizontal shaft; the other to fly. Both produced strong levitational energy — hence the second anecdote above.

As the velocities produced by the centripulsing process increase, the air molecules become cooler and more condensed through the interaction of both centripetral and centrifugal forces. The reduction in volume may reach 1/816, when air is converted into water, and produces a powerful vacuum inside that rapidly draws in larger amounts of air, creating a secondary vacuum above the saucer. The extreme centripulsion and densation not only produce an antigravity effect, but also raise the energy level beyond the physical, so that the electrons and protons are compressed back into their fourth dimension origins.

All of these actions contribute to the levitational affect, enhancing the principal upwards force provided by the densely compressed atoms passing through the aerofoil slits of the turbine blades ('t') before being thrust out between the outer cowl ('A') and

Fig.18.3 & 4. Repusaltor Prototypes.

the inner cowl ('E') with explosive force, hurling the saucer into the semi-vacuum above it (see Fig. 18.5, opposite).

Callum Coats in his fourth volume of the Eco-Technology series, *Energy Evolution,* brings together Viktor Schauberger's notes, comments and discussions that have survived the appropriation of the Soviet and American authorities. In that fascinating volume the machines discussed are the Air-turbine machine, Water-driven and Air-driven implosion machines, the Repulsator, the Klimator and the Repulsine. Sadly, the text often refers to sketches that are missing.

The Air-turbine machine created an artificial thunderstorm, operating on the principle of the tornado. Schauberger envisaged this as a fuel-less silent engine to power an aircraft by creating a vacuum in front to pull it forward. The Water and Air-driven implosion machines operated on the principle of a powerful vacuum; he designed a submarine using a water-driven implosion motor. The Klimator was a cooling or heating machine designed for domestic air conditioning.

There is no doubt that Viktor Schauberger produced a number of impressive and highly innovative machines for various purposes, and we have eye witness accounts of the operation of some, as well as some of his notes. However, any prototypes or working models were either destroyed in Germany during the war, or were expropriated from his flat by the Russians who first occupied Vienna, or confiscated by the Americans when they overran the Leonstein works at war's end, or by the Donner-Gerchsheimer consortium, who spirited him away to Texas in their ill-fated attempt to acquire his secret knowledge.

In the meantime it must be noted that there is no proof that any of them reliably produced over a significant period the power that was intended.

There are a number of people in America and Australia working on Schauberger's ideas, though the political climate has repressed development of their work. Let us hope that if these conditions improve, we might see modifications of some of Viktor's machines making their appearance. We shall be examining in the next chapter some of the new initiatives that have been inspired by Viktor's research.

The tragedy of Viktor Schauberger's life was of being born into a society with little interest in his dream of helping humanity become empowered and free. Instead, to his intense sadness and heartache

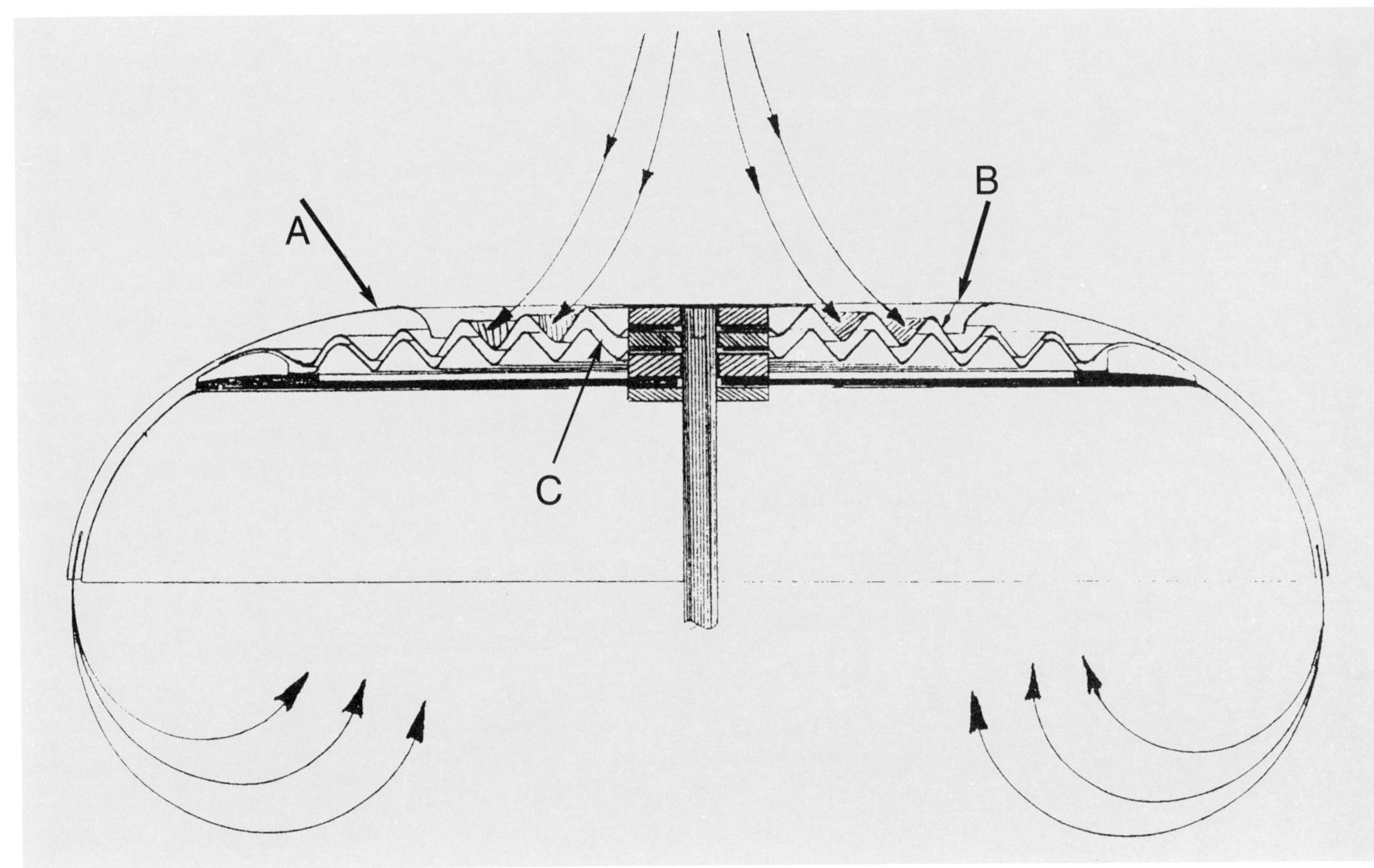

Fig. 18.5. Cross Section through Flying Saucer.
A = 1.2mm thick curved copper sheet, with central opening seen on Fig. 18.3. Between rilled plates B & C, air is drawn in due to the centripulser's high rate of rotation and subjected to powerful centrifugal and oscillating forces which cool and condense it. Transforming into water condenses air 816 times, causing a vacuum which accelerates the intake of more air. At revolutions of 20,000 rpm, vacuum and densification become intense, packing the molecules so tightly as to cause a levitational effect. The living vacuum thus created changes the atoms into a virtual state, compressing them back into their original 4th dimensional formlessness.

he found his inspired vision of working with Nature twisted towards the military aims of one of the most sadistic regimes of modern times.

American science could not take seriously someone with no education in science. Viktor Schauberger was hardly one to be considered as a contender for the stakes of space-age innovation. He merely observed Nature and talked about fish swimming in mountain streams, yet he was the one who cracked the anti-gravity challenge. As he himself remarked:

> Implosion is no invention in the conventional sense, but rather the renaissance of ancient knowledge, lost over the course of time.[15]

19. Viktor Schauberger and Society

The human legacy

We have been concerned in this study so far to give an overview of Schauberger's insights into how Nature works at the subtle level. Viktor also had strong views on where our society has gone wrong and where we might start to make changes. First we shall seek insights on the human level and, later, we shall mention some ongoing developments and research inspired by Viktor's work.

Viktor was a natural scientist and visionary who challenged the very worldview of a culture that considers itself to be at the apex of human achievement. His is not a political view, nor a particularly moral one. He was continually exasperated by the literal blindness of those in power, their inability to see what was before their very eyes.[1]

Viktor Schauberger's observations and vision have given us the keys to disentangling the environmental mess we have got ourselves into. His insights were not limited to technology and how we do things, but to all of life. If we were able to see that our education, social organization, philosophy, religions, medicine and science were all based on seeing only a part-world, we would have a sense of how much more exciting and fulfilling life could be on this wonderful planet, if we could escape from our materialistic worldview and accept our place on Nature's interconnected plane.

But, like the crowd in Hans Andersen's tale going along with the naked Emperor's fantasies, we are all accomplices in this tragic charade. Schauberger put it forcefully:

> If humanity does not soon come to its senses, and realize that it has been misled and misinformed by its intellectual leaders, the prevailing laws of Nature (with poetic justice) will reliably act to bring about a fitting end to this ineptly contrived culture. Unfortunately, the most frightful catastrophes or scandalous disclosures will have to happen before people become aware that it is their own mistakes that have led to their undoing. These can be rectified only with great

difficulty, precisely because it was those in power principally who committed them. Rather than question themselves, these institutions and individuals, ever protective of their own interests, would allow millions of their fellow human beings to perish before they would ever admit their errors.

A host of so-called experts is lined up against any systematic attempt to correct these errors. They are obliged to advocate the course they have championed, because it is their livelihood and they wish to be looked after until the end of their days. Yet, even this obstacle might be overcome if the mistakes could be restricted at least to a particular branch of industry. A thorough analysis of the most common mistakes made over the centuries reveals the enormous extent of the malaise arising from flawed principles and perverse practices. It reveals such grave cultural, technological and economic violations that no branch of industry is left untouched. Not even a partially unaware expert can absolve himself of blame, whatever his chosen field.

At the outset a powerful opposition must be reckoned with. It would be futile to expect any support from experts when, under these circumstances, it is obvious that nearly every one of them would be threatened. But this obstacle should cause no alarm, for we are not concerned here with the livelihood of a few, but with the survival of the whole of hoodwinked humanity. The attitude of many of our young people today certainly provides clear evidence that humanity is still morally healthy. They militate vehemently against the signs of decay emerging everywhere and refuse to continue to trot mindlessly down the road... that has led us into an economic and cultural cul-de-sac.

Opposition alone, however, achieves nothing. Our youth will achieve any practical success in their struggle only when the causes are identified and the errors are revealed that previous generations and we have made, so plunging the world into disaster.[2]

Schauberger wrote often of how balance is one of Nature's most urgent requirements. He would comment on how humanity is contravening Nature's law of balance. Amongst these imbalances are the enormous inequalities in wealth and opportunity in almost every country on the globe; a totally unacceptable level of persecution, abuse and lack of human rights; the pursuit of mindless, hedonistic and materialistic activities; and above all a lack of compassion or respect for fellow human beings of whatever origin, and for the animal and plant kingdoms. These are not *moral* observations of humankind, but part of a detached view of why we are violating the health of Nature or the planetary biosphere.

In Chapter Two, you may remember, when we discussed how all material objects are composed of atoms and particles in constant motion, it becomes possible to understand that everything is energy. There are different kinds of energy; thoughts and feelings are energy. Energy has qualities as well as frequency. Energies and actions of differing qualities affect each other favourably or adversely. For example, the crucial ingredients of the human being's gift of free will are *intention* and *commitment*. The quality of the intention (self-important/greedy *or* loving/compassionate) affects the quality of all our actions and their outcomes. Healing of any kind or at any level is affected by the quality of the healer's energy. In one's experience this becomes quite clear, yet apparently it is beyond the ken of contemporary science. Viktor Schauberger was amazed that this basic knowledge was not part of our education.

Viktor was attuned to the wider field of knowledge, and felt that our educational system greatly contributes to our society's limited worldview. He did not specifically write about this topic, but the following quote from a recent study very much sums up what he felt, and helps us to understand where things have to change:

> Our much-vaunted educational system specializes in instilling the known. There is a token and often grossly insufficient acknowledgment of the process of knowing. The knower is the Cinderella of almost every educational system. Self-awareness is actually obscured by conventional education, which cultivates a mentality of splitting, separating and compartmentalizing. Knowledge is gained of separate disciplines which are greatly divorced from the knower, isolated from each other and cut off from their connection to life lived in the world. As a result, by the time pupils leave school, if they are lucky their minds may have been fairly well-honed, but they are tuned to specialization and the particular, adept at putting things in boxes with labels, rather than being open to

the larger field of knowledge. Their energies may be well channeled, but they display only a fraction of the creative innocence and appetite for life and learning of a small child. (Ardui and Wrycza, *The Way of Unfolding*)[3]

What of the future?

Viktor Schauberger realized that the human community had little time to change its ways and begin to follow Nature's laws, before the inevitable reckoning that Nature will require of humanity. He had a rather touching faith in the ability of the younger generation to overthrow the oligarchies of power. However, in the last fifty years, the ability of a controlled media, especially television, to manipulate and undermine cultural behaviour, and the apparent irreversibility of the drug culture, have discouraged hope of initiatives coming from the young.[4]

The years since Schauberger's death have also seen the tentacles of multinational corporations reaching into every country in the world, capitalism at its worst. The capitalist system which has developed in the past 500 years or so, has brought unprecedented wealth to millions across the world. This increase in people's individual incomes (which admittedly expands their choices) has come at the appalling cost of pulling humanity as a whole out of balance with its environment; it is the enemy of biodiversity, and therefore of Nature. Until our human society has more interest in moral and ethical concerns than in making money, we are probably stuck with capitalism, for state ownership of industry has not always proved particularly workable.

The other structure with which we seem to be saddled is so-called democracy, which despite its name, has proved to be nearly as corrupt a way of centralizing power as any totalitarian system. If we wish to participate in society, we are committed to some extent to collude with these systems.

If more choices were made on moral and ethical grounds, rather than self-interest, the capitalist system might be doomed. However, if we can begin to see that the engine that drives Nature and its evolutionary processes has its origin in the supreme spiritual centre and source of all creativity (of which Nature is the mirror), then our moral principles would have a more stable foundation. Nature has no morality; but its laws seem to have been designed by the supreme consciousness to harmonize with the moral and ethical standards set by 'God' for humanity (e.g. The Ten Commandments). The most relevant of Nature's laws for us are perhaps the laws of Balance, of Biodiversity, and of Evolution towards higher consciousness.

On present performance, it is doubtful whether the human community can remain viable into the twenty-second century; the seeds of our self-destruction have been sown so widely. I have always felt that it would take a worldwide disaster to bring about the collapse of our corrupt systems, which could return decision making to the place where it really belongs – the local community, in respectful relationship to its natural environment; which, we must accept, has happened in the past.

Dr Dorothy Rowe, the distinguished psychologist, said in a recent interview: 'Ninety-nine percent of suffering isn't caused by natural disasters; it's caused by the ideas we hold. And if we believe these ideas are absolute truths, then we suffer and we force other people to suffer. But if we believe that our ideas are ideas we have created, then we know we're free to change them.'[5]

Implementing Schauberger's vision

It is clear that many are now responding to Viktor's call to become familiar with Nature's laws and to work with them. They are recognizing that this is the only way to start turning back from the terminal disasters that otherwise surely await humankind. As with any significant changes of consciousness in human history, a few pioneers become the leaven through which all of society starts to wake up and, like a cosmic shift, the awakening becomes unstoppable.

What follows are examples of what these pioneers are up to. For the most part these are very practical projects, often to do with water purification, river management or energy generation. What these innovations often have in common is the influence of the spiral or of vortex energy. The one area that is missing is that of implosive energy generation. Without Viktor's models and detailed drawings, it is hard to see how anyone can crack that nut, unless someone in American or Russian intelligence leaks some vital notes (as with Evgeny Podkletnov).

There is, however, the theory of spontaneous or synchronistic origination, which some claim accounted for the simultaneous discovery of electricity and other significant technical breakthroughs. When the time is right and the need is great, perhaps some higher intelligence with a concern for human evolution has cooperated through Nature to sow simultaneously the necessary seeds in a number of fertile minds.

Contact addresses and websites for individuals and groups mentioned here, and others, are found in Resources, on p.276.

SWEDEN

Olof Alexandersson is a Swedish engineer who became interested in Viktor Schauberger's research in 1956 and wrote the excellent introductory book *Living Water: Viktor Schauberger and the Secrets of Natural Energy*. He did not meet Viktor, but developed a friendship with his son Walter and met many of Viktor's old friends and colleagues. In 1963 he formed the Swedish Science Group for Biotechnical Technology which produced (among other devices) an "apparatus for biological synthesis of spring water," which was similar to Viktor's Repulsator.

This important research is being carried on today by the **Institute for Ecological Technology (IET)** in Malmö, Sweden. IET was formed by Olof Alexandersson as a foundation to continue the work of Biotechnical Technology. In the early 1980s IET organized an expedition to the Ouluanka Nature national park in Finland. Its aim was to verify Viktor's observations in an untouched natural environment. Later, IET replicated Schauberger's 'double water jets' experiment and (see p. 99) continued to work with the Repulsator.

Today IET is run as an association which evaluates, develops and applies Viktor Schauberger's ideas and theories. It operates a loose network, the IET-community, to help anyone who has an idea for a research project in the area, and runs networking seminars. IET helped with the organization of International Workshops for Natural Energies (IWONE 2001) in Leipzig and IWONE 2003 near Malmö, Sweden.

IET (which was known as the "Malmö group") has replicated Schauberger's Stuttgart experiments, interpreting them in the light of modern chaos and self-organizing systems research. Ongoing projects are mainly in three areas: for the purification, improvement and desalination of water; for energy production using ideas from the turbine in the Repulsine; and propulsion methods for air and water vehicles.

AUSTRIA

After his father died, Walter Schauberger set up, in 1962, the **Pythagoras Kepler School (PKS)** at Engleithen in the Salzkammergut mountains of Upper Austria. Walter was a physicist and mathematician, and set out to validate mathematically his father's research.[6] His particular interests were harmonic theories (the monochord) and conceptions of non-Euclidean geometry (plane sections of a hyperbolic cone). He never published his research; however, Callum Coats, who studied with Walter at the PKS, is currently writing up some of Walter's work. It was intended that Walter's eldest son, a physicist, Dr Tilman Schauberger should succeed him at the PKS but, in the event, Tilman died shortly after his father's death in 1994.

As a result, Walter's younger son Jörg gave up his work in the Austrian media to help save his grandfather's work. Aided by his wife, he runs courses at the PKS for those who wish to learn more about the Eco-technology heritage. Every year, there are usually about six seminars in German, with participants from Austria, Germany, Switzerland, but also from Italy, Hungary, the Benelux Countries or from Scandinavia. Less frequently they now also run international seminars in English, bringing together people from all over the world who are engaged in Schauberger-inspired research, to share their findings. Speakers at these seminars are specialists or technicians in water or environmental issues who are willing to follow unorthodox ways of studying how Nature works. Members of the PKS now give lectures in many different countries round the world.

Water and the vortex are the present main topics of study at the PKS. However, they intend to test Viktor's ideas for river balancing with energy bodies and flow guides to help rivers flow naturally and to protect valuable land and property from flooding.

The Schauberger Archives are open for research by appointment — see the PKS website. The PKS copper gardening tools, books, cards and videos are on sale by mail order.

GERMANY

Although Viktor's contemporaries have long since gone, and also most of Walter's, there are still some who knew them. Dr Norbert Harthun has re-formed his **Gruppe der Neuen** (the New Group),

Fig.19.1. Flowform.

Fig.19.2 Vortex energizer.

whose aims are to explore Viktor and Walter Schauberger's theories and to interpret them in contemporary scientific idiom.

In 1967 the terms "environmental pollution" and "environmental protection" were virtually unheard of. At that time nobody demanded a gentle technology, friendly to Nature. In that year Walter Schauberger, a scientist who was then a 'lone voice,' gave a lecture on "Biologically Oriented Technology," in the centre of the heavily polluted Ruhr (the main coal mining area of Germany). Inspired by Walter's message, Norbert Harthun, and a few other specialists, persuaded Walter to join the Gruppe der Neuen in Aachen to promote a technology that conformed with Nature's laws. The Group also decided to launch their own scientific bulletin *Mensch und Technik — naturgemäß* to publish articles about the possibilities of a new science for working with Nature. This innovative journal has now been a leader in its field for 26 years.

Members of the Group have given many lectures at home and abroad on the theme of how to restore good heart to Nature and the environment as part of a requirement for a high quality of life. The pioneering work of this and similar groups has initiated a change in awareness that was inconceivable thirty years ago. The "Gruppe der Neuen" has remained consistently independent from institutions and sponsors. It is still active, and its website gives details of its published articles.

Implosion is a quarterly magazine founded in 1958 by Aloys Kokaly, generally aimed at the lay reader, which is still published quarterly or semi-annually by Klaus Rauber. It has been, without doubt, the richest repository of Viktor Schauberger's writing (in German), and has been the source of substantial portions of the Eco-technology series.

BRITAIN

John Wilkes, an artist and sculptor at Emerson College in Sussex, has pioneered the **Virbela Flowforms**, which are a series of formed basins, arranged on sloping ground, to stimulate a water flow into figure-of-eight vortical movements, causing the water to pulsate rhythmically (Fig. 19.1). This movement simulates a mountain stream, energizing, restructuring and oxygenating the water. His first Flowform installed near Stockholm, Sweden in 1973, which is part of a biological sewage recycling system for a community of 200, has been a great success. The recently established Flow Design Research Institute, through the Virbela International Association, has contacts in 35 countries that have led to more than 1000 installations in over thirty countries, their purposes ranging from the aesthetic and educational to biological purification, farming, interior air conditioning and medical/therapeutic use. For further information, see Wilkes' *Flowforms: the Rhythmic Power of Water.*

Wilkes studied projective geometry under the distinguished mathematician George Adams, joining him at the Institut für Strömungswissenschaften (Flow Research Institute) at Herrischried in Germany, where he later collaborated with Theodor Schwenk (see *Sensitive Chaos*). It is tempting to believe that Schauberger's insights about water probably share a common source with those of Adams. Certainly people often tend to link Wilkes' Flowforms with Schauberger's vision of water.

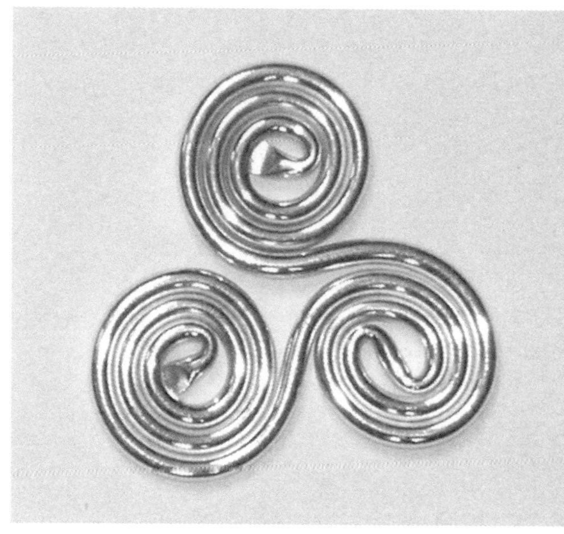

Fig. 19.3 Triple harmonizer.

Implementations, a British group which markets the Schauberger-inspired copper gardening tools is also developing a full-sized phosphor bronze "Golden Plough" in order to run tests to replicate the increases in fertility that Viktor found with his prototype.

A novel initiative combining healing techniques with the Schauberger vortex principle has been developed by the **Centre for Implosion Research** (CIR), in Plymouth. Specially imploded water is injected into a spiral-vortex cone-shaped copper pipe. The specific shape enables continual recharging of the imploded water from cosmic energy (the ether) always present in the environment, and is used to improve the quality of either standing water or drinking water supplies and to balance the energy in local environments (Fig. 19.2).

The CIR also produces much smaller, 'personal harmonizers,' flat spiral shaped tubular forms inspired from the spiral carvings found at the great Neolithic ritual site at New Grange in Ireland (Fig. 19.3). The small tubes contain imploded water, which is continually recharged by the environment because of their spiral form. Worn as ornaments or jewellery, they enhance the personal energy field and may be placed under a glass of water or a wineglass to improve the quality of the liquid. The great popularity of these devices is a compliment to their efficacy to improve energy or enhance individuals' sense of protection and of wellbeing (*see www.sulis-health.co.uk*).

Fig.19.4. Living Water Vortex Jug.

DENMARK

One of a number of vortex water treatment groups, Clean-Water has developed a very practical two-litre jug for home use. The **Living Water Vortex Jug** (Fig. 19.4) employs in its screw-down lid a small motor to drive a silver impeller that forms a splendid vortex in the water for 3½ minutes. It claims to erase impressions of the water's history of abuse, by superimposing more refined, constructive energies (see p.156). The water is restructured, cooled, softened and purified, and has been very well received worldwide.

USA

The pioneer spirit is still alive in the USA, and we expect to add many to our list of American Schauberger innovators. The interest in permaculture and biodynamic farming predisposes many towards Schauberger's vision.

One such is Dan Reese, who developed **Vortex Water Systems** in Texas, inspired by reading Alexandersson's *Living Water.* They are designed to solve the increasing problem of pollution of wells in the American South, by unwanted salts and minerals, and to restructure the water so that it feels smooth, uses less soap and tastes pure. The Vortex system (Fig. 19.5) has no moving parts or filters, does not use chemicals and is driven only by the force of the well pump.

Fig.19.5. Vortex Water System.

It was found that the system could be expanded to service as many as 76 homes from one well. A system is now being tested for removing mineral salts from a salt intrusion well and a larger farm system to help with the problem of cotton rot and to use less water to grow the same amount of crops. These will be major breakthroughs for the industry.

AUSTRALIA

As in the USA, many Australians are sympathetic to Schauberger's ideas. Many people depend on rivers for their water source. The author, Callum Coats, who has tested a number of Viktor's experiments, was inspired to design a well to receive water filtered from the river. A well should be dug about 5–10 metres from the river bank, depending on the size of the river, about 1.5 metres in diameter, the depth to correspond to the depth of the river bed. If the soil between the river and the well shaft is porous, the water will be filtered by the soil. If the soil is impervious, a channel connecting the river and well shaft should be dug and filled with fine sand to act as a filter. The well shaft must be entirely covered at the surface, to keep the well dark and cool and discourage the growth of pathogenic bacteria. The pump should be well away from the opening to avoid pollution, and the opening should be raised if there is any chance of the river flooding and pouring into the well *(see Living Energies, p.202.)* This system was first set up in 1972 and in recent contact with the present owner of the property (purchased in 1979) Callum Coats was told that the water supply had at all times functioned flawlessly, and still does.

Callum Coats is also involved in the making of a three-part video on Viktor Schauberger's theories in conjunction with Martin Selecki of 'Filmstream' in Byron Bay, NSW, as well as in the production of a 50 litre water cooling egg-shaped container in association with Phil Sedgman of 'Living Water Flow-Forms,' also of Byron Bay.

Endnotes

Introduction

1. *Living Energies*, p.28.
2. 'The Emergence of Biotechnology', by A.Khammas, *Implosion* magazine no.83, p.19.
3. The Schauberger Archives, Linz, Jan, 1952.
4. The scientific environment has considerably narrowed. Scientific research in the 1930s was largely government funded, and research for the most part was independent of commercial interest. Schauberger would be appalled by the present environment which, still identified with the material viewpoint, is now almost entirely dependent on industrial funding and the consequent demand that scientific research serves the needs of business and commerce. In addition, the anonymous 'peer review' system is a form of censorship against those who propose research that does not conform to convention, or which threatens the reviewer's own agenda.
5. *Living Energies*, p.9. His arch enemies, the Viennese Association of Engineers, had hatched a plot to dispose of him in a mental hospital, under SS observation. Schauberger was to go into the Vienna University clinic for a routine examination of his WWI wounds. Before this, by coincidence, he had tea with an old friend, Mrs Primavesi and told her he would return in twenty minutes. When he did not, and she found he had not returned home either, she went to the nearby clinic, whose director she knew well, refusing to leave until Viktor had been found. He turned up in the portion of the hospital reserved for the mentally insane, trussed up in a straightjacket waiting for the lethal injection (the standard practice for the disposal of undesirables in that regime). Needless to say, she quickly extricated him. (Another theory is that the plot against him was ordered by Hitler himself, who had met Schauberger.)
6. See also Chapter 18, p.252, for Richard St Barbe Baker's account.
7. Viktor Schauberger, *Our Senseless Toil.*

1. Schauberger's Vision

1. The Schauberger Archives.
2. Published in *Die Wasserwirtschaft*, no.20, 1930.
3. *Ancient Futures: Learning from Ladakh*, by Helen Norberg-Hodge.

2. Different Kinds of Energy

1. A few years ago, it was established by precise calculation that the bumblebee's body weight prohibits it from flying, according to the laws of aerodynamics. (Just as well the humble bee wasn't told.) Clearly there is much that conventional science does not understand about Nature!
2. Teilhard de Chardin, priest-scientist, was the first to propose this, in answer to his ongoing question: 'How can the two realms of our experience, the outer and inner worlds, be reconciled?' David Bohm went further, insisting that matter and energy are one and the same. He described two orders, the Explicate Order being what we can measure and to some extent describe; and the Implicate Order which we cannot measure, and in our present state of knowledge and evolution, cannot adequately describe.
3. The implication of this natural law is that compassion will triumph over selfishness, generosity over greed, a law more evident higher up the evolutionary ladder. This outcome may at present look distant, but if we believe that it is meant to be, then our small attempts to make changes should gain the cooperation of all-powerful Nature. This is similar to the Christian belief that God will cooperate if only we take the first steps. Also, see 'Opposites working towards Balance' (p.52).
4. The qualities of higher dimensions are: Fourth — Time (control of space/time); Fifth — Presence (outside of space/time); Sixth — Potential (the creative state which is non-dimensional); Seventh — Gateway to the Divine.
5. These diagrams are from *From Atoms to Angels* by Paul Walsh-Roberts, a very accessible introduction to these concepts.
6. Another important by-product of quantum physics research is the work of US physicist Hugh Everett, who in 1957 observed that when a measurement is performed on a quantum system, all possible outcomes of the measurement actually occur; this contrasts with the conventional view that only one of many possible states is ever observed. His proposal leads to the conclusion that the Universe is constantly dividing to give vast numbers of alternative universes that co-exist, but do not interact with each other, and that we live in a single one of these many universes.
7. For a good introduction to the dimensional shift and how it will affect us all, see Cori, *The Cosmos of Soul* (details in Bibliography).
8. See further particularly in Chapter 3. Callum Coats calls this resolution of apparently conflicting elements 'dialectic thinking,' by which unity is found (*Living Energies*, pp.61–64, esp. table p.63), and quotes Hegel defining this as, 'the process of thought by which such contradictions are seen to merge themselves in a higher truth that comprehends them.'
9. *Living Energies*, p.74.

3. The Attraction and Repulsion of Opposites

1. The ozone layer filters out the harmful ultra-violet rays known as UVa and UVb. The UVc, which have a different wavelength, are allowed through, and play a large part in the growth of organisms (for instance, helping to build healthy bones).
2. Viktor Schauberger once commented wryly that instead of asking himself what caused the apple to fall to the ground, Sir Isaac Newton should have asked how it got up there in the first place!

4. Nature's Patterns and Shapes

1. *Your Body Doesn't Lie* (Behavioral Kinesiology) by John Diamond MD, Harper and Row, New York, 1979.
2. This is the basis of the 'muscle test' to discover foods that may be toxic for someone. The subject holds the sample (maybe a bottle of wine) in the left hand, or to

their chest, while the 'tester' tries to push down the raised right arm of the subject, who tries to resist the pressure. If the arm has lost muscle tone, the food may have an undesirable effect on the subject.

3. *Living Energies*, p.42.
4. If they are above absolute zero (–273°C).
5. BBC *Wildlife* magazine, June 2001.
6. For an account of Backster's work, see Bird and Tompkins, *The Secret Life of Plants.*
7. *Cymatics: The Study of the Interrelationship of Wave-forms with Matter*, by Hans Jenny, Basilius Press, Basle, 1966.
8. Democritus (460–370 BC)
9. Callum Coats shows scores of examples from Nature in *Living Energies*, pp.51–53.
10. Harold S. Burr, *Blueprint for Immortality: Electrical Patterns of life Discovered*, Spearman, 1972.
11. Lawrence Edwards: *The Vortex of Life: Nature's Patterns in Time and Space*, Floris Books, 1993.
12. Earth's diameter is 7,920 miles; the Moon's is 2,160.
13. Named after a twelfth century Italian mathematician born in Pisa, Leonardo Fibonacci or Filio Bonaccio. The son of an Italian customs agent based in Alexandria, he helped to bring Arabic numbers to the Roman world and popularized the modern decimal system of numbers. The series bearing his name progresses by adding the two previous numbers to make the next, e.g. 1, 1, 2, 3, 5, 8, 13, 21, 34, 55, 89, etc. (It is said that he used it as a model for the growth of a population of rabbits.) Dividing a Fibonacci number by the number before it produces the Golden Mean proportion (the Golden Ratio) in increasing accuracy of decimal places, the larger the number.
14. Walter Schauberger's research of this phenomenon was groundbreaking.

5. Energy Production

1. There is controversy about whether human activities are the *cause* of global warming. Climate change goes through enormous cycles. In Britain, for example, from 1,000 years ago when it was much warmer than now (grapes were grown in Scotland), to 200–300 years ago when the ice on the Thames could support an elephant, with many fluctuations in between. We have insufficient records to say with certainty that the present accelerated warming world-wide is cyclical in its origin. However, there is little doubt that its increasingly severe impact is greatly compounded by the enormous output of carbon emissions (*Observer*, January 5, 2003). See also Chap.13, note 1.
2. The average fuel consumption of a typical car allows a journey of 620 miles (1000km) for an energy expenditure of 1000kW, or one person's annual energy consumption. In terms of oxygen consumed, a car driven at 50kph requires 22.25kg of oxygen, roughly 750 times the amount needed by a human being for the same period. In eleven hours, the car has consumed the oxygen one human being requires for a year. Callum Coats calculated that to replenish the oxygen devoured by the world's roughly 450 million vehicles would require a healthy productive forest of 38 million km^2, or 28% of the total world's total land area.
3. Kilowatt hours.
4. The ratio between created matter and the energies required to create it was established in 1984 by the Nobel awarded Swiss atomic scientist Dr Carlos Riebers as about 1:1 thousand million, effectively the proportion of the whole of reality of which we are aware.
5. Entropy has its counterpart — ectropy (sometimes called 'negentropy'). The laws of entropy or thermodynamics apply to the products of our mechanistic science as it is a 'closed' system. Nature, however, is an open system, and one finds in fact that entropic tendencies are held in check by the predominant ectropic ones, otherwise life could never have developed. Evolution is essentially ectropic or energy integrative rather than energy dissipative, as increasingly complex organizations harmonically stabilize more energy.
6. Weston Price: *Nutrition and Physical Degeneration*, 1938, 1945, 1998. As an experienced dentist, he noted the degeneration of jaw and bone structure, but also the deterioration in intelligence that ensued from a change to western diet.
7. *Living Energies*, p.35.
8. See *Living Energies*, pp. 50–55 for further illustrations of spiral forms in Nature.
9. H.H.Price, Wyckham professor of Logic at Oxford (Hibbert Jour, 1949).

6. *Motion — the Key to Balance*

1. Viktor Schauberger, *Implosion* magazine no.51, p.22.
2. Viktor Schauberger, *Implosion* magazine no.48, 1954.
3. A hyperbolic spiral represents the physically nonmaterial centre-less dynamic of Nature's outside>inward motion. The *phi* spiral is the dynamic of inside>outward physical and material growth.
4. *Ibid.* p.56.
5. Dr Tilman Schauberger, Viktor's grandson and an expert on his work, described his grandfather's ideal spiral-vortical motion, the 'Cycloid Spiral Space-curve,' as goal-oriented, structured, concentrated, intensifying, condensing, dynamic, self-organizing, self-divesting of the less valuable, rhythmical (cyclical), sinuous, pulsing, in-rolling, centripetal (and out-rolling centrifugal) movement. This applies also to Figs 12.1 and 12.2.
6. If the starting radius is 1 and the initial resistance is 1 on an inwinding path, when the radius is halved, the resistance is $[\frac{1}{2}]^2 = \frac{1}{4}$ and the rotational periodicity, frequency or velocity is doubled.

7. *The Atmosphere and Electricity*

1. High specific heat means that water is slow to heat up, but also slow to cool. Its heat retaining quality makes it good for heat storage systems.
2. The temperature neither decreases nor increases constantly, but fluctuates as we ascend through the various atmospheric layers, so that at a certain altitude, at around 7 miles (12km) for instance, the temperature is –76°F (–60°C), whereas around 31 miles (50km) it is 50°F (+10°C).
3. This increases by the inverse square of the separation. If, for example, the separation is 10mm, then the potential is 12. If the separation is reduced to ½, i.e. 5mm, then the potential is 22 (=4) and so on, as shown in Fig. 12.6. The smaller the separation, therefore, the greater the corresponding potential, which could be unleashed once the *permittivity* of the dielectric has been overcome. (Permittivity is the amount a substance can assist or resist the transfer of an electric charge.)
4. Pure water has a dielectric value of 81, which is 81 times greater than a vacuum

(=1). A thin layer of pure water vapour may therefore have the capacity to resist the transfer of enormous charges, permitting the accumulation of very large voltages and potential. The concentric layers of water vapour with a temperature of 4°C may thus act like a spherical condenser, formed of nesting spheres which charge the Earth with energy.

5. Being in a lower dynamic and more harmonically stabilized energetic state, the greater density of water vapour at increasingly lower altitudes may well correspond through resonance to the lower wavelengths of the incident radiation, whose frequency has been reduced by contact with the braking effect of the atmosphere, thus creating the medium with which radio-waves are reflected back to Earth.
6. For elaboration of how this can be demonstrated, the reader may read Coats' description of Lord Kelvin's and Walter Schauberger's experiments (*Living Energies*, pp.95–99).
7. Leopold Brandstätter, *Implosion statt Explosion*, self-publication, Linz 10, Fach 20, Austria.
8. *Living Energies*, p.100.
9. Kenneth David and John Day: *Water — The Mirror of Science*, p.149, Heinemann Educational, 1964.
10. A 1°C rise in temperature causes the retention, but not necessarily an even distribution, of an additional 1,000 million cubic metres of water vapour in the atmosphere *(Living Energies*, p.100).

8. The Nature of Water

1. *Our Senseless Toil*, Pt.I, p.11.
2. See *The Divining Hand* by Christopher Bird.
3. Davis, K.A. and Day, J.A., *Water — The Mirror of Science*, 1964.
4. *Implosion* magazine, no.8., 1945.
5. How to obtain safe drinking water is dealt with in Chapter 12.
6. Viktor first came to the attention of hydrologists in 1922 with his revolutionary water-flume design for transporting logs inexpensively from inaccessible untouched mountain forests without the usual high rate of damage of conventional methods. This, his first encounter with opposition from the scientific establishment, is well described in both *Living Water* and in *Living Energies*.
7. The extra 'e' enlarges the meaning of the usual 'carbon,' to include a whole range of elements used in forming the physical structures of life (see further on p.51).
8. Viktor Schauberger, *Our Senseless Toil*, Pt.I, p.4.

9. The Hydrological Cycle

1. *The Memory of Water — Homeopathy and the Battle of Ideas in the New Science* by Michel Schiff, Thorsons, 1995. Callum Coats has more on Benveniste's research and the controversy around it, in *Living Energies*, pp. 119–121.
2. The temperatures indicated on the following diagrams do not necessarily conform to actual temperatures, but are intended to demonstrate the process.

10. The Formation of Springs

1. The French for spring is *source*.
2. Callum Coats adopted an impeller design taken from Schauberger's 1936 patent for an air turbine.

11. Rivers and How they Flow

1. From Viktor Schauberger's treatise, 'Temperature and the Movement of Water' ('Temperatur und Wasserbewegung'): *Die Wasserwirtschaft*, No.20, 1930.
2. Schauberger also pioneered new designs and built fourteen such dams. For information on this, see *Living Energies* pp.159, 160, and *The Water Wizard*, pp.101, 121, 122–34, 209.
3. See also *The Water Wizard*, p.207.
4. Schauberger established that turbulence was a natural automatic acceleration-restricting brake in flowing water, in a treatise he published entitled 'Turbulence.'
5. Callum Coats in *Living Energies*, pp.176–7 describes one he saw.

12. Supplying Water

1. *The Ecologist*, May 30, 1999.
2. International Water Management Institute.
3. *Guardian Weekly*, March 14, 2001. The UN Department of Economic and Social Affairs estimated that six countries will account for half the increase: India, Bangladesh, Pakistan, China, Indonesia and Nigeria. Their startling projection is based on the assumption that fertility will continue to decline. The population explosion would be even more dramatic but for the HIV/AIDS epidemic. The report noted that increased international migration would be one consequence. The pressure on food resources will be enormous, but the impact on water supplies for the developing countries will be nothing less than catastrophic.
4. *National Geographic* magazine, 'Earth's Fresh Water under Pressure,' Sep. 2002
5. *The Ecologist*, May 30, 1999.
6. *National Geographic* magazine, ibid.
7. *The Ecologist*, May 30, 1999.
8. *Ibid.*, Caspar Henderson.
9. *Ibid.*
10. Viktor Schauberger, *Our Senseless Toil.*
11. *Fluoride — Drinking Ourselves to Death?* by Barry Groves is a well-informed source of factual information on this subject. (Gill and Macmillan, 2001)
12. *Ibid.*
13. Waldblott, McKinney and Burgstahler: *Fluoridation: The Great Dilemma*, Coronado Press, 1978: 288.
14. *Jour. Dent. Res.* 1990; 69:723–7.
15. 'Living in a democratic fluoridated country,' *Australian Fluoridation News*, Sep–Oct 1995; 31 (5).
16. Barry Groves, *Fluoride: Drinking ourselves to Death?*, p.227. Gill and Macmillan, 2001.
17. Viktor Schauberger, *Nature as Teacher*, p.5.
18. The best ones have a four-stage system: ceramic for bacteria, carbon for chemicals and organic contaminants, ion exchange for heavy metals, and block carbon for final cleansing; the filters being easy to change, every six months.
19. We discussed higher energies interpenetrating our physical world in Chapter 2.
20. *Our Senseless Toil*, Pt.II, p.14.
21. The energies are essentially dynagens, or growth-promoting, created by the biometal composition — silver (male), and copper (female); the silver also has bactericidal properties. Dynagens are also produced by the centripetal movement of the main water body flowing down the centre, raising the overall vitality, life-energy and wholesomeness of the water.
22. Callum Coats describes these experiments in detail in *Living Energies*.

23. *Our Senseless Toil*, Pt.II, p.34.
24. Heart specialists were recently astonished to discover that blood flow through the heart and arteries depended on a spiral movement (*New Scientist,* Feb. 6, 2001).
25. 'Hydrodynamics of Blood Flow,' by Dr. Ernst O. Attinger, Div. Biomedical Engineering, University of Virginia Medical Centre, Charlottesville, VA 22901, USA.

13. The Role of the Forest

1. From the Schauberger Archives.
2. 'The Dying Forest' ('Der sterbende Wald'), by Viktor Schauberger, Pt.1: *Tau* magazine. Vol.151, Nov.1936, p.30.
3. The Gulf Stream, which gives north-west Europe an exceptionally mild climate, might fail for two reasons: (a) the inability of the failing Amazonian heat engine to push the stream from the Caribbean; (b) the cold, salty waters around Greenland power two 'pumps' which draw the warm Gulf Stream towards Northwest Europe, and send cold water back southwards. The heavy cold water streaming down the coasts of Greenland pours into the abysses, propelling forward the lighter and warmer Gulf Stream. Fresh water from the melting Greenland icecap could weaken the pumps and close down the Gulf Stream. An important new theory is that, within a few years of the failure of the Gulf Stream pumps off Greenland, a new mini ice age would quickly spread in the North Atlantic, with temperatures dropping by 10°F in north-eastern USA and in Western Europe (Woods Hole Oceanographic Institute Report, *Nexus*, Feb.2003 and especially see www.whoi.edu). Interestingly, over seventy years ago, Viktor Schauberger predicted that over-clearing of forest and critical mismanagement of water supplies would lead to a new ice age (in *Our Senseless Toil*).
4. Soil under forest floors retains ten times more water than nearby grassland. The Amazonian basin was almost devoid of humid tropical rainforest in the last glaciations. Clearing the forest produces high contrast between day and night temperatures, gusty winds and dry soil. Clear-cutting and burning cause dieback in neighbouring forest; water table disappears and desertification ensues.
5. 1.5 to 2 million animal species live in the forest canopy. A profusion of epiphytes (ferns, orchids, and so on) takes up nutrients flushed down by heavy rain. All nutrients are retained within the entire system, and provide for the lateral expansion of the forest. Medicinal plants are common, many of which are as yet unresearched and may be lost forever. The tropical rainforest environment exhibits the highest levels of evolutionary development and biodiversity.
6. 'Destroy the Amazon — Destroy the World' by Peter Bunyard, *The Ecologist,* Jul/Aug 2002
7. The Amazonian Forest produces latent heat to drive air masses in three separate directions:
   1. Crossing the Caribbean to Florida, helps drive the Gulf Stream NE
   2. Over the Andes into the Pacific westerly, following the trade winds
   3. Southwards, towards Patagonia

   In the temperate latitudes, rainfall is derived from moisture-laden winds blowing in from the oceans. The tropical rainforests, on the other hand, particularly the Amazonian, actually create rainfall and recycle it. Only 25% of the Sun's energy heats the air. The remaining 75% is converted into 'latent heat' by evapo-transpiration, the mechanism through which water is pumped into the atmosphere from the leaves and stems of the plants. The humid air rises rapidly, forming cumulo-nimbus and layered clouds that irrigate areas further downwind, releasing the latent heat energy back into the atmosphere. Two-thirds of the world's rainfall is affected by these cloud systems that also produce most of the world's lightning in a narrow band on either side of the Equator, helping to power the outreach of surplus energy from Amazonia to neighbouring countries.
8. Except when the El Niño is operating a contrary wind system.
9. Permaculture Institute, P.O.Box 1, Pyalgum 2480, NSW, Australia. Permaculture International Ltd, P.O.Box 6039, South Lismore 2480, Australia.

14. The Life and Nature of Trees

1. Viktor Schauberger insisted that we must understand more about the vital importance of trees for our environment. This chapter, except for the last section, is relatively standard information about trees which, as the highest form of the vegetable kingdom, have a mediating role with the animal kingdom.
2. From *Design in Nature* by J. Bell Pettigrew, Longman Green, 1908, p.671
3. Adapted from *Health and Light* by Dr. John N.Ott: Devin-Adair, Greenwich CT, USA, 1973.
4. There is an intriguing exception to this rule. Balsa, the softest wood of all, grows in certain equatorial forests. This suggests that the wood-quality-determining frequency has proceeded past the point where hardwoods are created and has re-entered the resonant conditions of the softwood-generating frequencies, although one full octave below, because balsawood is a magnitude softer than the softest of normal softwoods.
5. Schauberger found that the quality of resonant timber could be improved by submersion in a highly energetic mountain stream. In fact, the timber for the famous Stradivarius violins that had superb resonance was from mulberry that had fallen into alpine streams.
6. See Wertheimer, N., 'Electrical Wiring Configurations and Childhood Cancer': *American Journal of Epistemiology* (Mar.1979). Also: Perry, S. and Pearly, L., 'Power Frequency Magnetic Fields and Illness in Multi-Storey Blocks,' *Public Health* (1988) p.102. See also: Dowdson, D. et al., 'Overhead High Voltage Cables and Recurrent Headaches and Depression': *Practitioner*, 1988, pp.435–6.
7. Cowan, D. and Girdlestone, R. in *Safe as Houses?* describe the German researcher Volkrodt's theory of the resonance similarity of some trees' leaves and needles to microwave receivers.
8. *Ibid.*
9. Girdlestone regards brief exposure to a microwave oven *in good condition* not to be dangerous. The problem, he says, is that acceptable emissions vary internationally; he quotes one German test in which nearly all the 101 ovens emitted more than the makers' guarantee, but passed the German requirements, while all would have failed the Russian standard.
10. Callum Coats gives a fuller description of photosynthesis in *Living Energies*, pp.218–220, from which our table is reproduced.
11. See Bunyard, *The Breakdown of Climate*, p.77.

15. The Metabolism of the Tree

1. Viktor Schauberger, *Our Senseless Toil,* Pt.II, p.34.
2. For greater detail on this experiment, see Viktor's description in *The Water Wizard*, pp.50–52, or Callum Coats in *Living Energies*, pp.131–32. Callum also describes another experiment designed by William Morgan in the 1860s that shows the action of true springs.
3. Diagrams from *Wurzelatlas; mitteleuropaischer Grunlandpflanzen*, Vol.1, 'Monocotyledoneae' 1982, and Vol.2, 'Pteridophyta und Dicotyledoneae,' 1992, by L.Kutschera and E.Lichtenegger: G.Fischer, Stuttgart, Germany.

16. Soil Fertility and Cultivation

1. *Tau* magazine, Vol.146, p.11, 1936.
2. *Our Senseless Toil*, Pt.I, p.13.
3. From the Schauberger Archives.
4. *Genetic Engineering,* by Mae-Wan Ho, Gateway 1998, Gill and Macmillan, 2000.

17. Organic Cultivation

1. *The Survival of Civilization*, self-published by John Hamaker and Don Weaver.
2. Further detailed information on rock dust can be obtained from any of the following: Don Weaver, P.O.Box 1961, Burlingame, CA 94010, USA; Joanna Campe, ed. of *Remineralize the Earth*, 152 South St., Northampton, MD 01060, USA; Barry Oldfield, president, 'Men of the Trees,' 3 Over Avenue, Lesmurdie 6076, W. Australia; *Das Buch von Steinmehl* by Helmut Snoek: Orac-Pietsch, Germany.
3. Alex Podolinsky's work is fully elaborated in *The Secrets of the Soil*, by Christopher Bird: Harper, New York
4. Austrian Patent No.265991.
5. *Implosion*, No.45, p.3.
6. Excerpt from a letter from Viktor Schauberger to Dagmar Sarkar in the mid-1950s; the diagram has been redrawn and annotated by Callum Coats for greater clarity.
7. An alternative egg-shaped amniotic liquid manure transformer is described on p.273 of *Living Energies*.
8. Viktor Schauberger, *Implosion* magazine.
9. Viktor Schauberger uses the prefix *ur-* to indicate what he called the 'first born' or basically primeval.
10. Schauberger Archives, Linz, January 1952.
11. Viktor Schauberger, *Our Senseless Toil.*
12. Excerpt from a letter from Viktor Schauberger to Dagmar Sarkar in the mid-1950s; the diagram has been redrawn and annotated by Callum Coats for greater clarity.
13. *Implosion* magazine, No.37, p.8.

18. Harnessing Implosion Power

1. *The Hunt for Zero Point*, by Nick Cook, Century 2001. Nick Cook is a veteran aerospace researcher; he is Aviation Editor and Aerospace Consultant to *Jane's Defence Weekly*, the world's leading military affairs journal, and Industry/Defence Editor of *Interavia*, the aerospace trade publication.
2. *Ibid.*
3. For background, refer to 'After 50 years the Cover-up Conspiracy goes on' by Hamish Mackenzie (*Sunday Express,* June 16, 2002), on Dr Stephen Greer's 'Disclosure Project' to persuade Congress to set up an open hearing on the secrecy surrounding the US government's UFO and alien contact and research programmes. The big US corporations like Boeing, Lockheed Martin, Northrop Grumman would benefit most from alien technology.
4. *The Hunt for Zero Point*, Nick Cook.
5. Viktor Schauberger, *Implosion* magazine, no.71, p.12.
6. Viktor Schauberger, *Implosion* magazine, no.83, p.17.
7. *Living Energies*, p.276. The Schauberger quote is from *Mensch und Technik*, year 24, vol.2, 1993.
8. Callum Coats cites Russian research published in 1992, which describes space as multi-layered (layers, if you like, belonging to different dimensions); and a vacuum, not a 'curved void' as usually understood, but to be composed of elementary vacuum particles resulting from the conversion of actual electrons and protons into virtual states which exist, not in our space, but in a complementary layer. (*Living Energies*, p.276)
9. Letter to Aloys Kokaly in 1953 — *Implosion* magazine, no.29, p.22.
10. From St Barbe Baker's Foreword to *The Schauberger Departure*, (September 28, 1980) which was the original title for what subsequently became *Living Energies.*
11. Callum Coats commented that the water she poured in was probably charged with silicates, which Viktor considered essential to healthy water. The natural oscillating concentrative vortical flow in healthy streams also produced Viktor's 'emulsions' from the fine dispersions of minerals and trace elements (including silicates) which endow the upstream-moving water with the levitational energies that enable trout or salmon to negotiate high waterfalls.
12. A. Khammas in *Implosion* magazine.
13. *Living Energies*, p.287.
14. These phenomena are discussed in greater detail in *Living Energies*, pp.275–93, and particularly in *Energy Evolution.*
15. Viktor Schauberger, *Implosion* magazine, No.36, p.3.

19. Viktor Schauberger and Society

1. Increasingly, one is drawn to Gurdjieff's dictum, that humanity is asleep, or to change the metaphor, the blind are leading the blind.
2. *Our Senseless Toil.*
3. Unpublished ms. The authors are NLP trainers. Peter Wrycza's book *Living Awareness — Awakening to the roots of Learning and Perception* was published by Gateway in 1997. A few pioneers in education have attempted to redress this overemphasis on absorbing discrete facts that have no connection to the student, by adopting a more holistic, inclusive, approach. The most successful of these have probably been Maria Montessori (Montessori schools for the younger ages) and Rudolf Steiner (the Waldorf Schools) for the whole age range.
4. 'Fast Forward into Trouble' by Cathy Scott-Clark and Adrian Levy (*Guardian Weekend*, June 14, 2003) on how murder, fraud, and drug offences are plaguing the peaceful Buddhist idyll of Bhutan, only four years after the introduction of 46 cable TV channels.
5. Interview by Ursula Kenny in *The Observer*, September 1, 2002, in connection with the publication of Dr Rowe's book *Beyond Fear*, Harper Collins, 2002.
6. A short biography of Walter Schauberger can be found on the PKS website.

Resources

Schauberger- and Ecotechnology-associated websites and addresses
The following list was compiled on publication of this book, so ongoing revisions are inevitable. It may be possible to update this list in a revised edition, but a more practical solution is to review the list kept on our website: *www.schauberger-books.org.uk*

The Schauberger Institute and Research Centre, known as the PKS (Pythagoras Kepler School), of which Jörg Schauberger, Viktor's grandson, is the director:PKS, Kaltenbach 162, A-4821, Lauffen, Bad Ischl, Austria. *www.pks.or.at*

Gruppe der Neuen, run by Dr Norbert Harthun, one of Walter Schauberger's colleagues: *www.gruppederneuen.de*

Callum Coats is the principal authority on Viktor and Walter Schauberger's research. He spent several years studying with Walter Schauberger and then, over a period of nearly twenty years, set about translating and editing most of the archive of Viktor's writing. He is the author of *Living Energies* and the editor of the four-volume *Eco-technology* series: *www.Schauberger-Ecotechnology.com*

The UK networking centre's website *www.schauberger-books.org.uk* is run by Alick Bartholomew. It keeps an up-to-date list of various Schauberger-related research projects around the world, and makes available English language Schauberger literature, CDs, videos and tapes.

The Living Water Vortex Jug and its little cousin the portable Aqua-Vortex, oxygenate and restructure the water, improving its energy and taste. These, a plumbed-in water filter that removes fluorides and the Personal Harmonisers may be obtained through Sulis Health, The Hollies, Wellow, Bath, BA2 8QJ, UK; *www.sulis-health.co.uk*

Institute of Ecological Technology (the Swedish Malmö group):
www.iet-community.org
An unofficial, but informative American website (though much of the text seems to have been drawn freely from *Living Energies*):
www.frank.germano.com/viktorschauberger.htm

The Schauberger Copper Gardening Tools are produced by Johannes Stadler at the PKS, Kaltenbach 162, A-4821, Lauffen, Austria. Email: stadler.cuprum@eunet.at

The UK agent is: Implementations, PO Box 2568, Nuneaton, CV10 9YR, UK *www.implementations.co.uk*

David Dennard has put on his website chapters of his useful book *The Pearl of Wisdom* which deals with the power of the Vortex: *www.whirl power.cc*

Water Vortex Systems, PO Box 1295, Bandera, Texas 78003, USA: *www.texashillcountrymall.com/vortex*

Dr Masaru Emoto's book *The Message from Water* (see Bibiography) may be obtained in the UK at : The Living Tree, Milland, Liphook, Hants. GU30 7JS, tel: 04428 741 572 (flower@atlas.co.uk); in the USA at: info@holisticnetworker.com. His website *www.hado.net* contains background to the research, some photographs and networking information.

www.altenergy.org: A good American site on the vortex and on implosion — professional and informative.

http//homepage.ntlworld.com: good elaboration of the principles of the vortex and of implosion.

www.vortrexscience.com: William Baumgartners's site; implosion-online newsletter.

www.sbu.ac.uk/water: Martin Chaplin of South Bank Univ. on water structure.

www.flantech.com: a good source on Dr. Patrick Flanagan's microclusters in water.

www.digibio.com: Dr Jacques Beneviste's research on memory in water.

www.whirlpower.cc: David Dennard has put on his website chapters of his book *The Pearl of Wisdom* which deals with the power of the Vortex, which are worth reading.

www.frank.germano.com/viktorschauberger: An unofficial, but informative American site about Viktor Schauberger, (though much of the text seems to have been plagiarized from *Living Energies!*)

Bibliography

Abram, David *The Spell of the Sensuous*. Random House, 1996; Vintage 1997.(*A visionary view of humans' connection with the Earth and with Nature.)*

Alexandersson, Olof *Living Water.* Turnstone, 1982; Gateway 1984; Gill and Macmillan, 2002.(*Good accessible portrait of Viktor Schauberger and his ideas about water; first published 1977 in Swedish.)*

Ardui, Jan and Wrycza, Peter *The Way of Unfolding* (unpublished ms).

Ash, David and Hewett, Peter *The Vortex*. Gateway, 1990.(*Many superstitions and mysteries may be explained in terms of energy. Good introduction to vortex theory.)*

Bartholomew, Alick *The Schauberger Keys* (Schauberger-books.org.uk). *A summary of Viktor Schauberger's worldview, originating as notes made during the writing of* Hidden Nature.

Baker, Richard St Barbe *Dance of the Trees*. Oldbourne, 1956.

—, *I Planted Trees*. Lutterworth, 1944.

—, *My Life, My Trees*. Lutterworth, 1970; Findhorn, 1979.(*One of the great pioneers of restoring our forests.)*

Bellamy, David *101 Ways to Save the Earth*. Lincoln 2003.

—, *The Bellamy Herbal*, Century 2003.

—, *Bellamy's New World: Botanical History of America*. BBC 1983; Smithmark 1985.

—, *The Changing World: The Forest*. Simon and Schuster Educ. 1991, Lincoln, 1999.

—, *The River*. Simon and Schuster Educ. 1991, Lincoln, 1999.

—, *The Rock Pool*. Random, 1988; Simon and Schuster Educ. 1991.

—, *The Road Side*. Random, 1988.

—, *How Green are You?* Random 1991; Lincoln, 1991.

—, *Jolly Green Giant*. Century, 2002; Arrow 2003.

—, *Tomorrow's Earth: A Squeaky-Green Earth*. Courage, 1992.

Bird, Christopher and Tompkins, Peter *The Secret Life of Plants*. Harper, 1989.

—, *Secrets of the Soil*. Harper, 1989.(*Two classics in the area of alternative science.)*

Blair, Lawrence *Rhythms of Vision*. Croom Helm, 1975.(*The changing worldview of science.)*

Blossfeldt, Karl *Urformen der Kunst*. Wasmuth, 1935.(*Superb photogravure plates of plant growth.)*
Bunyard, Peter *The Breakdown of Climate*. Floris Books, Edinburgh, 1999.(*Excellent description of how climate works and of the human causes of climate change.)*
—, (ed.) *Gaia in Action*. Floris Books, Edinburgh, 1996.
Burr, Harold *Blueprint for Immortality: Electrical Patterns of Life Discovered*. Spearman, 1972. (*A classic in its field)*
Carson, Rachel *Silent Spring*. Houghton Mifflin, 1962; Collins, 1964.(*The book that inspired the environmental movement.)*
Coats, Callum *Living Energies*. Gateway, 1996; Gill and Macmillan, 2001.(*The most authoritative study of Viktor Schauberger's research; took eighteen years to write.)*
Cook, Nick *The Hunt for Zero Point*. Century, 2001.(*A veteran aeronautical editor investigates how the US military/defence programme might have befitted from German WWII secret weapons development. A fascinating story of the search for anti-gravity and powerless flight which indicates that Schauberger was its pioneer.)*
Cori, Patricia *The Cosmos of Soul*. Gill and Macmillan (Gateway), 2001.(*An introduction to cosmic science.)*
Cowan, David and Girdlestone, Rodney *Safe as Houses? Ill Health and Electro-stress in the Home*. Gateway, 1996.(*A well-researched and useful guide to electromagnetic and geopathic stress.)*
Edwards, Lawrence *The Vortex of Life*. Floris Books, Edinburgh, 1993.(*Fascinating research into Nature's patterns, particularly on the geometry of bud growth.)*
Emoto, Masaru, *The Message from Water*. Hado Publishing, Vol.1, 1999, vol.2, 2001. *(Remarkable photographs of ice crystals demonstrating water's ability to record resonances (*hado*) of different energy qualities, of thoughts, emotions and of music. Vol. 1 is more general, of social icons, vol. 2 more personal (e.g. family life). See* Resources*)*
Gelbspan, Ross *The Heat is On*. Perseus, 1997. (*A study of global warming issues.)*
Grohman, Gerbert *The Plant*. Steiner, 1974.(*An anthroposophical study of the plant.)*
Groves, Barry *Fluoride, Drinking Ourselves to Death?* Gill and Macmillan, 2001. *(Readable and a reliable authority.)*
Ho, Mae-Wan *Genetic Engineering, Dream or Nightmare?* Gateway, 1998. *(Widely regarded as providing the most sustained and reasoned*

challenge to many of the scientific assumptions underlying genetic modification.)
—, *The Rainbow and the Worm, The Physics of Organisms.* World Scientific, 1993.(*A holistic, campaigning biologist.)*
Hageneder, Fred *The Spirit of Trees.* Floris Books, Edinburgh, 2000.
—, *The Heritage of Trees.* Floris Books, Edinburgh, 2001. (*Impassioned and inspiring study of the lore of trees — spiritual, symbolic, historical and scientific.)*
Jenny, Hans *Kymatik/Cymatics.* Basilims, 1945.
Johnson, Steven *Emergence.* Scribner; Allen Lane, 2001.(*How complex systems can arise naturally as part of Nature's evolutionary imperative.)*
Lattacher, Siegbert *Viktor Schauberger — Auf den Spuren des legendären Naturforschers* (On the track of the legendary Natural Researcher). Ennstaler, 1999.(*The first significant biography of Viktor Schauberger. It concentrates on his wartime activities.)*
Lovelock, James *Gaia, A New Look at Life on Earth.* Oxford, 1979.
—, *The Ages of Gaia.* Oxford, 1988.
—, *Gaia, The Practical Science of Planetary Medicine.* Gaia, 1991.
—, *Healing Gaia, Practical Medicine for the Planet.* Gaia, 1991; Harmony, 1991.(*The scientist of Gaia who will never get his deserved Nobel prize because the Establishment doesn't like pioneers.)*
Lusar, Rudolf *Secret Weapons of World War II.*
Manning, Jeane *The Coming Energy Revolution.* Avery, 1996.(*A good overall assessment of alternative sources of energy)*
Marks, William *The Holy Order of Water.* Bell Pond, 2001.(*A passionate study of water lore and science, from ancient Greece to our present challenges of pollution and ecological destruction.)*
Michel, John *City of Revelation.* Garnstone, 1972.(*A classic of sacred geometry.)*
McKibben, Bill *The End of Nature.* Random House, 1989, 1999.
Milner, Edward *The Tree Book.* Collins and Brown, 1992.
Ott, John *Health and Light.* Devin-Adair, 1973.
Pedler, Kit *The Quest for Gaia.* Souvenir, 1979.
Price, Weston *Nutrition and Physical Degeneration.* Price-Pottenger, 1935; Keats, 1989.(*In the early 1930s, Dr Price and his wife recorded the degeneration of health in indigenous communities all over the world which were experiencing the impact of modern culture and diet. A remarkable and seminal study.)*

Russell, Peter *The Awakening Earth*. Routledge, 1982.
Schauberger, Viktor (Callum Coats, trans. and ed.), *The Eco-technology series:*
—, *The Water Wizard*. Gateway, 1998.(*A selection of Viktor's writings about the qualities of water in its natural state, problems with water supply and delivery, much on river flow and river regulation.)*
—, *Nature as Teacher*. Gateway, 1998.(*Thoughts about environmental catastrophe; correspondence with contemporaries and frustrations with establishment science.)*
—, *The Fertile Earth*. Gill and Macmillan (Gateway), 2000.(*Schauberger's writings on trees and forestry practice; fertilization of the soil, biodynamic agriculture, failure of contemporary farming; fertility and subtle energies in Nature.)*
—, *Energy Evolution*. Gill and Macmillan (Gateway), 2000.(*Viktor writings about some of the principles behind the different kinds of suction and implosion machines he developed, for producing spring water; an air conditioner and free energy generation.)*
—, *Our Senseless Toil (Unsere Sinnlose Arbeit)*. Krystall, 1933; PKS, 2002.(*A new German edition is now available from the PKS Institute in Austria — see www.pks.or.at)*
Schell, Jonathan *The Fate of the Earth*. Pan, 1982.
Schwenk, Theodore *Sensitive Chaos*. Steiner, 1965.(*A brilliant and original study of the behaviour of water; beautiful photographs.)*
—, and Wolfram Schwenk *Water, Element of Life*. Anthroposophic Press, 1989. (*A more philosophical father and son co-authorship.)*
Sheldrake, Rupert *A New Science of Life*. Blond and Briggs, 1981.
—, *The Rebirth of Nature*. Rider, 1990.
Steiner, Rudolf *The Nature of Substance*. Steiner Press, 1966.
Stevens, Peter *Patterns in Nature*. Penguin, 1974.
Thomas, William (ed.) *Man's Role in Changing the Face of the Earth*. Chicago, 1956.(*Celebrated international anthropological symposium co-chaired by Carl Sauer, Marston Bates and Lewis Mumford.)*
Walsh-Roberts, Paul *From Atoms to Angels*. Gill and Macmillan (Gateway), 2001.(*Very readable introduction to a spiritual study of the human.)*
Wilkes, John *Flowforms: the Rhythmic Power of Water.* Floris Books, Edinburgh, 2003.
Wright, Machaelle Small *Behaving as if the God in All Life Mattered*. Perelandra, 1981, 1997.

—, *Co-Creative Science: Revolution in Science with real Solutions for Today's Health and Environment*. Perelandra, 1997.(*Machaelle Wright founded Perelandra, a Nature research centre in Virginia, in 1977. She works with Nature intelligence with a conscious, coordinated programme and as an educational effort, demonstrating a new approach to health, horticulture and environmental balance.)*

Young, Arthur *The Reflexive Universe*. Delacorte, 1976. (*A pioneer of holistic cosmological thought.)*

Zuk, Bill *Canada's Flying Saucers. The Story of Avro Canada's Secret Projects.*Boston Mills Press, Ontario.

Index

Note: entries in *italic* signify illustrations